Blackening
of the Bible

AFRICAN
AMERICAN
RELIGIOUS THOUGHT AND LIFE

This series provides opportunity for African American scholars from a wide variety of fields in religion to develop their insights into religious discourse on issues that affect African American intellectual, social, cultural, and community life. The series focuses on topics, figures, problems, and cultural expressions in the study of African American religion that are often neglected by publishing programs centered on African American theology. The AARTL program of publications will bridge theological reflection on African American religious experience and the critical, methodological interests of African American religions studies.

SERIES EDITORS
ANTHONY B. PINN, Macalester College, St. Paul, Minnesota
VICTOR ANDERSON, Vanderbilt University, Nashville, Tennessee

Blackening of the Bible

THE AIMS OF AFRICAN AMERICAN BIBLICAL SCHOLARSHIP

Michael Joseph Brown

TRINITY PRESS INTERNATIONAL
A Continuum imprint
HARRISBURG • LONDON • NEW YORK

Scripture quotations are taken from the New Revised Standard Version of the Bible, copyright 1989, Division of Christian Education of the National Council of the Churches of Christ in the United States of America. Used by permission. All rights reserved.

Trinity Press International, P.O. Box 1321, Harrisburg, PA 17105

Trinity Press International, The Tower Building, 11 York Road, London SE1 7NX

Trinity Press International is a member of the Continuum International Publishing Group.

Cover design by Trude Brummer

Library of Congress Cataloging-in-Publication Data

Brown, Michael Joseph.
    Blackening of the Bible : the aims of African American biblical scholarship / by Michael Joseph Brown.
        p.   cm. – (African American religious thought and life)
    Includes bibliographical references and index.
    ISBN 1-56338-363-2 (pbk.)
    1. Bible – Black interpretations – History. 2. Afrocentrism – Religious aspects – Christianity – History. 3. Womanist theology – History. I. Title. II. Series.
BS521.2.B76 2004
220.6'089'96073 – dc22

                                                                    2004010257

Printed in the United States of America

04   05   06   07   08   09   10   9   8   7   6   5   4   3   2   1

To Max
(1990–2003)

Contents

Preface

This book began as a conversation I had with a very dear friend and colleague, Victor Anderson. As you would guess, the subject was African American biblical interpretation. We both lamented, to some extent, the absence of a single volume work that presented and offered a critique of the enterprise. A few months later, I found myself writing a proposal for such a thing.

To be honest, I attempted to convince Victor and Anthony Pinn, the editors of the African American Religious Thought and Life series, that I was not the person for the job. My scholarly work has not focused directly on this specific form of cultural hermeneutics. Nevertheless, they encouraged me. They believed that the fresh perspective I would bring to the task would allow readers unacquainted with African American readings of the Bible to see it in a less partisan light. I hope I have accomplished, at least, this goal. Thus, this book is intended to serve as an introduction to the enterprise of African American biblical hermeneutics. It assumes that the reader has a basic knowledge of biblical interpretation as an academic field, as well as some acquaintance with the debates that accompany it.

In writing this book, I have been guided by three organizing principles. First, the book focuses on African American biblical scholars. I point out several times in the book that African Americans in other theological fields have written on the Bible and biblical themes. For example, James Cone's essay "Biblical Revelation and Social Existence" was a landmark contribution to the relationship between black theology and biblical interpretation. However, Cone is not a biblical scholar. He is a theologian. If this book is in any way an exposition of the academic enterprise of African American biblical scholarship, then it must confine itself to those voices in the discipline who have been trained in the field of biblical studies. Of course, many will now point to the inclusion of Cheryl Kirk-Duggan and Ron Liburd as grounds for claiming that I violate my principle of disciplinary exclusivity. Let me respond. I added Liburd because he raises an issue regarding the theological grounding of the enterprise that others appeared reluctant to raise initially. I added Kirk-Duggan because she represents a strand of development in womanist interpretation that had to be included, at least from my perspective. I pray that my readers, instead of criticizing my shortcomings here, would remember the dictum of Robert Burton, "No rule is so general, which admits not some exception."

Second, this book is representative of the work being done in the field of African American biblical hermeneutics. It in no way pretends to be an exhaustive analysis of every scholar and every writing in the field. I purposely attempted to balance the book between scholars in both testaments in order to give the reader a suitable introduction. At times, I fall short of this goal. Still, however, the organization of the book lends itself well to the comparison of somewhat contemporary scholars who are in conversation with each other around a core set of issues. Of course, some will question the exclusion of so-and-so from the discourse. Let me say that no attempt was made to exclude any scholar on grounds other than the limitations of space. I wish I would have had space to discuss thoroughly the exemplary work of R. Cottrell Carson, Hugh Rowland Page, Gay L. Byron, Abraham Smith, and others. Maybe I, or someone else, will pursue their work in another volume. As it stands, this book gives the reader an overview of the various modes of engagement used by African American biblical scholars.

Third, I decided early on in this project to make the book more descriptive than argumentative. I do not think the purposes of introduction are fulfilled when one takes an entirely critical posture to the material one is explaining. Of course, I do offer a critique. There is much about African American hermeneutics that needs clearer explanation and theoretical grounding than I have found in the field. At the same time, I have operated under the premise that the reader will be unable to understand the critique if an impassioned argument is not made for the proposal. Again, I hope I have achieved this goal. I have confined my own criticisms of the various scholars in this book to the ends of their sections. Moreover, I intentionally avoided reading outside critiques of African American hermeneutics until after I completed the chapters. I did not want to be unduly influenced by what other scholars claim is being performed in the field. Having written one short article addressing this issue in the past, I recognize now how influenced I was by the statements of other scholars about what they believed to be occurring among African American interpreters — criticisms that were not always a fair representation.[1] Thus, what one finds here is an honest appraisal by one biblical scholar of a form of biblical scholarship that he finds intriguing. Let me outline the book briefly.

Chapter 1 introduces the topic of African American biblical hermeneutics by placing it within the larger context of the contemporary debates surrounding biblical interpretation as such. Looking at four criticisms leveled against the historical critical enterprise, I explain how the acknowledgment of the need for contextual readings of Scripture arose. Then I examine three contemporary forms of contextual reading in South America and Africa. The purpose behind this examination is to contextualize the type of biblical engagement commonly referred to as African American. I point out that, in contrast to these other forms of contextual reading, African American hermeneutics is decidedly academic in its situatedness, audience, and aims.

Chapter 2 looks at what I perceive to be the foundation of African American hermeneutics, the enterprise of corrective historiography. I argue that the initial purpose for promoting a distinctive form of an African American reading of Scripture was to correct the historical biases that Euro-Americans perpetuated in their various discourses on Scripture. Focusing on the work of Charles Copher and Cain Hope Felder, I outline the strengths and weaknesses of this approach — its greatest strength being, I argue, its use of the conceptual paradigm of Afrocentricity.

Chapter 3 examines what I believe to be the next stage in African American hermeneutics: a movement from the acceptance of an African presence in the Bible to the consideration of how African Americans have engaged the text historically. Focusing on the work of Randall Bailey and Vincent Wimbush, I demonstrate how scholars moved quickly away from the barely defensible position that black-skinned people occupied the pages of the Bible to an approach that moved the area of focus more to the New Testament and the present.

Chapter 4 examines the work of womanist biblical scholars. I decided to present the womanist approach to interpretation in a chapter all its own for a couple of reasons. First, womanists are attempting to develop a distinctive hermeneutical voice in contrast to their male colleagues, and I was afraid their perspective would be lost if mixed in with others. Second, they represent another advance in Afrocentric interpretation. Their hermeneutical method is not represented in what precedes in chapters 2 and 3, but it does influence what follows in chapters 5 and 6.

Chapter 5 examines the work of the latest generation of African American biblical scholars, that is, those who have only recently completed dissertations. Brian Blount, of course, is an exception to this characterization. His work is foregrounded in this chapter because he represents the shift that is occurring in the field away from a singular or intracommunal conversation to a pluralistic one, a shift I believe to have been influenced by the womanist approach to interpretation. The scholars discussed in this chapter represent the trends found in the latest writings of African American hermeneutes.

Chapter 6 accomplishes three aims. First, it lays out my assessment of the aims of African American biblical interpretation. As the reader will see, I have developed a distinctive perspective that seeks to account for its flourishing. Second, I offer four critiques of the enterprise garnered from the various criticisms that have been leveled over the years. Finally, I offer four proposals for African American biblical interpreters to consider. Each is provocative in its own way. I believe practitioners of African American hermeneutics will find these proposals a source of continued conversation and reflection for the near future.

As a final expression, I would like to thank various individuals who assisted immeasurably in the writing of this book. First, I owe a great thanks to Victor Anderson and Anthony Pinn, who encouraged me to take on the project. Second, I owe a debt of gratitude to Henry Carrigan, the senior editor at T&T Clark International, who not only encouraged me in the project but also waited patiently for its completion. A word of deepest thanks to Shively T. S. Jackson, my research assistant, whose many hours of research and reading made the completion of this book a viable possibility in the first place. Her insights and suggestions can be found throughout this work. I would be remiss not to thank the students of my Introduction to the New Testament class for being attentive during lectures that were in reality drafts of these chapters. Also, I would like to thank the New Testament Colloquium, both faculty and students, for giving me feedback on chapter 4 of this work. Finally, I would like to thank Randall Bailey, Teresa Fry-Brown, and Herbert Robinson Marbury for discussing the manuscript with me at various points and for reading some of the chapters in their initial stages. The insights of these scholars have helped me immensely. I am reminded of the words penned by Peter of Blois, "We are like dwarfs on the shoulders of giants, by whose grace we see farther than they." I pray this to be true. Of course, all shortcomings in this work are the result of my own limitations. My sight is not always as acute as I would hope.

As usual, my most sincere appreciation must be given to Alvin Tyrone ("Imani") Gridiron and Michael Anthony Brown for their patience and support. Because writing has occupied so much of my time, especially this year, I know I have not been the partner and parent I should have been. Further, I appreciate how much Imani has continued to support my work even after we have suffered some devastating medical setbacks. His unceasing encouragement for me to finish this book has demonstrated to me the depth of his appreciation for my vocation.

MICHAEL JOSEPH BROWN

Atlanta, Georgia
Palm Sunday 2004

Abbreviations

For references to ancient and biblical texts, I generally have used the abbreviations of *The SBL Handbook of Style for Ancient Near Eastern, Biblical, and Early Christian Studies* (Peabody, Mass.: Hendrickson, 1999); and John F. Oates, *Checklist of Editions of Greek and Latin Papyri, Ostraca, and Tablets* (Atlanta: Scholars Press, 1992).

Chapter 1

The Eclipse of a Eurocentric Enterprise

Those groups less sure of their access to privilege and ability (women, racial minorities, the disabled, the aged, children), those very groups who may have been, or may still be subservient to the privileged elite, are not always quite so sure either of their ability to be understood or of their ability to communicate with dominant groups. Faced with miscomprehension, there has been a tendency for such groups, in their understandable frustration, to deduce that their discourse is self-referential and incomprehensible outside their group. They may even feel that this incomprehensibility places on them a type of cultural aphasia. Such aphasiac exclusion is not always tolerated. When it is not, it is an easy step, utilizing this very incomprehensibility as a political lever, to insist upon the uniqueness of their own voices and to require that their voices, perceived as separate from those of the ruling elite, receive privilege. Uniqueness, otherness, becomes the characterizing quality of the "disenfranchised."[1]

The Interested Character of All Readings

To some, the art of biblical interpretation is transparent. As one old adage goes, "The Bible says what it means and means what it says." In an earlier work I expanded on that saying by adding the qualification "except when it doesn't."[2] In truth, the Bible can be a confusing document. On top of the differences in historical situation, biblical and modern languages, ethno-religious allegiances, and cultural and theological presuppositions, there is the problem of communication itself. As literary and philosophical critics have pointed out repeatedly, language frequently lacks a coherent

1

origin or centeredness that would allow us to read the Bible, as well as other texts, with complete clarity. In fact, such ambiguity is the basis for the interpretive enterprise itself.[3] Whether through historical reconstruction, literary analysis, or some other means, biblical scholars have come to this ancient sacred text repeatedly as a source of theological authority for the modern faithful.

African American biblical scholars, like their counterparts all over the globe, approach their craft as a vehicle for exploring and disseminating the biblical witness in our specific modern context. Such an examination, and the methods it employs, says something substantive about our modern culture in light of biblical proclamation.[4] Nevertheless, the complexities of modern Western life have forced biblical scholars, especially those who are African American, to approach Scripture from an interpretive angle that is radically different from that of their intellectual predecessors. Frequently European or Euro-American males, who often unwittingly wrote out of their own culturally defined contexts, believed their interpretations to be universally applicable. In the twenty-first century, such an air of universality has been challenged and overthrown with relative effectiveness. More recent philosophical inquiries have demonstrated that all readers, who are not otherwise apathetic, are "interested" in the interpretation and appropriation of texts.[5]

This place is probably as good as any to begin our study. All readings are interested readings. This observation, the product of decades of philosophical reflection, is at the heart of all contextual readings of texts. Whether we approach readings from a Latino, liberationist, Filipino, or Asian perspective, or some other perspective, there is a sense in which all of us bring nearly canonical perceptions and experiences to our reading and appropriation of texts, especially when they are deemed sacred texts. These readings are contextual in that many of our perceptions and experiences are the harvests of countless crops of socially situated and culturally derivative plantings in our minds.

African American biblical interpretation, even in its academic manifestation, is one such contextual reading. Based on the dual theological foundations of liberation and black theologies, African American biblical interpretation looks for the potentially liberatory reading of biblical texts, the kerygmatic proclamation, behind what otherwise presents itself as a repository of patriarchy, ethno-religious exclusion, and heterosexism.

Eclipsing the Historical-Critical Enterprise

The historical-critical method of biblical interpretation arrived in the United States sometime in the late nineteenth and early twentieth centuries.[6] It was the product of the German Enlightenment and its use of the Cartesian tool of methodical doubt.[7] This method of interpretation was revolutionary because it broke the chains the church once had over the Bible and its explication. Rationalism was the cornerstone of the method. It had triumphed over dogmatism in Europe and was now seeking to conquer North America. In this milieu, the human being was at the center of rational inquiry with its disestablishment of tradition and trumpeting of reason as the sole criterion of truth.[8]

The effects on our understanding of the Bible were astounding. Biblical scholars were now listening for the voice of the writer and first audience with every linguistic tool at their disposal. The reconstructive technique has been called the *sensus literalis sive historicus*, the literal or historical sense of the text. To accomplish such a feat, scholars took four steps: collected, evaluated, related, and presented. Edgar Krentz makes this process clear when he says, "[Historical criticism] is a method for *collecting* all possible witnesses to an era or event, *evaluating* what they say, *relating* the findings to one another in a coherent structure, and *presenting* the conclusion with the evidence."[9] In essence, the historical-critical method has been about establishing a narrative.

History is a narrative constructed from the data of experience, evaluated by its narrator; this narrative is presented to an intended audience for the purpose of providing meaningfulness to otherwise random phenomena. Historiography has its limitations. For example, it cannot account for phenomena for which there are no surviving witnesses. Moreover, in its popularly accepted form, it operates according to principles that are grounded in a distinctively European rationalism. At the end of the nineteenth century, Ernst Troeltsch addressed many of these principles in his essay "On Historical and Dogmatic Method in Theology."

According to Troeltsch, historical criticism rests on three principles. The first is the principle of methodological doubt. Going back to René Descartes, this mode of investigation posits that nothing should be accepted as true simply because it is in the tradition. Accordingly, the biblical canon, the product of prolonged Judeo-Christian reflection on the nature and activities of God, is the result of a theological decision rather than a full and objective account

of what happened. It is tradition. This does not automatically dis-
credit it as a source of history, but it does remove the shroud of
mystery and authority many attribute to it. In a similar manner, it
tempers all historical narratives as the products of probability and
not indisputable fact.

The second principle is analogy. It maintains that all events are
similar in principle. That is, we understand the past by relating
it to our experiences in the present. The final principle is mutual
interdependence. Also known as the principle of correlation, this
rule implies that "all historical phenomena are so interrelated that
a change in one phenomenon necessitates a change in the causes
leading to it and in the effects it has."[10] Simply, it is the application of
the idea of cause and effect. Historical criticism assumes that every
event is related in some way to an event that precedes it, as well as
to one that follows. All totaled, these principles made Christianity
and its Bible the objects of disciplined inquiry and investigation.
Deemed scientific by many of its earliest practitioners, historical
criticism marked a new era in biblical investigation, one that sought
to communicate the biblical narrative unfettered by the theological
orientations of its canonizers and ecclesiastical interpreters.

Although a revolutionary approach, the historical-critical method
faced resistance from its inception. So-called dogmatic scholars criticized the method as undermining the rightful place of Scripture
in the church, a place above reproach. This position can be found
among many in the United States who reject the idea that the Bible
can be understood as anything other than entirely sacred. More recently, dissenting biblical scholars have criticized historical criticism
on other grounds. John Barton outlines four.[11]

The first is the historical-critical concern with genetic questions.
Historical critics ask when and by whom the books of the Bible
were written. They want to know their intended readership. In
addition, they often are interested in the various stages that contributed to the final product. Historical critics have long suggested
that many of the books in the canon are, in fact, composites. They
were put together out of a number of originally separate source
documents, including oral stories. Critics have attacked the method
as more interested in the sources underlying the biblical books
than in the books themselves. Once historical critics determine the
origin of a passage or passages, they soon lose interest.

The second criticism leveled at the historical-critical method
regards its pursuit of original meaning. Historical critics are interested in determining what a text meant to its first readers, its

original and intended audience. They are not concerned, it is supposed, with what a biblical passage might mean to a modern audience. By placing the Bible in a decidedly historical context, practitioners argue that we misunderstand Scripture if we take it to mean something it could not have meant for its first readers. In this paradigm, the original meaning is equivalent to the true meaning. The third area of criticism is its interest in historical reconstruction. Historical criticism often has been concerned with historiography in a straightforward sense, with what happened in the past. Biblical scholars have examined the so-called historical books of the Hebrew Bible, the Gospels, the Acts of the Apostles, and others to determine what actually happened. Looking past the biblical authors and their theological agendas, historical critics have repeatedly examined the Bible to determine as best as possible the historical parameters that influenced the narratives, prophecies, poetry, rhetoric, and visions that constitute Scripture.

The final area in which the historical-critical method has been criticized is its claim to disinterestedness. It was meant to be a value-neutral method of biblical investigation. Historical critics traditionally attempt to approach the Bible without prejudice. They are interested not in what the text means for the modern individual, but in what it *meant* (original meaning). To do this, the critic must be neutral, renouncing any kind of faith commitment for the sake of truth.

All of these orientations are related in one way or another to the ideals of the Enlightenment, and arguably before that to the ideals of the Protestant Reformation. Taken together, they constitute a method of biblical engagement that strives consistently to distance itself from outside influences, whether from the church or the interpreter herself. It is an ideal mode of engagement for freethinking people, another indication of its relationship to the Reformation and Enlightenment. Echoing Luther's famous dictum, "Here I stand, I can do no other," historical critics refuse to bend their knees to any god other than truth.[12] At least, that is the ideal.

According to its critics, historical criticism rarely, if ever, reaches this ideal. They charge that the "neutral, scientific pursuit of truth by a disinterested scholar has been shown ... to be bankrupt."[13] Particularly vulnerable in the second and fourth areas, critics, particularly postmodern ones, assert that no reading is disinterested and original meaning is specious. Historical critics have conceded the former but remained staunch on the latter. This concession on behalf of the practitioners of historical criticism, however, opened up the possibility of considering the interpreter in front of the text; namely, the role historical context or social location plays in the act of interpretation.

Rooted in a Rich Black Soil

Once biblical scholars allowed for the possibility of contextually oriented readings of Scripture, Pandora's box could not be closed again. As Walter Dietrich and Ulrich Luz attest, the context of academic biblical studies has changed from a pseudoscientific engagement with the Bible to one that recognizes the subject as a central figure in the act of interpretation.[14] From the Brazilian rain forests to the teeming metropolises of Asia, scholars began to acknowledge and take seriously the role played by the reader in biblical interpretation. As Dietrich and Luz describe it, global society is going through a "cultural crisis."[15] Europeans have abandoned reading the Bible for the most part. "It can be found everywhere [in Europe] indeed: standing on the shelves in everybody's home as a relic from studying the subject 'Religion' in school, or as a memory of one's wedding ceremony in church," yet it no longer plays a pivotal role as the foundation of truth or the source of piety.[16] In contrast, North Americans, particularly those in the United States, read and relate to the Bible as "alive and effective not only in fundamentalist or evangelical circles, but also within the mainstream churches."[17] In Africa and South America, groups and reading communities are discovering the Bible to be a powerful tool. In times of crisis, Dietrich and Luz contend, interpretations matter. In these communities,

> the people . . . read the Bible — torn between capitalism and extreme poverty, between individual, indigenous cultural roots and imported Western culture and science, fascinated by the never-ending task of adopting the Christian faith, which became homeless in western and northern Europe. For them, it [is] a new, alien faith, and they [have] turned it into their own.[18]

In Asia, the Bible "is read among the intellectuals" of various nations.[19] Although in general these readers are not Christian, they see reading the Bible as necessary and fruitful. Dietrich and Luz attribute this interest to a search for identity.[20]

Addressing what they consider the central problem with the Western approach to biblical interpretation, Dietrich and Luz point to the abstract nature of the enterprise: "It is carried out abstractly and therefore leads to abstract results and truths, which are not related to any context."[21] By abstract, they mean "unattached to the life and reading of 'ordinary' people" and to the present conditions that constitute their lives.[22] Western biblical scholars, including those in the United States, would rather flee to an imaginary textual world than confront the stark reality of this one. In contrast, Africans and South Americans, generally in community, are finding the Bible to be a rich resource for language to describe their daily struggles and a source for their common identity. Although they frequently struggle with the abstracted exegesis of European and American scholars, these communities find their greatest hermeneutical resource to be their own contextual situation. As Dietrich and Luz assert, "Only because of their contextual situation are there a meaning and a value in the way they read the Bible, in their research and in their hermeneutical efforts."[23] We shall briefly examine three of these contextual approaches.

The Discourses of the Dominated

Gerald West, a South African biblical scholar, acknowledges that the Bible has been both oppressor and liberator for his people. He gives this anecdote as an illustration: "When the white man came to our country he had the Bible and we had the land. The white man said, 'Let us pray.' After the prayer, the white man had the land and we had the Bible."[24] He goes on to say that this situation is further complicated by the response given by Desmond Tutu: "And we got the better deal."[25]

West argues that South Africa illustrates the problem that arises when the oppressor and the oppressed share the same sacred text. The Bible has been used by the perpetuators of racial oppression to justify the marginalization of the indigenous population. Yet, as Archbishop Tutu's response illustrates, to many South Africans the "Bible is a symbol of the presence of the God of life with them."[26] For many South Africans, including those who are not Christian, the Bible serves as the people's book, the only source of theology for many. Its dual status, therefore, as tool of the oppressor and resource for the oppressed makes reading and interpreting the Bible a precarious task for South African biblical scholars.

Pointing to a crisis in culture, West says that *The Kairos Document,* a statement developed during the struggle against apartheid, functions as a model by which South African biblical scholars can engage effectively the contemporary task of interpretation. As he describes it, "[The] crisis that was shaking the foundations of our country [under apartheid] was both political and interpretive."[27] The struggle against apartheid demanded that biblical scholars develop new readings and theologies for the liberation of the masses. Now that apartheid, the political crisis, has passed, the problem of interpretation persists and is more critical than before. As West relates,

> While it is no longer necessary for the church to represent the liberation movements, as it was in decades of their bannings, this does not mean that the readings and theologies forged in the struggle ought to be abandoned in order to "go back to being the church," whatever this might mean.[28]

Pointing to the violence that erupted in KwaZulu-Natal in the 1980s, West argues that a retreat to the Western model of biblical interpretation cannot address the existential concerns that confront many South Africans. If the Bible is to continue to function as the presence of the God of life in the lives of a people continually confronted with crisis and death, what is needed is not a retreat but an advance in the readings developed during apartheid. West says, "As the South African context constantly reminds us, biblical interpretations have life and death consequences; they shape the type of response the state, the church, and ordinary people make to particular social realities."[29]

Another model of biblical engagement is needed. West acknowledges that many biblical scholars, although socially committed, felt powerless in the face of the violence that confronted the populace of KwaZulu-Natal and elsewhere. Through dialogical engagement with the poor, these scholars began to realize that certain reading strategies would not work. They recognized, first, a tendency either to romanticize or to minimize the contributions of common people to the task of hermeneutics. West dismisses this strategy of "listening to" the poor, a product of such romanticism, as an unattainable ideal, because it presupposes a fully realized "self-knowing subject free from ideology."[30] Likewise, he dismisses the strategy of "speaking for" the marginalized as paternalistic, because it denies the ability of the poor and oppressed to speak for themselves.[31] The form of biblical engagement West advances is one of "speaking with." Such engagement induces the development of two critical capacities. The first requires that the biblical scholar remain ever

vigilant of his own context as well as that of his reading partners. Each context influences the process of interpretation, such
that it is impossible to say that individuals approach the text in a
value-neutral manner. The second requires that the biblical scholar
accept as legitimate the contributions, as well as the context, of
her reading partners. Unless these two capacities are developed, the
scholar can be said only to be "listening to" or "speaking for" the
marginalized.

Of course, the interpretations of scholars often will be different
from those of the marginalized. West not only acknowledges this
fact but also celebrates it. Difference, he maintains, must be seen
as the basis upon which any fruitful interpretation can emerge. In
a direct challenge to the historical-critical belief that meaning is
"found" in the text through the examination of historical context,
West argues that meaning is, in fact, "produced" by readers engaging the Bible from different social locations.[32] He believes that
by reading in community and taking seriously the contributions of
marginalized readers, biblical scholars can develop a hermeneutic
that will maintain the presence of the God of life in South Africa.
By espousing this viewpoint, he is not abandoning a critical engagement with the Bible. The critical aspect of his hermeneutic is
rooted in the dialogic relationship that occurs when scholars and
ordinary people read the Bible together, one that allows each party
to be influenced and partially constituted by the other.

A Grassroots Approach

The Brazilian scholar Carlos Mesters offers another complementary
discussion of the importance of context in the process of interpretation. As a Catholic, he recognizes that other forms of biblical
engagement are occurring in the Brazilian context, and so offers
this approach as only one example of contextual interpretation.

As he describes them, reading communities in Brazil approach
the Bible foremost from the perspective of their own existential
concerns: "We want to know whether the Bible is on our side or
not!"[33] In other words, Mesters argues that the central concern for
any sort of legitimate hermeneutic is not what the text *meant* but
what it *means* in the daily struggles of people. In this sense, the
Bible serves an important, although secondary, role in the process
of "meaning making." Mesters likens the Bible to the motor of
a car: It is indispensable to the driving experience, although it is
rarely the direct focus of the driver's interest.[34] To put it another

way, people read the Bible as a way of interpreting their own experiences.[35] As Mesters says, "The Bible is supposed to start things
off, to get them going; but it is not the steering wheel. You have
to use it correctly. You can't expect it to do what it is not meant
to do."[36]

The purpose of biblical interpretation, according to Mesters, is
discovering the Word of God in our own reality. Whether individuals understand the historical context of the Scriptures is not
particularly relevant. And yet Mesters identifies three obstacles that
confront ordinary readers of the biblical text: literacy, literalism,
and linearity. By literacy, he really means the problem of illiteracy — the inability of many in the community even to be physically
able to read the Bible. In order for the Word of God to reveal itself
in their midst, the marginalized often must revert to stories, songs,
and other means to communicate the biblical message. By literalism, he means disassociating the Bible from the everyday lives of its
readers. He points out, "If [the Bible] is treated like a finished mon-
ument that cannot be touched, that must be taken literally as it is,
then it will be an oppressive force."[37] Mesters believes that through
a creative reading of Scripture, and through the assurance that God
is on the side of the poor, the marginalized can be liberated from
the error of bibliolatry. By linearity, he means the cultural construction of time by marginalized people — a construction that views
time as circular — rather than the linear construction advocated by
most scholars. When community members recognize that the Bible
is really a collection of stories "people told to others about their
history," they realize that it is a repository of collective memory
and identity. Instead of emphasizing difference, this orientation,
along with a circular conception of time, emphasizes the similarities, the recurrences, between biblical characters and the lives of
their modern readers. As members of the community say, "God
speaks, mixed into things."[38]

Mesters addresses the presence of the biblical scholar in the
life of the grassroots interpretive community. He recognizes that
the aims of a biblical scholar often are quite different from
those of an ordinary reader. Moreover, he attributes the difference to the educational experience of the scholar. He says, "We
are awfully 'Europeanized' in our training."[39] The recognition
of his own Eurocentricity allows Mesters to distinguish between
his educationally oriented concerns and those that arise from the
community. Instead of emphasizing the differences between the historical context of the Bible and that of the present, as a scholar

would do, Mesters says, "[The people] are mixing life with the
Bible, and the Bible with life. One helps them to interpret the other.
And often the Bible is what starts them developing a more critical awareness of reality." Instead of instructing the marginalized
in their faith, Mesters says the biblical scholar must allow and encourage the poor to read the Bible in a way that permits them to
claim their own faith experiences.[40]

In examining the reading practices of grassroots communities
in Brazil, Mesters observes seven shifts in his biblical orientation
and encourages others to embrace these shifts. First, the Bible is on
the side of the poor. This change from tool of the oppressors to
guidebook for the oppressed involves the recognition that common
people discover things in the Bible that others, particularly scholars, do not find. Second, the Bible is a model for salvation and not
an explicit and unique history of salvation. Against such an exclusivist reading of the biblical materials, Mesters says, "Each people
has its own unique history. Within that history it must discover
the presence of God the Liberator who journeys by its side."[41]
Third, the Bible's function is to provide meaning for the reader. By
this, Mesters does not mean that we should abandon the historical-
critical approach entirely. His experience dictates that people will
become interested in the material conditions of biblical figures, but
only after they have critically engaged the Bible as a resource for
understanding their own lives. Fourth, the Bible is a community
document. It is not the exclusive property of the scholar. Mesters
argues that by reading the Bible in community, the sacred text can
reclaim its rightful place as a document of the church — the *sensus ecclesiae*. As he describes it, "Now the common people are
helping us to realize that without faith, community, and reality
we cannot possibly discover the meaning God has put in that ancient tome for us today."[42] Fifth, biblical interpretation is not a
neutral act. Mesters rejects the so-called disinterested and scientific
engagement of the Bible attributed to historical critics. Recognizing that the Bible has been the tool for the historical oppression of
many, especially when considered in light of how technology also
has been used to alienate the masses, he responds, "Technology is
not neutral, and neither is exegesis."[43] Sixth, the Bible addresses
concrete experiences. Mesters argues that one of the tricks biblical
exegetes have used to marginalize the masses has been the over-
spiritualization of biblical concepts. He argues that ideas such as
grace, salvation, sin, justification, and mercy point to concrete actions in the biblical text and are not meant to be relegated to a

netherworld — what African Americans frequently refer to as the
"by and by." Finally, the Bible's role is to facilitate people's lives.
It is not meant to be an end in itself. Mesters does not subscribe
to the idea that the Bible should be considered a theological relic
to be engaged apart from the ongoing life of the believing community. When viewed in this manner, the Bible becomes a document
written by people in a different time and place, which only dis-
tances it from the community it is supposed to inspire. In effect, the
Bible subjugates them. Through a contextual reading, the Bible can
be liberated by and liberatory for people of faith. He says, "[The]
common people are putting the Bible in its proper place, the place
where God intended it to be. They are putting it in second place.
Life takes first place!"[44]

Rooted in Black Culture

Justin Ukpong, a Nigerian New Testament scholar, begins with the
premise that the Western biblical interpretive tradition is intellectu-
alist, while the African tradition is existentialist.[45] By existentialist,
he means limited to a particular social and cultural context. He
explains:

> African readings are *existential and pragmatic* in nature, and
> *contextual* in approach. They are interested in relating the
> biblical message to contemporary and existential questions,
> and lay no claims to a universal perspective.[46]

Valid for its context, and possibly valid for other contexts as well,
interpretation, according to Ukpong, is the stage upon which an
ethics of transformation is erected.

This transformation is effected by ordinary people. Ordinary
people, according to Ukpong, are "a social class, the common
people in contradistinction to the elite."[47] And, as he goes on to
say, "[It] is the ordinary people that are accorded the epistemological privilege." Thus, the Bible is not neutral. It is avowedly on the
side of the poor.

Yet the elite are not excluded entirely. They are invited to
adopt — "be converted to" — the perspective of the marginalized.
This ethics recognizes that the Bible is not a neutral or innocent
text, and so must be read critically in light of its historical conditioning. It also involves appropriating the proper meaning for this
context, the contemporary perspective of the poor.

Ukpong says that three elements are involved in this inculturated reading process: (1) the people, (2) reading from their perspective, and (3) using their frame of reference. He advocates biblical scholars reading with the ordinary people as a means of producing critical readings that retain the privileged insight of the marginalized. In his view,

> Reading "with" means that the reading agenda is that of the community and not of trained readers, that trained readers do not direct or control the reading process or seek to "teach" to the community the meaning of the text that they have already known. Rather, they read as part of the community, and facilitate the interactive process that leads to the community producing a critical meaning of the text.[48]

If done properly, this reading practice will uncover and bring to the fore "the 'voices' of the unimportant characters that may sometimes be present only thematically in the text."[49]

Out of the three approaches discussed, Ukpong probably best describes context and the role it plays in interpretation. He says,

> The reading operation itself is not just the application of a reading method to read a text; it involves the *implementation* of the regime of the method in a particular way directed by particular interests and concerns of both the method and the readers. Readers, most often unconsciously, go to texts with some questions in mind reflecting the interests they have unconsciously imbibed over the years as well as some expectations derived from their preunderstandings, and are influenced by their status in society, denominational affiliation, gender, and so on, in the way they understand texts.[50]

According to Ukpong, even using the same method does not guarantee arriving at the same interpretation. Every reader brings to the text her ideals and conceptual frame of reference. In Ukpong's own approach, he embraces what he designates to be African ideals, those that affirm their social location, including a strong belief in the presence of the supernatural in the Bible. This is indicative of what he calls their conceptual frame of reference, the worldview they have "acquired imperceptibly," either through culture or through the use of a particular reading method.[51] Ukpong is critical of Africans, or anyone else, who adopt reading methods without reflecting on the conceptual frames of reference that go along with them.

Every reading is contextual. It can make no legitimate claim to universal truth because it is rooted by necessity in a conceptual frame of reference, which is always historically, socially, and culturally conditioned.[52] Yet Ukpong does not abandon the historical investigation of the Bible entirely. He uses it, but critically. Agreeing with other contextual readers that meaning is "produced" and not "found" in the interaction between the text and the reader, Ukpong argues that the purpose of any legitimate form of interpretation "is to appropriate a text's meaning in a contemporary sociocultural context."[53] Thus, he views the Bible as a "plurivalent" text rooted in its own set of historical contexts with the potential to speak to contemporary persons in their particularized historical contexts.

Logically, such an approach opens up the possibility of a multitude of readings that may be in conflict. In this case, he argues that readings should be in conversation with one another. If they cannot be reconciled through this means, Ukpong says that their validity must be adjudicated "by their faithfulness to the ethical demands of the gospel that include love of neighbor, respect for one another, and so on."[54] He admits that individuals, as products of a process of historical and social conditioning, hold worldviews that are both positive and negative with respect to liberation. This is why it is important for them to read in community. Through communal interaction, individuals can reflect critically on their own worldviews as well as those found in the text. Unless the Bible is understood as "good news" for all, it cannot maintain its moral authority. Thus, biblical interpretation is guided by the theological norm of liberation.

With liberation as its guiding norm, the act of reading the Bible with ordinary people has as its goal the transformation of readers and their society. As Ukpong says persuasively,

> They seek to appropriate the biblical message not in abstract theoretical terms but within the context of a commitment to action in concrete human situations. The goal is not merely to acquire knowledge about the Bible but to facilitate the living of the Christian faith in concrete life situations and to provide answers to questions of practical life concerns from the perspectives of the questioners.[55]

Transformation and liberation through an inculturated act of reading, one that privileges the insights of the marginalized as a basis for understanding and action, is the final and appropriate aim of Ukpong's hermeneutic. As a whole, these new contextual approaches to interpreting Scripture reveal six themes. (1) First and foremost, these approaches are guided by the dictates of a theology of liberation. Unlike the historical-critical approach, which attempts to be theologically neutral, this contextual mode of biblical engagement makes no attempt at neutrality. It is theologically situated. It is, in effect, a form of advocacy. These contextual readings promote a form of biblical interpretation that seeks to make real the ideals of the liberationist worldview. Having discarded the air of neutrality, these contextual interpretations place the Bible and its ostensible core message in the hands of the marginalized. Instead of classifying the Bible as a book to be examined by scholars or wielded by social and religious elites, these contextual approaches argue that the rightful interpretive locus for the Bible is among the marginalized. (2) Consequently, their method of interpretation is one grounded in and made operative by the existential concerns of the poor.

(3) Instead of emphasizing difference, these approaches emphasize similarities. They have, in effect, covered up Gotthold Ephraim Lessing's "ugly ditch," the chasm that stands between history (the ancient text) and faith (its modern appropriation).[56] (4) This sort of interpretation, which takes seriously the context of the reader, is not without its obstacles, however. Enumerated by Mesters and Ukpong, the social locations of the marginalized often can impede their liberatory readings of Scripture. (5) This explains why such interpretations are explored in community. In the communal context, the individual worldviews of Bible readers can interact with and be transformed by the readings of their partners. (6) The result is a produced meaning, one that does not feign to be neutral or without theological content. It is an interpretation, a mode of biblical engagement that purposely lends itself to an ethics of social transformation.

The Darkening, or Advent, of African American Interpretation

Transformation has not been confined to the shores of Africa and South America. Breaking the chains of colonialism and apartheid prompted persons of African descent in the United States to develop their own hermeneutical strategies for liberation. Drawing on a long tradition of biblical interpretation going back to slavery, African Americans in the post–World War II era vocalized more than ever before their understandings of a liberated and liberating hermeneutic.

The Eclipse of Eurocentric Theology

Black theology, a form of liberation theology, came explicitly out of the crucible of the 1960s and its social and political tumult. Its real roots go much deeper, however. According to its practitioners, black theology goes back to the slaves' original appropriation of Christianity. As African theologian Edward Antonio describes it, "Black theology represents not just a faddish attempt to redefine Christian teaching in the light of the demands of the social and political forces of the 1960s but a critical search for a historically black Christian form of reflection on issues of racial justice and liberation."[57] As such, it represents a form of social struggle rather than simply an intellectual exercise.

James Cone, arguably the most influential thinker in black theology, has been credited with formulating the basic categories that inform this mode of theological discourse.[58] According to Cone, black theology entails black people reflecting on the black experience.[59] Within the confines of this posited experience, black theologians seek to articulate the historic effects of racism on the lives and psyches of dark-skinned people.

Racism, another intellectual product of the Enlightenment, is not engaged by black theologians as a fallacious intellectual construct, which it is. Instead, because it is a form of social struggle, black theology engages racism as a mode of behavior that privileges the white few at the expense of the colored many. As Antonio persuasively maintains,

> [For] Black theology racism is not just a set of beliefs which say that inherited biological traits determine moral and intellectual dispositions so that some races are not only biologically but, therefore, morally and intellectually better than others, it is also a mode of behaviour which prescribes discriminatory policies intended to work against those considered to be biologically less better off.[60]

In this sense, black theology represents a socially located form of theological reflection. What black theologians seek to address, generally, is the paradox between the continuing influence of racism and the inclusive proclamation (and presumed practice) of the Christian gospel. Contextually stated, black theologians explore the discontinuity between white American claims to be Christian and their seemingly unrelenting racism. More important, black theology is a response to such a situation. If racism constitutes the negative social structure that black theology seeks to address, an affirmation of black humanity is its positive corollary.

As a method of intellectual engagement, this form of Christian reflection operates using the dialectic of "context" and "gospel." That is, it is a movement between essentially two contexts, the situation of the thinker and the situation of the revelation. Neither can be considered a universal perspective. Thus, the theological claims advanced by black theologians are always shaped in interested language, eschewing any pretense of universal application.

Individuals, following Cone's logic, are the products of an effective history of experiences. By this, I mean an individual is (at any given moment) the sum total of all her own experiences as well as those that preceded her, what might also be called a "collective self-understanding."[61] For example, slavery, Jim Crow, and desegregation are part of the effective history of persons of African descent living in the United States. Regardless of the ways each individual has incorporated these experiences into his or her own life, they are part of who he or she is. Cone calls this an individual's biography. It is, in his view, the most determinative factor in the formation of a theological perspective. Given, however, the historical situatedness of such a theological perspective, it would be impossible for black theologians to make claims that pretend to be universally valid. In fact, black theologians adamantly deny the possibility of divine, universal truth claims.[62]

Grounded in the African American experience, or blackness, as its historic and formative context, black theology seeks to make this peculiar, but fundamental, datum of human experience the raw material of its theological reflection, as well as the basis for its hermeneutic of liberation. In this way, black theology has a somewhat different existential grounding than other theologies of liberation that elucidate the structures of oppression through concepts such as "class," "gender," "global capitalism," and so on. Blackness is the central symbol employed in this mode of theological reflection. It should not, however, be reduced to the element of skin color. In this way, black theologians have been able to address other forms of oppression while staying focused on the symbolic center.

According to Cone, "authentic human existence means 'being
in freedom.'"[63] By freedom, he means a concrete negation of oppression. Because freedom must be experienced in the lives of
individuals living within the confines of historically conditioned social structures, it is actually a socialized understanding of human
existence as such. Cone affirms the inescapable relationships individuals have with each other in the present as well as their
collective relationship to the past. Consequently, black theology
also involves the critical appropriation of the effective history that
informs and impinges upon the present.

Two of the most important resources for black theologians
in their critical appropriation of effective history are the biblical witness and tradition. Each serves its own critical role in the
construction of theological claims. I use the term "biblical witness" rather than "the Bible" because black theology considers
the Bible revelatory only insofar as it functions as a witness to
God's ultimate liberatory self-disclosure in Jesus Christ. In this
respect, black theology has been drawn repeatedly to two paradigmatic biblical events: the exodus from Egypt and the ministry of
Jesus Christ. These form, as it were, "the 'objective core' of its
hermeneutic and express God's concern for those in social and political bondage."[64] The other resource for black theology, tradition,
can be subdivided into the main Christian tradition — the historic
process of Christian self-interpretation that shaped the canonical
biblical witness and gives us access to it — and the tradition of re-
bellion, protest, and self-affirmation that characterizes the African
American experience in the United States.

Black theology has made considerable use of the African American tradition as a source for constructing its theological claims
(e.g., the slave narratives). It has been not nearly as effective in using the biblical witness for the same purposes. Unlike the other
contextual approaches to interpretation examined above, black
theology has suffered from two somewhat related problems. The
first is the traditional disinterest among American biblical scholars in theologies of liberation. Although Cone, as a follower of
Karl Barth, believed in the biblical grounding for his theological perspective, confirmation was not to be found in the writings
of mainstream biblical scholarship. In response, Cone wrote his
own biblical interpretation of black theology. Entitled "Biblical
Revelation and Social Existence," it emphasized the historic liberatory activity of God in the Hebrew Bible and preeminently in the

ministry of Jesus Christ.[65] The second problem has been the traditional absence of African Americans in the guild of biblical studies. When black theology emerged, very few African American biblical scholars were practicing in the academy. As Cone and Gayraud Wilmore, the editors of *Black Theology: A Documentary History*, attest,

> By the mid-sixties when Black theology came on the scene there were four or five serious Black students of the Bible, most of them uncredentialed, at Black colleges and theological seminaries, but no predominantly White theological seminary or university department of religion in the United States or Canada employed a single Black person in the biblical field.[66]

For the enterprise of black theology, this absence was critical. Because of the contextual character of black theology, it would be impossible for anyone other than an African American biblical scholar to interpret Scripture through the symbol of blackness. Thus was born a critical need for black theologians: African American scholars of the Hebrew Bible and New Testament — scholars who could explicate the scriptural basis for this liberatory theological enterprise.

The Dark Roots of African American Interpretation

The first few doctorates awarded in biblical studies to African Americans go back to the mid-twentieth century. When Leon Wright received his doctorate in New Testament studies from Howard University in 1945, there were no African Americans with earned doctorates in biblical studies. Of course, scholars in other areas of theological studies wrote extensively on the African American appropriation of the Bible. These studies, mainly sociological in orientation, were not the same as a constructive engagement with the Bible itself. By the 1970s, when a small group of African American Bible scholars began to engage the interpretive implications of black theology, seeds were being planted for a growth in the number of African Americans in the discipline. The last half of the twentieth century would experience a considerable rise in the number of doctoral degrees awarded to African Americans. It may be premature to say that we soon will see the emergence of a critical mass of African Americans engaged in the academic study of the Bible, but positive change is evident nevertheless.

The number of African Americans presently in the academic field of biblical studies is still small. Out of the more than six thousand members of the Society of Biblical Literature (the national organization to which the majority of biblical scholars belong), fewer than fifty are African American. And although their numbers almost doubled from twenty-six in 1995 to forty-five in 2000, they still constitute less than 1 percent of the number of biblical scholars teaching in American colleges, universities, and seminaries.[67] Randall C. Bailey, a Hebrew Bible scholar, laments the history of exclusion that has plagued African Americans' pursuit of doctoral degrees:

> Given the long-standing interests on the part of African Americans in the study of the Bible, one might easily be led to a long pattern of racism and sexism on the part of individuals, academic institutions and the guild in discouraging and even preventing African Americans from pursuing academic doctorates in the field as explanation of the current situation.[68]

Given the phenomenal advances African Americans have made throughout American society, and particularly in the academic study of religion, since the *Brown v. Board of Education* decision in 1954, the influence of systemic racism *in their recruiting, training, and hiring of black Bible scholars can be felt to this very day*. Nevertheless, as African Americans made strides in the attainment of academic doctorates in biblical studies, they increasingly began to challenge the orientation and methods employed by their Euro-American colleagues.

African American biblical scholars have taken seriously, for the most part, the call of black and other liberation theologies for intense engagement with the Bible. Exploring ways in which they could assist the cause of liberation, many African American scholars of the Hebrew Bible and New Testament began to pursue the possibilities for a liberated and liberating reading of Scripture. According to Bailey, they have pursued essentially four different tasks.[69] This taxonomy, although extremely helpful, will not serve as the primary basis for this investigation of African American biblical interpretation. Still, Bailey's outline should serve as a helpful introduction to the enterprise.

The first task of African American interpretation has been to demonstrate an African presence in the Bible. As Bailey says,

"These works take literally all references in the Bible which re-fer to Africans (Egyptians and Cushites) and treat the text as a reliable historical document from which 'historical truth' can be discerned."[70] Beginning with the Table of Nations in Genesis 10, these studies have served as a major corrective to traditional academic interpretations that either implicitly or explicitly excluded Africans from the biblical world. Of course, they also have recognized and addressed the negative portrayal of the descendants of Ham propounded by mainly nonacademics, an interpretation that justified slavery in the United States and elsewhere. Looking at individuals and locations, this mode of engagement sought to inspire a sense of racial pride among persons of African descent living in the United States. Bailey says, "[Once African Americans] realize that these characters in the Bible are not white, but rather black, we will feel better about ourselves, because [Africans] are valued in the Bible."[71]

The second task of African American hermeneutics has been to challenge Eurocentric interpretations of the Bible. As in the case of the Hamite curse, African American biblical interpreters have demonstrated consistently the ways in which their colleagues have erased the African presence from the Bible or stigmatized it as secondary or unimportant. In a similar manner, black scholars have charged the discipline with thoroughgoing Eurocentrism. By this, they mean a mode of biblical engagement and presentation that privileges things European to the detriment of other sociocultural orientations and methods. Yet another related charge has been the de-Africanization of the Scriptures, that is, the obfuscation or erasure of clear African influences in the biblical texts. In all, the African American challenge to the discipline and its procedures has marked a second way in which black voices have intruded into a previously Eurocentric conversation.

The third type of research being done by African American scholars is in the assessment and review of biblical interpretation in the black community. These scholars look at the history of African American interpretation as well as potential new interpretations according to contemporary cultural constructs. As one of its practitioners recently argued, one of "the problems with black religious scholarship is the assumption that the Bible is a major resource in the history of black people without examining in what ways this has or has not been the case."[72] Investigations along these lines have examined the various ways in which African Americans have appropriated the Bible and its many messages. According to Obrey

Hendricks, a New Testament scholar and novelist, African American biblical scholars pursuing this type of research must examine and appropriate their sources carefully, "not just buying into them for their cosmetic value, but to assess them for their liberation potential."[73] Using the dual sources of the Bible and tradition, this task of interpretation has yielded, and most likely will continue to yield, fresh insights into how African Americans can engage the Bible on their own terms.

The last task of African American interpretation has been in the area of ideological criticism. Bailey explains that this mode of engagement involves "trying to discover our story and how to use it as a strategy for reading."[74] Following the lead of the South African biblical scholar Itumeleng Mosala, the practitioners of this form of engagement are not confined to one method of biblical interpretation. They use historical, literary, socio-rhetorical, and other methods in their attempt to unmask the ideologies of the biblical writers. Frequently these scholars assess and critically engage the ideologies of the Bible's readers as well.

Of course, it would be an overstatement to say that all African American biblical scholars pursue an interpretive agenda along the lines of the black theological paradigm. Those who do, however, share much in common with their colleagues in South America and Africa. For example, they agree that interpretation can and should proceed according to a liberatory model. They agree that the existential concerns of readers should play a critical role in the analysis and appropriation of texts. They agree that the Bible is not neutral. As we shall see, however, African American biblical scholars do not always agree with their communally oriented counterparts on the particulars of textual engagement. African American biblical interpretation, like black theology itself, is a distinctive form of theological reflection situated in the North American context.

The title of this chapter suggests that African American biblical interpretation has taken center stage in the program of academic biblical studies in the United States. This is not the case by any means. So few African Americans are involved in the project that, on the surface, such a suggestion would appear laughable. What I am suggesting, however, is that this form of biblical interpretation, guided by the norms of black theology, has become a central disciplinary concern for African American biblical scholars in their quest to develop a distinctive hermeneutical voice. Using primarily Eurocentric methods of biblical interpretation as a backdrop,

African American scholars have begun to explore the implications of taking seriously the role of the reader in front of the text. Like black theology, African American biblical hermeneutics is a largely academic enterprise. That is, for the moment at least, it is a form of theological reflection used by scholars. It has not found a place among the larger African American populace yet. Many people, academics and nonacademics alike, often are confused by this situation. They think that this form of scriptural reading is guided by the contemporary interpretations of ordinary African Americans, as in the contextual interpretations sampled above. Although African American biblical scholars envision this approach as influencing the reading practices of those in the pulpit and pew, and are working hard to bring about this aspiration, one would be mistaken to think that she or he will encounter the modern interpretations of ordinary African Americans in what follows.

Chapter 2

Dark and Prophetic Voices in the Wilderness

The Negro has a history of which he need not be ashamed, but he will wait a long time for a White man to write this history in fairness, for the consumption of the great White public.[1]

A Corrective Historical Lens

As I pointed out briefly in the last chapter, the development of historical criticism as a tool for biblical interpretation is long and varied. Many scholars have already written on this subject, so there is no need for me to rehearse further its development here.[2] The ongoing quest to understand and appreciate the various communities and traditions that gave rise to the Bible is not a simple matter of collecting data. It involves the construction and propagation of a narrative. Although the majority of contemporary historical critics would concede that the task of historical reconstruction is not a purely objective endeavor, the discipline has been unable to distance itself completely from the air of neutrality that has long enshrouded it. The recognition that historical-critical studies, as practiced in the West, are deeply entrenched in Euro-American cultural values came about through the influence of those whose voices had been previously marginalized. Women, African Americans, Latinos, homosexuals, and others have argued persuasively that the dominant narrative of Western civilization, including that propounded by biblical scholars, is deficient insofar as it has neglected the lives and histories of persons who do not fit a narrowly constructed Eurocentric depiction of reality.

Among the first to challenge the dominant narrative were Africans in America. Their exclusion from the dominant cultural

discourse in their diasporic homeland compelled several generations of African Americans to question the validity of the narrative
itself. I will not focus on the long history of African American attempts to subvert the dominant historical paradigm, since that is
a substantial study in its own right. I will confine my discussion
to more recent attempts by African American biblical scholars to
complicate and, at times, undermine the historical-critical enterprise.

Looking at the World through White-Colored Glasses: Charles B. Copher and the Black Presence in the Old Testament

Trained as a historical critic, Charles Buchanan Copher spent
his academic career at Gammon Theological Seminary, a part of
the Interdenominational Theological Center in Atlanta, Georgia,
teaching African American seminary students. An African American scholar teaching in a historically black theological institution,
this context provided the impetus for Copher's explicitly contextual rereading of the Hebrew Bible. As he once wrote, "Granted
that the Bible, along with interpretations of it, have proved to be
and continue to be sources of blessings to millions of people. It is
also true that these have been and continue to be sources of some
of the greatest curses humankind has known."[3]

Using historical-critical tools, Copher reexamines the biblical
narrative put forward by European and Euro-American scholars and concludes that they have attempted to occlude the black
presence in the text. In stark contrast, he asserts, "In the veins
of Hebrew-Israelite-Judahite-Jewish peoples flowed black blood."[4]
Such a provocative statement is the result of Copher's continued
reading and analysis of the Old Testament with respect to its use
of various forms of racial and ethnic identification. Copher lays out
his argument in two key essays.[5]

In his essay "Three Thousand Years of Biblical Interpretation
with Reference to Black Peoples," Copher examines biblical, Jewish, Christian, and Islamic sources with respect to their use of color
designators and other terms for persons of African ancestry.[6] He
argues that before any examination can take place regarding the
way in which later interpreters have understood the Bible's color
designators, one must consider how the biblical authors used the
terms in their own writings. According to him, the Hebrew terms

shahar, hum, kedar, cush, and *hoshek* were used as indicators of
blackness.[7] After examining the use of these terms in various Hebrew Bible texts, Copher concludes, "[The] most probable original
text of the Hebrew was free of pejorative statements about peoples
regarded as Black by the original authors."[8]

Moving on to the Septuagint, Copher points out that it places a
curse on Ham rather than Canaan. Ham, supposedly related to the
Hebrew *hum,* could be understood as a color designator of Noah's
son. Dismissing such a view, Copher says, "What this one manuscript may show at best is a move in the so-called intertestamental
period towards a curse-on-Ham position in some circles or by a
translator or scribe, even though *ham* may not necessarily at the
time refer to blackness."[9]

Copher acknowledges, however, a stream of thought in rabbinic Judaism that provides extensive and pejorative commentary
on black-skinned people.[10] He says,

> Upon these statements will hang later interpretations of the
> Bible with reference to Black persons and peoples among
> Jews, then Muslims, then Christians; and through them they
> will be spread around the world as a deadly poison. There-
> after all the children, not only of Canaan, but also of Ham,
> will be considered to be black: Cushites (Ethiopians), Mitz-
> raimites (Egyptians), Phutities, and Canaanites.[11]

Having established the association between Ham's descendants
and a black skin complexion as a creation of the rabbinic tradition,
Copher examines the portrayal of Africans in early Christianity.
He looks first at the apocryphal and pseudepigraphal texts, and
concludes that they do not contain any negative interpretations of
biblical texts with regard to black-skinned people.[12] After a cur-
sory examination of the rest of early Christian literature, Copher
arrives at the same conclusion. He does acknowledge, however,
that some assertions in Christian texts "do contain statements pejorative in nature with respect to Ethiopians."[13] The vast majority,
nonetheless, are similar to Clement of Alexandria's line of reasoning in *Protr.* 2.36.5.1, where he discusses the role Ethiopia played
in Greek mythology as the place where Zeus feasted (see also, e.g.,
Origen, *Princ.* 4.3.9.22).[14]

Islam is another matter. Relying on the work of Bernard Lewis,
Copher says,

> [A] common explanation of the slave status of the Black
> man among Muslims is that the ancestor of the dark-skinned

people was Ham the son of Noah who (according to Muslim legend) was damned black for his sin. The curse of blackness, and with it that of slavery, passed to all Black peoples who are his descendants.[15]

Copher posits a genetic relationship between the rabbinic materials that characterize blackness in a negative manner and similar interpretations found among Muslim scholars. As he understands it, such negative stereotyping occurred within Judaism well into the Middle Ages and likewise continued to influence Islam and subsequently Christianity. Saadya Gaon's Arabic translation of the Hebrew Bible perpetuated this negative view, and Rabbi Solomon ben Isaac of Troye's exegesis of the Noah story also contributed to this trajectory of misinterpretation.[16] And although it would become a cornerstone of pro-slavery and segregation argumentation, the Hamite curse, subsequently also related to Cain, became, according to Copher, "common in the seventeenth century as an explanation of the Negro's color rather than as a support for slavery."[17]

Many Africans in America resisted such an understanding. Others accepted it. Copher points to Phillis Wheatley, who identified herself as "black as Cain," as one example of such acceptance. In fact, he concedes that "up to a generation ago Black writers boasted proudly of Negroes' being the children of Ham."[18] Such an attitude, Copher points out, was often an occasion of creative cultural adaptation. Instead of emphasizing the so-called curse on Ham, African Americans used him as a symbol of a glorious and ancient African connection to the Bible.[19]

With the advent of historical criticism in the United States, the already questionable Hamite curse was attacked decisively as incredible. And while many would rightly regard this as an advance in biblical historiography, it did have a negative consequence. As Copher points out, when Euro-American biblical scholars refuted the connection between Ham and persons of African descent — "and thus not subjects in the biblical accounts about Cain, Ham, Canaan, or any other biblical character" — they removed African people from the biblical historical narrative altogether.[20] Instead of white masters and black slaves, critical scholarship, perhaps unwittingly, transformed the biblical world into a virtual extension of Europe.

At the end of his essay, Copher observes:

Not to be excluded in an essay of this kind is an aberrant type of Black biblical interpretation that has existed for some two generations and is increasing among several groups. This type goes beyond Black identification of Black peoples with the biblical Hamites and claims that Black peoples are to be identified with the ancient Jews; or with the ancient Hebrew-Israelites, as different from Jews of modern times. For these the Old Testament especially is a collection of writings by and about Black peoples.[21]

This statement, which appears to contradict Copher's earlier declaration, will be examined in more detail below. For now, it is appropriate to say that Copher welcomed the reintroduction of an African (or black) presence in the Bible. He believed that the use of critical methods to read the Bible from an African American perspective would correct some of the historical misinterpretations found both inside and outside academic institutions.

Copher's arguments in this essay are mainly judicious. He makes no effort to push the philological evidence beyond what it can bear. He stops short of making any modern-day application of his findings other than to assert that the history of European and Euro-American noncritical interpretation has been marked by misreading and misapplication. Further, he points out the deficiency of the critical interpretations of this same group of exegetes. Rather than giving persons of African descent their rightful place among biblical peoples, scholars have all but erased their presence entirely. This situation marks no real improvement upon the first. Thus, Copher points the way toward a method of interpreting the biblical texts that places Africans and their descendants in a more positive light.

The sensitive reader might be concerned about Copher's presentation of Jewish and Muslim scholars as opposed to Christian ones. Specifically, Copher places blame for the Hamite curse at the feet of the rabbis and the sheikhs. He speaks of Christians as being almost passively influenced by such readings of Scripture. A fairer assessment of the relationships between Jewish, Islamic, and Christian interpretive practices regarding the curse would allow, in my estimation, for a more active Christian acceptance and application of the Hamite curse.

Copher dismisses the interpretive practices of groups such as the Church of the Living God and the Royal Order of Ethiopian Jews as "aberrant" because they are noncritical and seek to distance modern Jews from their hypothetical ancient predecessors in particular. Ignoring the fact that most modern Jews have a significant amount of European blood running through their veins, Copher fails to draw a distinction between ancient Israelite and Second Temple religion and its modern successor.[22] To be frank, I am not suggesting that the two are unrelated. Still, to posit a genetic relationship between the two would necessitate complex historical argumentation. Copher dismisses the claims of these untraditional interpreters as specious, that is, attractive but devoid of any real substantive content.

Perhaps the most serious question that can be raised against Copher's arguments in this essay has to do with the putative connection between Africans in the Bible and African Americans. The vast majority of Africans one encounters in the biblical world are Cushites/Ethiopians and Egyptians. On the one hand, Copher is correct that both groups are undeniably Africans. His argument then implicitly binds all of Africa together into a presumed cultural unity or, better, relationship. According to this framework, Ethiopia (i.e., all of Africa that is not Egypt) and its preponderantly positive presentation in the biblical texts means that all persons of African descent can read themselves into the biblical narrative as positive figures. On the other hand, such an assumption fails to prove any actual historical contact between ancient Israelites (and Jews) and persons from sub-Saharan Africa, the part of the continent from which the undeniable majority of Africans were exported to Europe and the plantations of the New World. What binds these geographically differentiated groups together, at least according to Copher's presentation, is skin color.

Copher's second essay, entitled "The Black Presence in the Old Testament," takes up many of the same arguments made in the first.[23] In contrast to the first essay, Copher outlines the black presence in eight successive Old Testament periods. After acknowledging five difficulties related to his analysis, he provides an equal number of historical, ethnographical, literary, and academic issues that must be settled for his argument to be persuasive. They are: (1) the color of Hamites and Elamites in the Table of Nations, (2) the modern Euro-American ethnic category of "black," (3) ancient discussions of "race," (4) the use of color designators in ancient Hebrew literature, and (5) modern scholarship's understanding and use of all four.

As in the last essay, Copher examines the so-called Hamite curse. He also discusses the relation between this curse and the curse on Cain. Also discussed briefly in the first essay, but not in my analysis of it, was the pre-Adamite view. According to this perspective, Africans "belong to a black race created before Adam and from among whom Cain found his wife, and thus in this way Cain became the progenitor of black peoples."[24] Copher traces this idea back to the sixteenth century.[25] Criticizing what he calls the New Hamite view — "the opposite of the older view" — Copher points out their inability to read without bias, since its advocates argue that "if there is any such [black] presence [in the biblical texts], it is only that slight bit that may be attributable to the Cushites or Nubians — terminology differing according to particular scholars."[26] Thus, scholarship appears driven to extremes with regard to Africans: If they are present, they must be cursed. If they are not cursed, they must not be present. Copher argues for a more realistic engagement with the Hebrew Bible and the presence of Africans in it.

Once again, Copher uses terms designating color as one way of identifying an African presence, but this time he adds the term *pinehas*. Of it he says, "*Pin^{e}h^{a}s*, from the Egyptian *Pa-Nehsi,* means the Negro or Nubian, depending on a given translator."[27] He observes that Phinehas was the name of Aaron's grandson, suggesting a black presence in the Mosaic genealogy.[28] He notes, in addition, that *ham* was the poetic name of Egypt.[29] This marks a reversal of his earlier stance that *ham* did not refer to blackness.

Focusing specifically on the various periods, Copher describes an appreciable black presence in each: Nimrod in the pre-patriarchal period, and the Sumerians, Hagar, Ishmael and his wife, Kedar, and others in the patriarchal one. He considers the term *Hebrew* indicative of a social status rather than an ethnic classification.[30] Thus, it tells us nothing about the ethnic or racial characteristics of those involved in the exodus. He then argues that Moses' family was black based on (1) the name of his brother's grandson and (2) his identification as an Egyptian by Jethro's daughters in Exodus 2:19. Copher concludes this section of his overview by saying, "[All] of them were black."[31]

In the period from the judges to the exile, he finds several indications of African presence. In the period of the Judges, Copher points to, among other things, the names of Eli's sons, Hophni and Phinehas, both of which are Egyptian.[32] During the united monarchy, he points to the "Cushite," one of the two messengers to King David presumed to be a slave. Challenging this view, Copher says that his status is not given in the text and that ancient slavery would have involved Caucasians rather than blacks.[33] Further, he observes that Solomon's favorite wife was black.[34] He also points to prophecies and historical records in the divided kingdoms period that illustrates a black presence. In fact, prophetic activity predominates Copher's discussion of the later period of the kingdom of Judah.[35]

In the exilic and postexilic periods, Copher points to the depictions of Egypt in, primarily, Ezekiel and Zechariah. He says, "It is not without historical interest to note that according to Ezekiel, Egypt's origins lay in the land of Pathros, Upper Egypt, and that it is there that it will be restored, albeit as a lowly kingdom."[36] The implication is that Ezekiel believed Egypt's origin to be in the south, the area closer to Ethiopia and the rest of "dark-skinned" Africa. Copher concludes the essay by saying, "From slaves to rulers, from court officials to authors who wrote parts of the Old Testament itself, from lawgivers to prophets, black peoples and their lands and individual black persons appear numerous times. In the veins of Hebrew-Israelite-Judahite-Jewish peoples flowed black blood."[37]

Laying aside this provocative conclusion for the moment, we shall examine further Copher's claims by following the unfolding of the argument. First, he contends that Israelites and Greco-Romans would have understood Ethiopians and Egyptians to be black.[38] What warrants his claim, notably with respect to Egypt, is a particular "modern Euro-American ethnic category [designating such persons as] black"; namely, the antebellum notion that even the smallest amount of black blood in one's ancestry makes one black. Moreover, since the idea of Egypt's commingling with its southern neighbors is an accepted axiom in modern scholarship, their Egyptian "blackness" is assured. Copher goes on to say of Nimrod that at least one ancient Hebrew writer "believed civilization in Mesopotamia to owe its origin to a son of Cush, the black one."[39] From a different perspective, however, such racial classification is misleading at best.

Abraham was probably black, according to Copher, because his original home was Ur of the Chaldeans, whose inhabitants included blacks. He classifies the Sumerians as black based on their self-designation as the "black-headed ones," which he maintains really refers to skin color.[40] Continuing this line of reasoning, he links the Sumerians and Abraham, and says, "[There] is reason to believe that black blood flowed in the veins of at least some of the original Hebrew inhabitants, who, many scholars have argued,

were very mixed from the beginning."[41] The veracity of mixed ethnicity is demonstrated undeniably for Copher by the presence of
Hagar, Ishmael, Kedar, and others in the Abrahamic lineage.
Copher appears to accept the accuracy of the biblical narrative. He makes no distinction between the African presence in the
narrative world of the Hebrew Bible and its likely relationship,
if any, to the historical world. In other words, Copher makes a
mistake common to historical critics of the Hebrew Bible: He accepts the biblical narrative on its face and uses it as a basis for
writing history. There continues to be great debate on the his-
toricity of the patriarchal narratives. Thus, Copher's arguments,
as long as they assume historical accuracy, would fail to convince
many. In addition, Copher's argument regarding ethnic classification needs to be analyzed and refined further. Take Moses' family
as an example.

Moses was black, according to four interrelated arguments put
forward by Copher. First, *Hebrew*, as used specifically in the exodus narrative, was a designation for a social class rather than
an ethnic group. Second, Moses was identified as an Egyptian by
Jethro's daughters (Exod 2:19). Third, Moses' wife, Zipporah, was
a Cushite. Finally, the name Pinehas, which means Nubian, gives
the reader a clue to the ethnic origin of the entire family line.
These four things tell us something substantive about the ethnic
makeup of Moses' family. In the accompanying footnote, Copher
emphasizes the existence of Cushites in Asia as well as American
definitions of race as proof for his claim. While conceding that the
most that can be said of the Israelites is that they were of mixed
ethnicity, Copher believes that the vagaries of their ethnicity make
them black in American eyes. Thus, Moses and his family were
black, at least according to how Americans have defined the term.
This argument is far from historically convincing, however. First,
names rarely give us insight into ethnicity, much less skin color, in
antiquity. Second, the fact that Moses looked like an Egyptian tells
us nothing more than how he was dressed. Third, the ethnic origin
of Moses' wife says little about Moses and may only serve to prove
if anything the mixed nature of his subsequent lineage.

Copher makes a provocative statement in his discussion of the
united monarchy. He says, "The truth of the matter...is that in
the ancient biblical world, most slaves would have been what today are called Caucasians rather than Negroes."[42] Copher grounds
this claim on an article entitled "Slavery in the New Testament,"
from *The Interpreter's Dictionary of the Bible Supplement*. The

real complexities of reconstructing a reliable picture of slavery in the ancient world notwithstanding, on its face there is reason to question Copher's assessment. First, the data upon which his claim rests is anachronistic. The differences between the New Testament world and the Old Testament world are ample enough that any information a scholar can draw from slavery in the first century CE could not convincingly correspond to that in the time of Abraham. Second, I take the term *Caucasian* in Copher's statement to mean "white" in a general sense and European specifically. Outside of the fact that the notion of a Caucasian race itself is mythic, there is little evidence to suggest that Europeans played a prominent role as slaves or anything else in the Hebrew Bible narratives.[43]

Turning to the subject of academic bias, Copher highlights Amos 9:7a, which reads, "Are you not like the Ethiopians to me, O people of Israel? says the LORD." He comments, "Typical of much Euro-American biblical interpretation with respect to black people, many commentators give a pejorative interpretation to Amos's comparison, viewing the Ethiopians as a distant and despised people."[44] Copher is undoubtedly correct in his assertion that far too often Euro-American scholars have injected even unwittingly their own cultural and racial biases into their interpretations of biblical texts. Copher places confidence in unbiased historiography as a foil to such continued academic misappropriation. Yet one wonders how much historical weight should be placed on a poetic text such as Amos. When prophets and psalmists compare Israel to other nations, especially Egypt and Ethiopia, are we not to wonder why those nations were chosen? In other words, a variety of motives are at work in these texts that we may not be able to recapture fully. Copher points to history as a way of adjudicating between ideological motives that may have belonged to the original historical setting and those that arose subsequently. And while this may be acceptable when it comes to texts that purport to convey historical data, such a method may not possess the same interpretive value when applied to a text of another literary genre.

Copher points to the "historical records" and the "prophetical books" as objective referents to a black presence in the ancient Israelite world.[45] Yet one must question the degree of sustained, critical historical dissection these texts can withstand. Few, if any, independent historical accounts exist that support the biblical witness. For example, Copher points to Zerah, an Ethiopian, as an example of a black presence during the period of the two king-doms. Following 2 Chronicles, he maintains that Zerah invaded Judah. Yet Copher must concede that there is "no other reference to an Ethiopian ruler with his name."[46] This raises significant issues about an argument that purports to provide proof for a historical presence in the ancient world.

Another example of disputed historical accuracy is Copher's claim regarding the prophet Zephaniah. He argues that Zephaniah was black. He grounds this in the context of the book's super-scription: "The word of the LORD that came to Zephaniah son of Cushi son of Gedaliah son of Amariah son of Hezekiah, in the days of King Josiah son of Amon of Judah" (1:1). Copher clas-sifies Zephaniah as black based on two interrelated arguments: (1) One of Zephaniah's parents was black, or (2) both of Zepha-niah's parents were black. The argument for the African ethnicity of Zephaniah's father resides in his name, Cushi. He points out that some scholars have argued that there is no ethnic significance to the father's name at all.[47] Copher, believing that names convey ethnicity, argues that Cushi informs the reader of the subject's skin color. Others argue that Zephaniah's mother was black. The main proponent of this view has been Gene Rice. It has been disputed as well. Copher appears to accept Rice's argument nevertheless. He concludes unflinchingly that Zephaniah was "indeed a native Ju-dahite, black in color."[48] Following the logic Copher has developed thus far regarding ancient Israelite ethnicity, such an argument ini-tially appears valid. Again, however, we must question the relative historical weight that can be placed on the prophet's hypothetical self-description. As I pointed out, serious questions of method and proof (independent or otherwise) lie behind any such attempt to make historically valid ethnic claims.

Returning to Copher's conclusion, we must say that the claim that the ancient Israelites were black is based on a particular read-ing and appropriation of the Hebrew Bible. As it stands, there is little or no verifiable connection between the literary forms and world of the Hebrew Bible and the historical one to which a claim such as this by necessity refers. Copher is correct when he says that in the various narratives, poems, and prophecies of the Old Testa-ment there is an incredible amount of mixing between Israelites and Africans, specifically Egyptians and Ethiopians. And although the real historical questions surrounding this literature are in dis-pute, Copher's arguments are undeniably correct with respect to the biblical story.

A Book by Africans for Africans: Cain Hope Felder and the Black Presence in the New Testament

Cain Hope Felder, who teaches at Howard University Divinity School, has been instrumental in advancing the program of African American biblical interpretation. Like Copher, his context has involved preparing African Americans for ministry. His book *Troubling Biblical Waters: Race, Class, and Family* has functioned as a landmark in this emerging method of biblical criticism. Although trained as a New Testament scholar, Felder writes on subjects in both testaments.

Quite often in his writings, Felder expresses his adherence to the black liberation perspective that undergirds his entire interpretive project.

[The] rise and proliferation of liberation theologies (Black, Latin American, or Asian), feminist theologies, and contextual theologies that we have witnessed in the last two decades have come to represent profound impatience with Bible scholars who have been perceived as less than helpful in clarifying important but complex hermeneutical issues.[49]

Quieting such impatience is at the core of Felder's work. His liberatory framework allows him to advocate a political vision of emancipation for persons of African descent in the United States. Although he challenges an Eurocentric vision, Felder does not advocate the superiority of Africans and their descendants over their European, Asian, or other counterparts. He embraces multiculturalism as a core component of a just society. Moreover, to create this society, Felder embraces explicitly an ethics of transformation.[50] Such transformation interpretively involves seeing the biblical world, with all its diversity of ethnicities and cultures, as paradigmatic for modern life in the United States and elsewhere. To effect transformation he attempts to dismantle the dubious modern notion of prejudice by reclaiming the black (African) presence in the sacred narratives.

Felder's writings represent a considerable body of work on the subject of African American critical engagement with Scripture.[51] Because of his prolificacy, we will concentrate our analysis on *Troubling Biblical Waters* and incorporate Felder's other writings into the discussion where applicable.

Felder begins *Troubling Biblical Waters* with a statement that reveals his analysis to be one of corrective historiography. He says,

The purpose of this book is to provide some sorely needed correctives regarding the Bible in relation to ancient African and Black people today. Despite the fact that the Bible has a favorable attitude about Blacks, post-biblical misconstruals of biblical traditions have created the impression that the Bible is primarily the foundational document of "the White Man's religion."[52]

Persons of African descent have been excluded from the biblical narrative or maligned by racially motivated readings of the text because of a "quiet consensus" among biblical scholars that when the Bible speaks of Africa, it does not mean black Africa. Felder describes this interpretive "sleight of hand" as an attempt to consider "the mixed stock of ancient Afro-Asiatics as somehow 'nonblack.'"[53] Given the construction of American culture in particular, Felder appears offended that such a racialized culture would neglect its own construction of blackness. Since "racial classification" in the United States defines "a person as black... on the basis of the most miniscule amount of traceable African descent," American academics and religious leaders are hypocritical in their blindness toward the biblical narratives.[54] If Americans were true to their racialized readings of sacred texts, they would be forced to acknowledge that the people who inhabited the ancient biblical story world were black.

Felder's book is divided into three broad sections. The first concentrates on race. Two of the three chapters devoted to this topic discuss explicitly Old Testament issues. The second section focuses on the topic of class. Chapter 4 addresses the biblical mandates regarding justice. Chapter 5 focuses on how the Bible is used in historically African American churches. Chapters 6 and 7 discuss class issues in Galatians and James. The final section concentrates on family. Chapter 8 is an explicit consideration of black women and ordained ministry. Chapter 9 looks at the construction of family in the biblical world and its parallel construction in contemporary Christian discourse. The last chapter addresses family in a broad sense as a basis for Felder's discussion of the possibility of nuclear annihilation.

Felder enjoys employing technical terms and concepts as a mechanism for structuring his arguments. For example, the discussion in chapter 1 is structured around the idea of recontextualization. By this, Felder means a "process of rediscovering some essential features of the Black religious experience in Africa, including, but not limited to, African traditional religions, and doing this as one enters a new dialogue of liberation and spirituality as found in the Bible."[55] It further means "self-perpetuating liberation and the perpetual self-critique of those who would lead in the process."[56]

Felder begins chapter 1 with a discussion of the black religious experience, something he believes to be a coherent part of the overall culture. This leads in turn to a discussion of the role of the Bible in that experience. Felder argues that "biblical stories, themes, personalities, and images have inspired, captivated, given meaning, and served as a basis of hope for a liberated and enhanced material life [for African Americans]."[57] He credits the experience of enslavement for the allegiance of persons of African descent to the Bible. Their recognition of biblical authority came, he maintains, from an "experiential sympathy" with the stories of the Hebrew Bible and New Testament.[58] With this he implies that African Americans in particular understand biblical authority in a manner that is distinct from the Euro-American dogmatic statements that form the basis of even many historically black denominations.[59] The same is true for the Bible as such; African Americans relate to it differently.

Felder contends that the biblical canon — the product of centuries of Jewish and Christian reflection on God's purported communicative presence in their communities — is in truth an arbitrary creation of persons with various theological motives. Consequently, African Americans have never believed in or accepted the Bible in the same way as many of their Euro-American counterparts. Seeing the Bible as authoritative, African Americans traditionally have bypassed the related issue of its normativity. Acceptance of the canon as such as normative by African Americans would only validate a certain "triumphalism" that promotes a self-serving and predominantly European understanding of the tradition.[60] In contrast, Felder argues for another norm for determining the Word of God amid the words of Scripture: liberation. He says, "People must seek to liberate themselves from the popular tendency to deify the Bible as *the* definitive and exclusive Word of God, as if God's entire revelation only exists in the canon of biblical literature."[61] In effect, he raises a concern central to many modern critiques of bibliolatry.[62] Felder would most likely agree with Schubert Ogden, who said, "The theological authority of Scripture, great as it may be, is nevertheless a limited authority, in that it could conceivably be greater than it is — namely, as great as that of the apostolic witness by which it itself is and is to be authorized."⁶³ Using liberation as his hermeneutical lens, Felder points to this notion of recontextualization as a means to correct a narrow Eurocentric bias in canonization and interpretation.

One aspect of the Eurocentric bias in biblical studies has involved the exclusion of serious black scholarship from the general disciplinary discourse. Incorporating the "knowledge of subjugated peoples," as Felder likes to identify it (quoting Michel Foucault), into the mainstream of biblical studies would mean reorienting the discipline radically. Pointing to the results of over a century of scholarship, beginning with the efforts of Henry Sylvester Williams in 1900, Felder concludes that (1) writers of African descent have recognized the implicit racism in much of the Western intellectual tradition and that (2) Africa can serve as a focal point for a renewed type of scholarly inquiry. This is the essence of what scholars call Afrocentrism: placing Africa rather than Europe at the center of any analysis of the black religious experience.⁶⁴ If this approach is pursued, according to Felder, then persons of African descent, as well as others, can carve out a new international African identity that moves toward liberation and King's vision of the beloved community.⁶⁵

Marking the rise of Egypt as the impetus for the recorded black religious experience, Felder advances three claims. First, the growth and development of Egyptian civilization had more to do with African cultural resources than with those from the outside. Second, Egyptian religion as a subset of the larger cultural experience is a reflection of African cultural influence as well. Third, Egypt's leaders, the pharaohs, were black Africans. The importance of these arguments resides in Felder's effort to point out systematic racial bias in Western scholarship that overlooks the obvious. He protests, "[The] West has invented a hypothetical white Pharaonic [Egypt] that imported [its] civilization from Asia."⁶⁶ Each of Felder's three claims is complicated by the racialized lens he uses to support specifically his strong suggestion that Egypt's leaders were black. He says, "The point is that there is evidence to suggest, that, *by modern standards of race,* the indigenous Pharaohs of the Eighteenth to the Twenty-fifth Dynasties (ca. 1500–653 BC) were for the most part probably black."⁶⁷ Although it is a less than robust historical assertion, if Felder's claim for Egyptian racial classification is correct, then his two other claims gain credibility as a matter of course. Independently of one another, however, Felder's claims raise serious questions. Take, for example, his assertion about religion. It argues implicitly for a black African cultural unity. This unity, I contend, does not reflect actual circumstances. It is a heuristic rule that fails to clarify the real relationships, if any, between the various African civilizations.

Felder's description of Egyptian religion, like his description of sub-Saharan African religion, betrays an attempt to force African religious traditions into a now dominant Western religious model. In his description of Egyptian religion, Felder attempts to draw authentic relationships between ancient Egyptian theology and subsequent Jewish, Greco-Roman, and by implication Christian theological understandings. Despite the fact that Egyptian religion consisted of a wearying diversity of local gods and temples, Felder does the same thing Greco-Roman writers did; namely, attempt to force Egyptian religious views and practices into a nationalistic pantheon that is analogous to those of the Greeks and the Romans.[68]

Likewise, Felder describes sub-Saharan African religion as if it were one step away from Christianity. He says, "The New Testament world, particularly as reflected in the canonical Gospels and Acts of the Apostles, is in many ways congenial to the world of the ancient Black religious experience, despite Bultmannian demythologizing."[69] It is an appealing picture without question. The problem, however, resides in the nature and substance of the analogies between African religions and Christianity that Felder puts forward (i.e., what exactly he means by "in many ways"). Generalized similarities between the two religious systems are not sufficient proof to carry Felder's claim. Such analogies between religious systems often are used by scholars as a way of uncritically forcing polytheistic systems to conform to the dominant Western religious ideology. When this is done, the distinctive character of each polytheistic system becomes distorted and caricatured for the sake of advancing an arguably triumphalist religious and cultural agenda. At most, such analogies are strongly suggestive.[70] Their truth-value can extend only so far. Felder's argument regarding the congeniality of Christianity and African religions, like those of most Euro-American scholars regarding Christianity and antiquity, cannot go far beyond the level of the superficial. As such, it can be accepted only with a great deal of historical qualification.

Felder, like Copher, lays out a program of corrective historiography in his discussion of the African (black) presence in the Bible. Outside of Egyptians and Ethiopians, Felder agrees with Copher that those liberated from bondage in the exodus were "a racially mixed stock of people — Afroasiatics."[71] He goes on further to

argue for the blackness of the Messiah by reading Matthew from
a distinct liberation perspective. From his perspective, the commitment, suffering, and liberating activity performed by the Messiah
render him, by nature, a person of liberated stock; that is, of the
same ethnicity as his exodus ancestors. Felder maintains that the
Hebrew Bible and ministry of Jesus not only form the core of African American theology because of their liberatory content, but also
serve an ethno-cultural purpose in that the biblical characters are
also black.[72]

These and other historical claims highlight Felder's idea of
recontextualization. A self-perpetuating liberation, along with a
decidedly epistemological privilege, is the only way to fulfill the
Bible's vision of a just human community. Through the rule of in-
ference, Felder claims that the ethnicity of the majority of biblical
characters, even arguably the most important biblical character,
is Afroasiatic or black. Let us focus specifically on his claim for
the ethnicity of Jesus, an argument Felder elaborates on in other
articles.[73]

Felder begins his argument by claiming that Jesus' mother,
Mary, must have been of the same ethnic stock as her ancestors
and had an appearance similar to that of the typical "Yemenite,
Trinidadian, or African American today."[74] He is forced to focus
on the ethnicity of Mary because of Christian traditions regarding
the nature of Jesus' birth. That is, if one accepts the traditional
Christian claim that Jesus was conceived by a mysterious relationship between Mary and the Holy Spirit, then the entirety of
Jesus' ethnicity derives from his mother. If one takes a more critical
perspective and accepts the likelihood that Jesus was the product of a union between Joseph and Mary, then, accepting the
claim that both his parents were of Afroasiatic descent, the ge-
nealogical narratives in Matthew and Luke serve to substantiate
Felder's view, at least paternally. If, however, one concedes the possibility of the truthfulness of extra-biblical materials, and Jesus
was the product of a union between Mary and a Roman, then
Jesus was both Afroasiatic and European (i.e., given the idea that
"Roman" stands as an ideological representation for Europeans
in ancient rabbinic literature).[75] At any rate, whether of mixed or
"pure" Afroasiatic stock, according to Felder's perspective, Jesus
was black. This conclusion then serves to substantiate the plausibil-
ity of the flight to Egypt in the Matthean narrative (Matt 2:13–15).
Only Afroasiatics could successfully hide among other Afroasiatics,
according to Felder's reasoning. This does overlook, however, the

fact that Greco-Romans (what Felder would call Europeans) also lived in Egypt and that ancient methods of espionage were not nearly as sophisticated as they are today. In chapter 2 of *Troubling Biblical Waters,* Felder discusses the ethnicity of the Queen of Sheba. After a considerable amount of analysis and discussion, he proves at least four points: (1) The actual place of origin for the Queen of Sheba is in dispute. (2) The amount of historical data on this matter is scarce at best. (3) Several modern groups have conflicting claims. (4) The African American claim regarding her ethnicity is just as valid as any other claim. As with arguments involving ethnicity in general, who defines the terms and how they are manipulated pretty much determines the persuasive outcome of the discourse. Thus, Felder's corrective historiographic program challenges and dislocates the now dominant Western historical narrative by offering an alternative reconstruction of events.

Along with the often compelling character of his historical claims, Felder is successful in achieving his goal of Afrocentricity. The complexities of the inferences he uses notwithstanding, Felder displaces European or Western history as the locus for biblical historiography and puts Africa squarely at the center. Under his hermeneutical lens, the characters who inhabit the biblical world are predominantly Afroasiatics. The Bible then becomes a collection of works about persons of African descent with a particular message for modern African descendants and others. In taking on the scholarly community, Felder says, "It was a sign of academic racism that thoroughly sought to de-Africanize the sacred story of the Bible along with the whole sweep of Western civilization."[76] What Copher only suggests, Felder states bluntly. He blames academics and their minions for perpetuating a systematic exclusion and distortion of the African presence in the Bible. Felder's program of interpretation releases Euro-American scholars (and others) to envision a new liberative human community by forcing them to see themselves on the margin rather than at the center. The sheer level of discomfort, he believes, will convict, convert, and conform the Eurocentric to a new standard of social existence.

A renewed collective existence lies behind Felder's push for a pluralistic social vision. When he examines the ancient theories of race in chapter 3 of *Troubling Biblical Waters,* Felder agrees with Copher's assessment that the ancients did not possess any elaborate definitions of the idea. Yet they did have a color consciousness, although such a consciousness was not ideologically motivated. The Israelites in particular do not seem to have gone beyond superficial color recognition in the Hebrew Bible. Felder suggests that part of the reason for this positive racial attitude involves the mixed ethnicity of the persons who escaped from Egypt. As he points out, the term *Semite* does not denote an ethnicity as much as it does a language family.

Again, Felder clusters his arguments around two key technical concepts: sacralization and secularization. Sacralization means "the transposing of an ideological concept into a tenet of religious faith in order to serve the vested interest of a particular ethnic group."[77] In contrast, secularization means "the diluting of a rich religious concept under the weighty influence of secular pressures (social or political)."[78] In the secularizing process, a powerful religious concept, such as that of gender equality, becomes weakened by cultural and ideological influences outside the religious sphere. In other words, the radical message of the gospel is undermined by the efforts of a nonliberatory social structure. What binds both concepts together is their common effect: the subjugation and marginalization of certain social groups.

Felder points to the Hamite curse of Genesis 9:18–27 as one example of sacralization. He calls it an "ethnological etiology."[79] Working through the form critical issues surrounding the passage, he concludes that the earliest version of the story referred only to Ham, but its later version reflects political developments in Palestine that attempted to justify the subjugation of Canaanites and Philistines.[80] It also reflects a sacralist move by interpreters of the Hebrew Bible, as this curse sanctioned the enslavement of sub-Saharan Africans. His second example involves Israelite genealogies, which he labels "theologically motivated."[81] He says, "Critical study of these genealogies illuminates theological motives that inevitably yield an increasing tendency to arrange different groups in priority, thereby attaching the greatest significance to the Israelites as an ethnic and national entity, greater than all other peoples of the earth."[82]

To highlight his claim that the genealogies are an imperfectly developed form of racism out of line with the fundamental thrust of Scripture, Felder puts forward Moses' wife, Zipporah, and says, "God's stern rebuke of Miriam's and Aaron's incipient racial prejudice is a perpetual reminder of the extraordinarily progressive racial values of the Bible in comparison to the hostile racial attitudes in the medieval and modern period."[83] Felder suggests in *Troubling Biblical Waters* that the ethnocentric attitude expressed by Aaron and Miriam reflects a bias against Zipporah based on skin color, but in "Race, Racism, and the Biblical Narratives," he rethinks this position and argues that the bias was based on class. Surprisingly, he contends that Zipporah was of a higher social class than Moses and the other Hebrews.[84]

In his last example of sacralization, Felder points to the development of the doctrine of election in the Deuteronomic period. He contrasts this understanding of election with the later use of the term "the elect" in the New Testament. The author concludes that the idea of election strengthened the perception of Israel as a "race," but such an exclusivist vision rightly fell apart under the universalist vision of the gospel in the New Testament. If Felder is correct, this would be an example of an idea coming full circle: an idea that was sacralized and then rejuvenated as potent religious doctrine. Election, which began as a component of a universal divine scheme, became an indicator of ethnic superiority under the influence of the Deuteronomist, but later was destabilized by the church in its proclamation of an election free of ethnic or racial bias.

Felder points to secularization in the New Testament by examining the motives of its authors first. On the one hand, he argues that the New Testament's vision of human society is one of "racial inclusiveness and universalism."[85] On the other hand, he concedes that the New Testament tendency to prioritize Rome over Jerusalem constitutes a first step toward Eurocentrism. It is perplexing, however, to fathom that an author or authors would both advance and dilute a vision at the same time. If Felder is correct in his assertion that the New Testament authors embrace pluralism, then they are responsible for its advancement and proclamation even today. Yet he says they compromised. They diluted the very vision for which they are largely accountable. He gives an example to prove his point.

Looking at the Ethiopian official as an example of secularization, Felder says that Luke intended to place more importance on Cornelius's baptism than on the Ethiopian's.[86] Along with envisioning a racially pluralistic community in Acts 11, Luke also advocates a "Roman-centered world," an idea that allows his "vision of universalism to be undermined."[87] By giving Cornelius priority, the author of Acts suggests a divine preference for Europeans.[88] In this instance, Felder contends, the biblical author allows secularization to determine the limits of his kerygmatic witness.

Both sacralization and secularization present the modern interpreter with problems. How can one separate a valid religious concept from a sacralized ideology, or how can one detect the weakening of a religious ideal, without making a priori decisions regarding what the ideal should be? Indeed, Felder embraces certain theological tenets that inform his examination of these texts. And, as he deftly points out, others do as well. All historians construct their narratives entirely, or in part, on data that should be amenable to verification. This does not remove, unfortunately, the influence of the historian from the process. Her attentiveness to certain matters, or lack thereof, strongly determines the final form of the historical narrative. And since subjective bias cannot be banished, one is left to adjudicate between competing claims. For example, in his discussion of the priority of Cornelius's baptism in Acts, Felder claims that Luke, perhaps unwittingly, displayed a preference for Europe over Africa. Another way to interpret the differences in these episodes would be to say, as Felder does, that Luke displayed a preference for Rome. As a political, historical, geographical, and ideological construct, Europe did not exist in the first century CE. What one had, to oversimplify the matter, was the Roman world and the non-Roman world. Various ethnic groups comprised the empire, including northern Africans and Europeans. In fact, outside of his name, which was common, and his occupation, we know very little about Cornelius. We certainly cannot make any determinations regarding ethnicity from Acts 10:1, unless we assume that the Romans excluded all non-Europeans (although I am being anachronistic) from the armed forces. And there is more than ample evidence to prove the opposite.[89] Whatever factors may have influenced the author of Acts, it does not seem appropriate to say that he, even unwittingly, displayed a preference for Europeans over Africans. Clearly, later interpreters, especially those of European descent, may have constructed such an interpretive paradigm, as Felder also indicates, but then the blame resides with them and not with Luke.

In part 2 of *Troubling Biblical Waters*, Felder takes up the issue of class. As Felder situates the discussion, the Bible represents "a distinctive body of ancient literature with particular regard for the problem of social class as a religious problem, whether in ancient Palestinian Judaism or in the life of the early Church outside Palestine."[90] After working through Platonic and Aristotelian ideas of justice, he takes up the topic in the Old Testament and intertestamental literature. According to Felder, what distinguishes the Israelite and Jewish idea of justice from that of their ancient neighbors is the strong horizontal orientation of its ethics. Justice and righteousness became synonymous in the Hebrew mind. Further, Felder says there is an identifiable trend in the Hebrew Bible toward "more equitable humanitarian measures extended to all members of the community or to others within its confines."[91]

When it comes to the New Testament, Jesus is the paradigmatic figure and advocate for the justice of God. When Jesus speaks of love for one's neighbor, Felder says this applies to any human being, regardless of ethnicity, social standing, or communal affiliation. It is expressed most succinctly in tangible acts — acts that bespeak an unqualified love, or agape. He explains, "The significance of these forms of love in relation to Christian justice is that the interest of others is stressed as a norm for Christian social relations."[92] Whenever the ethical mandates for justice in the gospel are overlooked, Christianity becomes anemic and otherworldly. Felder believes that African American hermeneutics is one of the best ways to keep Christians acutely aware of their ethical responsibilities.

Felder outlines five forms of justice present in the New Testament. The first, reciprocal justice, is the mandate for fairness in Christian social relations. It is empathetic. As defined by Felder, the recipient of reciprocal justice is "obliged to become a medium of empathy, mercy, and forgiveness for others."[93] To illustrate, Felder points to the judgment scene in Matthew 25. At the same time, this text points to another form of justice identified by Felder: eschatological justice. To be meted out on the Day of Judgment, this form of justice is reckoned by God on believers and their actions. Interestingly, Felder argues that punishment is not an effective goal of eschatological justice; rather, it symbolizes a hope for repentance. The third form of justice is compensatory. It is the moral process of restoring persons to wholeness. As he says, "Through healings, acts of mercy, and forgiveness, or direct confrontations with the conventional authorities, the ministry of Jesus in each gospel constitutes the paradigm of divine compensations."[94] The final two forms of justice, commutative and charismatic distributive, are closely linked in Felder's writing to the Apostle Paul. The first involves the prevention or reduction of potential injury to others. The second involves what is normally understood as distributive justice, except in the charismatic realm. In both cases, Felder points to some situation confronted by the apostle as an illustration of his point. Contrary to one's expectation, Felder does not include women in his list of the recipients of justice. Contradicting the work of Elisabeth Schüssler Fiorenza and other feminists, he maintains, "[I]t would be an exaggeration to say that in these teachings Jesus advocates *full equality* between men and women."[95] At most, Felder allows that the New Testament encourages more equitable treatment of women, including allowing them some leadership in the fledgling church.

The last two chapters of this section address the issue of class in Galatians and James. Felder picks up the concept of freedom as central to the class discussion in Paul's letter to the churches of Galatia. He begins with a provocative hermeneutical claim:

> Over the centuries, the New Testament has affirmed the desirability of freedom for all persons and highlighted the impropriety of discriminating against people because of outward appearance and social standing. Nevertheless, especially since the African slave trade, Western churches have had great difficulty allowing themselves to be guided by the biblical visions of freedom and human equality.[96]

He goes on to advance his claim by raising concerns about the African American context: "[There] are indications, even within the Black Church, of a resurgence of a class consciousness that imitates patterns of the dominant culture."[97] In short, Felder wants to examine and criticize Western class consciousness, particularly in the United States, by looking at what he believes to be an analogous situation in first-century Galatia.

In his examination of the concept of freedom, Felder charges that the American notion of freedom is parochial and self-interested. In contrast, he maintains that biblical notions of freedom point toward the attainment of authentic human existence. Yet he recognizes that there are problems. First, the Old Testament, which proclaims the liberation of Israelites, also allows for the enslavement of non-Israelites. Second, the New Testament writers appear to sanction, or at least tolerate, the practice of slavery in the Roman Empire. Nevertheless, Felder argues that Jesus serves as the paradigm for a praxis of freedom. To illustrate his point, the author uses the temptation story in the gospels of Matthew and Luke as an indication of Jesus' rejection of potentially enslaving human situations (see Matt 4:1–11; Luke 4:1–13). Felder further augments his view of Jesus by saying that he identified with the marginalized. What he overlooks, however, are the parables of Jesus. Many of them use slaves as their main actors. Contrary to the expectations implied by Felder, the concern of Jesus' slaves is not freedom. In none of the parables is the institution ever even questioned. Moreover, the parable of the wicked tenants presents a particular problem, because in it Jesus sides with the absentee landlord against the tenants (Matt 21:33–46; Mark 12:1–12; Luke 20:9–19). In other words, Felder's argument for a biblical notion of freedom that represents a clear and convincing rejection of all forms of discrimination cannot hold up under examination. Even Jesus, Felder's paradigmatic embodiment of freedom, contradicts the epistemological privilege he advocates.

Looking directly at Galatians, Felder characterizes the historical situation as one of a crisis in values and identity. The churches of Galatia fall prey to a radically Jewish presentation of the gospel because of an abuse of their Christian freedom. By accepting this Jewish understanding of Christianity, the Galatians appropriated a class distinction inherent in its message and practice. Paul's inclusive vision of the Christian community — one without distinction between Jew and Gentile believer — is undermined by these missionaries and their Galatian followers. As Felder says, "There can be no preference to those of high social and economic-class status in Paul's teachings, and he carefully applies the principle in Galatians when dealing with the Jewish Christian leadership in Palestine."[98]

Felder detects a political dimension to Paul's message of inclusiveness in Galatians. It entails active resistance "to any form of human bondage as part of the cost of freedom."[99] This radical understanding of Christian freedom appears to be based primarily on statements Paul makes in Galatians 3:27–28 and 5:1.[100] Felder connects this idea of freedom to an Enlightenment view of human nature when he calls it "an inalienable right."[101] Thus, the gospel's call to freedom is a matter of the restoration of humanity to its primordial condition, an idea others have detected in Paul's thought as well.[102] In sum, Felder reads Galatians as a political statement for the acceptance and inclusion of all persons into the Christian community irrespective of race, class, or ethnic background.

Felder's vision of an inclusive Christian community is a worthy goal without question. However, I am not convinced that his reading of Galatians can carry the full weight he places on it. First, Paul's argument in Galatians is political only insofar as it reflects ecclesial disputes. Arguing for anything more than that would be

a misrepresentation of the text. Second, the presence of such a disagreement within the church calls into question Felder's idea that
the gospel as manifested in the ministry of Jesus and the subsequent preaching of the apostles was always one of inclusion. In
fact, Paul's purpose for writing Galatians was to argue for the
acceptability of his particular presentation of the gospel message
against those who understood it differently — some of whom were
the original disciples and even family of Jesus. The tacit acceptance
of Paul's gospel, as evidenced in his recitation of the apostolic con-
ference, demonstrates that the notion of inclusivity may have been
novel to the early church (Gal 2:1–10). Third, although Galatians
is most certainly an argument against a certain ethno-religious construal of human relations, especially the status consequences that
can be derived from such a construal, its acceptance into the Christian canon is as much a result of the failure of the Jewish mission
as it is a result of the validity of Paul's arguments. The erosion and
death of the Jewish Christian movement meant that the Pauline
argument for real inclusivity was in effect moot. The final point
that complicates Felder's argument has to do with his portrayal of
Galatians as a class argument. While it is not entirely inconceivable
that Jewish Christians saw themselves as holding a superior status
in the early community, it is not clear that that status should be
translated into class any more than it could be equated with ethnicity or culture. Felder appears to be most correct when he says that
the crisis in Galatians is predicated on the loss of a clear identity
among the believers. Identity in antiquity appears to have con-
gealed around practices related to one's ethno-religious allegiances.
Paul's gospel of radical freedom from such allegiances must have
posed a problem for the Galatians because it promoted exclusive
religious allegiance without the usually attendant ethnic identifiers.
Paul's opponents offered a clear identity because they worshiped
a Jewish messiah and lived according to a Jewish paradigm that
included the observance of dietary rules, circumcision, and other
ethnic practices. Whether such an identity constitutes a class is not
readily apparent.

   Felder is on much better ground in his argument on James. Here
a clear argument against class bias is put forward in James 2:1–
13. When James questions the community's practice of favoritism
and argues that "God [has] chosen the poor in the world to be rich
in faith and to be heirs of the kingdom that he has promised to
those who love him" (Jas 2:5), he is clearly manifesting a strong
position against the class consciousness that pervaded the social

structure of the Roman Empire. Of course, Felder is not content to allow the text to speak solely on the issue of class discrimination. He wants to push it to include a critique of racial discrimination insofar as race is an aspect of outward appearance. Again, Felder points to the Hebrew Bible and the Jesus tradition as the grounding for James's stance on class preference. Here the vision of inclusiveness as an ethical mandate upon the Christian community shines through most vividly.

What is not so clearly seen in Felder's interpretation of James is his Afrocentricity. In fact, outside of the few punctuated remarks in the essay regarding the resurgence of class consciousness among African Americans, this interpretation of James represents a more traditional approach to the project of biblical hermeneutics. The fertile ground that Felder does not exploit in his argument can be found in James 2:6: "But you have dishonored the poor. Is it not the rich who oppress you? Is it not they who drag you into court? Is it not they who blaspheme the excellent name that was invoked over you?" The idea of a group of people who are oppressed in turn oppressing others and imitating the pretensions of those who despise them is dealt with only lightly in Felder's analysis. Here the idea of identity, as well as social or ethno-religious allegiance, could have been exploited fully. Instead of a robust argument in favor of epistemological privilege, what one encounters in Felder's essay is a rather anemic evaluation of the contemporary American social situation in light of a clear ethical mandate.

Felder ends his analysis of class discrimination by arguing that James shares with other New Testament authors "an ancient vision of the Church as a socially concerned paradigmatic 'family.' "[103] This statement serves as an introduction of sorts to the third major section of his book. By family, Felder means "a biblical metaphor of kinship patterns and obligations that characterizes the Household of God in general."[104] Outside the metaphor, he points to the family structures portrayed in the biblical materials and finds an "astonishing variety of household arrangements."[105] His main concern is to address a problem in the African American community surrounding the issue of family obligation. Particularly, he is concerned that the black church no longer functions as a family.

The section begins with a discussion of women, specifically the issue of African American women in ministerial leadership. As he has many times before, Felder commences with a provocative statement: "[Everything] begins with Mary."[106] This recognition

that women are foundational to the process of human creation itself, and therefore the cornerstone of familial existence, calls into
question centuries of Western and biblical rhetoric regarding their
subordinate status. Somewhat oddly, Felder chooses not to examine the roles of black women in the Bible, admitting that "such
a procedure might lead to unproductive and unnecessary squab-
bling," although he does make reference to the Queen of Sheba as
black.[107] After admitting the male dominance of the biblical narrative, Felder argues that the ministry of Jesus provides evidence that
women began to be viewed as "entitled to greater rights as human
beings."[108]

Of course, Felder begins his analysis with Mary, the mother of
Jesus. Pointing specifically to her portrayal in Luke, he concludes
that Mary is paradigmatic of the socially concerned woman. He
then moves on to various other women contained in the gospel
narratives, including the Syrophoenician woman. In this case, he
concludes that Luke's goal is to emphasize the work of the Holy
Spirit in the early church to include women among the legitimate
members of the community.

Moving to Paul, Felder draws a distinction between disputed
and undisputed Pauline texts. This allows him to dismiss the majority of statements on the status of women in the New Testament
corpus as being late and unreflective of the apostle's personal position on the matter. The few passages that are left to consider
come from Galatians, Romans, and 1 Corinthians. Calling upon
the statement found in Galatians 3:28, Felder concludes that this
was a challenge to emancipate women within the church, not the
larger society. He follows up this assertion with a discussion of
the women named in Romans 16. He believes that this list demonstrates that Paul had no problem with women in ministerial
leadership. He dismisses the statements regarding women in 1 Corinthians as interpolations. Yet Felder appears to understand that
the New Testament canon cannot be relied upon to give a clear
and consistent view of women as liberated members of the early
community. He therefore concludes,

> The most substantive challenge offered by the New Tes-
> tament is to take full cognizance of its rich diversity and
> simultaneously develop the kind of hermeneutic that recog-
> nizes the mundane or human character of the struggles on the
> part of ancient communities of faith in transition as preserved
> in the New Testament.[109]

This historically critical and sensitive statement made by Felder blunts his argument regarding women, rendering it no more than a liberatory suggestion. Still, this essay on women, although somewhat superficial, reflects a concern among liberationists for the emancipation of all human beings. One may wonder, however, whether Felder's emphasis on the church as a family may not imply unwittingly the continued subordination of women as participants in the domestic sphere and not the civic one.

This concern rises when Felder turns to his discussion of families. Again, his discussion of women is muted. Admitting that both monogamous and polygamous family structures are found in the Bible, Felder does little to advance an alternative to the traditional nuclear family structure advocated in modern American society. He does advocate the acceptance of extended families and fictive kinship arrangements, but little consideration is given to the implications of their acceptance. Moreover, in his hypothetical ten commandments on the family, Felder gives credence to the continued subordination of women in the social structure. And although he says that the New Testament advocates "increased mutuality" in the domestic sphere, he spends no real time reflecting on what that may mean for modern African Americans.[110]

In sum, Felder's discussion of African American families is light on analysis of the ancient context, heavy on rhetoric against conservative Christianity, and almost completely lacking in substantive alternatives. His attack on the conservative Christian advocacy of the nuclear family model is understandable, because this model does not reflect the fullness of the biblical evidence. However, Felder does not marshal the evidence available to him. For example, he does not reflect seriously on the meaning of Mary's pregnancy outside of wedlock. Although a scandalous event both in antiquity and arguably in our modern context, the gospels of Matthew and Luke argue that God uses such scandal as a means of advancing the history of salvation. Indeed, in his genealogy Matthew appears to be saying that such scandals have always been part of the providential plan. One implication of such a statement could be that modern African American Christians should not be quick to judge or stigmatize women who have children outside of marriage. At any rate, Felder fails to exploit the hermeneutical potential available to him.

It is clear that corrective historiography is at the heart of his interpretive program. The central functional premise of this corrective agenda appears to be an attempt to play the race "game"

and win. The notion of Afrocentricity in itself participates, at least initially, in the construction of an ontological category that is without objective merit. On the subjective level, the construction of an Afrocentric identity and perspective may serve a verifiable psychosocial purpose. Any attempt, however, to cast "race" as a legitimate category for universally accountable historical analysis must be rejected based on the inability of the worldview to maintain under scientific scrutiny. As I indicated in my historical critique above, Felder, as well as Copher, is on shaky ground when it comes to the possibility of identifying black-skinned people in the biblical data. This does not mean, to be sure, that black-skinned people did not inhabit the world of the ancient Israelites and early Christians. The cumulative anthropological and historical evidence would invalidate such a conclusion. The central problem that confronts the reader is that biblical authors did not believe in and concern themselves with the concept of race as it has been advanced subsequently. Thus, they may not serve as the best witnesses to any conceived black-skinned presence in their daily lives.

Another Subtle and Somewhat Hidden Lens

The vast majority of African Americans are Protestants. As a consequence, they tend to have a higher notion of the authority of Scripture than do many of their non-Protestant counterparts. Felder and Copher, as well as other Afrocentric writings in this vein, demonstrate a fear of challenging a high view of biblical authority. Ron N. Liburd at Florida A&M University has challenged the uncritical acceptance of *sola scriptura* by African Americans, and specifically those involved in the academic interpretation of the Bible. He calls the ideology of unquestionable biblical authority oppressive. He says, "A fundamental flaw in black biblical hermeneutics is the authority invested in the Bible as the Word of God in order to posit a theology of liberation."[111] He goes on to say, "An African American biblical hermeneutic in the sense of calling the Bible the Word of God is counterproductive, in that it has to allow for the oppressors' legitimate use of certain biblical texts to maintain their position of dominance."[112]

Pointing to the work of Cain Hope Felder, Liburd says that Felder should have given up the notion of biblical authority as the primary locus for liberatory reflection. He argues for a vigorous

application of an Afrocentric perspective as a remedy for the deficiencies inherent in the idea of *sola scriptura*. For Liburd, accepting the all-too-human bias of the Bible for Liburd means "we must resist and dismiss as naïve or suspicious all attempts to tell us that the Bible transcends ideology." In sum, Liburd calls any historical interpretation of a presumably fundamental sacred text, even as practiced by corrective historians such as Copher and Felder, flawed and misleading. "We must banish from our vocabulary the idea that the Bible is God's Word for all people in all ages and, therefore, has applicability for every human condition."[113]

Other scholars have attacked *sola scriptura* as well. Roy Bennett, in his essay "Biblical Theology and Black Theology," foregrounds the African American experience at the expense of a vigorous acceptance of *sola scriptura*. Looking over attempts to make the task of biblical theology relevant to modern readers, Bennett concludes that a dialogue between black theology and biblical theology would invigorate the possibility of constructing a meaningful theological interpretation of the Bible as well as a strong biblical hermeneutic for black theology. He says, "The point is that the cultural awareness and perceptions of the black religious community, as in the Tillichian method of correlation, pose vital questions to Scripture and also bring with the question some new insights (revelations) in the encounter."[114]

Likewise, Thomas Hoyt, Jr., attacks the exclusive use of the historical-critical method, a by-product of scriptural primacy, and argues for the inclusion of other theological sources, including imagination. He says, "The authority of Scripture is displayed not so much in the answers that are given but in the questions that are raised...the question of biblical authority for African Americans, it appears to me, relates to the issues of culture and imagination."[115] Hoyt points to the importance of "the story" in African American culture as the grounding for any notion of biblical authority as well as a theological source in its own right. Because it is rooted in suffering, "the story" transcends the parameters of a purely Christian appropriation. In short, Hoyt, Liburd, and Bennett all question the implicit primacy of the Bible to the construction of a liberatory perspective. Along with their questioning, these scholars pave the way for an approach to the Bible other than the corrective historical-critical method employed by some.

Chapter 3

Afrocentrism and the Blackening of the Bible

A culture-specific, African-American reading of the Bible is not only recognized but embraced and celebrated.[1]

Reading Darkly: Placing Africa(ns) at the Center of the World

In the last chapter, I described how African American biblical interpretation began primarily as a means of corrective historiography. Depending on the modern Euro-American notion of race, this strategy for biblical hermeneutics attempted to use race as a tool for reenvisioning the landscape of the biblical world. In addition, although I pointed out that this form of revisionist history was ultimately unsatisfying, it succeeded in advancing a concept that would form the basis of other more recent forms of African American biblical interpretation. Afrocentricity, the idea of placing Africa as an ideological construct at the center of biblical investigation, would become a useful tool for African American biblical scholars in their endeavor to create a hermeneutic that speaks to the needs of a historically marginalized community.

Looking for a Place in the Sun, or a Darkly Subversive Reading of Oppressive Ideology? Randall C. Bailey and an Afrocentric Reading of the Old Testament

Like Copher, Randall Bailey teaches at the Interdenominational Theological Center in Atlanta. He has been instrumental in the development of African American biblical hermeneutics, not only through his various writings, but also through editing and encouraging up-and-coming African American biblical scholars. As I did

with Felder and Copher, I will focus on a couple of his key texts as a way to introduce readers to Bailey's hermeneutical program. Bailey generally accepts, rather than defends, the African presence in the Bible. This marks a point of departure from Copher and Felder, as well as others. And although he argues for the African character of Cush and Sheba in "Beyond Identification: The Use of Africans in Old Testament Poetry and Narratives," he does not emphasize, as the others have, the issue of skin color.[2] He begins this essay by criticizing previous, notably Euro-American, scholarship on the African presence in the Hebrew Bible. These scholars have either argued that the ancient Near East does not include Africa in any substantive way or restricted the African presence to that of Egypt, which they often have placed in the so-called Middle East rather than Africa. Bailey argues strongly that Egypt cannot be separated from its African geographical location. Likewise, he argues that Cush, whose location has been disputed, also should be placed in Africa. The identification of African nations serving one aspect of his program, Bailey sets out the particular purpose of his essay. He seeks to "examine the significance of the presence of African individuals and nations within the text [of the Bible]."[3]

Notice that Bailey wants to look at the significance of the African presence. For him, an African presence in the Hebrew Bible is indisputable. Egypt, Cush, and Sheba are African nations. He determines this fact based primarily on geography. "*African* refers to those nations that are located on the continent of Africa and that ancient Israelites designated as related to them," he explains.[4] Of course, Egypt is geographically situated on the African continent. Cush, according to Bailey, could be divided only into an African nation and an Arabian nation in the minds of biased scholars. The effort to locate Cush in Arabia is an example to Bailey of a conscious desire on the part of biblical scholars to de-Africanize the Bible. By this, he means the effort to obscure or deny the African presence in and influence on the sacred text. Bailey goes on to point out that Sheba is consistently mentioned with African nations in the famous Table of Nations text in Genesis 10. He admits, however, that most "geographers place it in the Arabian Peninsula because it is mentioned in the records of Tiglath-Pileser IV and because of similarities between the names Sheba and Sabeans."[5] Ultimately, Bailey conflates the two arguments and then reasons for the de-Africanizing of Hebrew Bible scholarship by ideologically motivated scholars of Euro-American descent. What Bailey does successfully in his discussion is point out that the evidence against the African placement of Cush and Sheba is just as equivocal as his is. Thus, the final decision to place Cush and Sheba in part or overall in Arabia is a matter of bias or, better, ideology, and not merely careful historiography. We should be mindful, however, that the identification of African nations in the biblical text is not the main purpose of Bailey's argument. His focus is significance, the implication of such a presence for interpretation.

Bailey concentrates on poetic and narrative passages in the Hebrew Bible as a means of assessing the significance of the African presence in those texts. Examining the characteristics of the portrayal of Africans in the Hebrew Bible, he places them into five broad categories. First, Africa represented the "ends of the earth." Pointing to the poetic texts of Isaiah, Jeremiah, and Zephaniah, Bailey argues that African nations represented the farthest places to the south to many Hebrew Bible authors. Second, Africa represented military power to the Israelites. Here Bailey points to statements made in Hosea, Isaiah, and Ezekiel as proof that ancient Israelites saw the Egyptians in particular as a formidable military force. Israel came to rely, he says, on Egyptian military might. "This reliance was based upon Egypt's ability to withstand external invasion and its long history of independence."[6] Third, Africa represented wealth. In his illustrations, Bailey draws on a number of preexilic, exilic, and postexilic sources to prove his point. Psalm 68 is a prime example to Bailey of this grand view of African nations. Egypt and Cush are mentioned explicitly in the psalm as nations that will worship the Lord. He reasons that the psalmist must be implying that Egypt and Cush are wealthy and faraway nations with statements such as the one found in 68:31: "Let bronze be brought from Egypt; let Ethiopia hasten to stretch out its hands to God." Fourth, Africa represented wisdom for the Hebrew Bible authors. Looking primarily at Isaiah 19, Bailey contends that African wisdom was paradigmatic for the development of Israelite wisdom. Finally, Africa represented normativity for ancient Israel. Drawing on the work of other scholars as well as his own, Bailey determines that African nations were paradigmatic in the Israelites' conception of themselves. To end his discussion, Bailey says, "Whether it is to give the example of the vastness of territory to be considered, military might and power, wealth, wisdom, or as a point of comparison for Israel in which its esteem is boosted, these nations are cited as paradigmatic."[7]

Bailey then turns to the employment of Africans in the narratives of the Hebrew Bible. Here he concentrates primarily on their significance for raising the esteem of the often-vulnerable Israel. He cites three examples: Zipporah, the daughter of Pharaoh, and the Queen of Sheba.

Cain Hope Felder addressed Zipporah in his work. Bailey constructs another reading of the narrative in Numbers 12:1–10. He argues that the criticism of Zipporah, the wife of Moses, was due to her high status rather than to the often biased reading that she was somehow inferior. Moses thought himself better than other Israelites because he was married to a Cushite, according to Bailey's reading. Miriam's argument to the contrary is based in her belief that status in the liberated community resides in one's connection to God rather than to any higher-status ethnic group. Interestingly, Bailey does not address the implications of his reading of the text. By rebuking and punishing Miriam, is God justifying Moses' feeling of superiority based on his marriage to Zipporah? If so, does this lend credence to the idea that some ethnic groups are better than others in the biblical text? Can such a determination be used in a liberatory reading of Scripture that stresses human equality? As I said, he does not address these concerns. His only aim is to argue for a positive assessment of Africans in the Hebrew Bible, and although his reading does accomplish this goal, it does not advance a liberatory agenda in its potential appropriation.

In his discussion of Solomon's marriage to the daughter of Pharaoh, Bailey claims something revolutionary for the ancient Israelite king. He argues that contrary to normal Egyptian royal marriage practices, which favored the creation of alliances through marriage to one of the pharaoh's sons, Solomon was able to create such an alliance by marrying one of his daughters. Moreover, Bailey argues for a strong identification between the Solomonic kingdom and Egyptian governing practices. The suggestion is that, at least in the Solomonic period, ancient Israelites saw Egypt and its governmental practices as normative for their own lives and governing practices. As Bailey sees it, the writers of the Solomonic history saw him as a diplomatic genius because he was able to do what other national leaders could not.

Solomon is again portrayed positively by his connection with the Queen of Sheba. Solomon was renowned as a wise ruler both in the Hebrew Bible and in subsequent postbiblical texts, and his connection with the Queen of Sheba, Bailey claims, was meant to underline his wisdom. Her esteem of Solomon only further emphasizes for Bailey "the high value ancient Israel placed upon African wisdom."[8] Taking up again the argument that Sheba was an Arabian nation and not an African one, Bailey dismisses such a view by saying "there was no ancient Israelite veneration of Arabian wisdom."[9] In sum, Bailey pushes the notion of Afrocentricity in this essay beyond the identification of black-skinned people in the biblical texts.

At least five improvements upon the corrective historiographical argument can be detected in Bailey's analysis. First, he accepts an African presence in the Hebrew Bible and tends to avoid the historiographical arguments that characterized the work of Copher and Felder in the last chapter. A subtler but important improvement can be seen in Bailey's avoidance of arguments regarding skin color. He does not claim that the ancient Israelites were Afroasiatics, nor does he argue skin color from the narrow definition put forward by authors in the last chapter. Bailey takes the more defensible position of arguing for an African presence as opposed to the determination of skin color. Third, Bailey confines his arguments primarily to the literary world of the Old Testament. Recognizing that little evidence exists outside the canon for the historical events purported by its authors, he chooses to take the more defensible route of talking about the significance of Africans as literary figures. This approach protects him from the criticisms that can be leveled against those who simply accept the historical veracity of the Hebrew Bible. Fourth, the author argues persuasively for a clear and positive African influence on, at least, the creation of certain Old Testament documents. Where others assumed an influence, or pointed to it consequentially, Bailey demonstrates graphically the places where Africans are employed in the biblical text as positive figures. Consequently, he avoids a prolonged discussion of the Hamite curse partially because others deal with it, but also because he recognizes that it only serves to continue a negative identification of Africans and their descendants. Bailey's pro-African stance leads to the final detectable improvement upon the historiographical program. His promotion of Afrocentricity moves the discussion beyond the bounds of historical reconstruction and places it within a more culturally defined context. He promotes Afrocentricity by using the significance of Africans as a tool for increasing the self-esteem and consciousness of African descendants, including African Americans. By reading these texts through an Afrocentric lens, Bailey demonstrates to his readers the hermeneutical possibilities inherent in the poetic and narrative materials. In turn, Bailey offers African Americans another resource for understanding their heritage and its relationship to the biblical materials.

This may be a good point of departure for raising some lingering questions with regard to Bailey's approach. First, is it possible to posit any substantial relationship between the Africans portrayed in the biblical texts and African descendants living in America? Bailey, like others, appears to view Africa as a cultural unity. Unlike Felder, he does not argue for analogies between sub-Saharan African cultures and those mentioned in the Bible. The absence of such argumentation makes the connection appear even less viable. West Africa with all its cultural diversity is not represented in the Bible, at least as far as the casual observer can tell. African presence in itself is not sufficient to posit a relationship between those portrayed in the Hebrew Bible and those whose ancestors were displaced from their homeland.

Second, were the ancient Israelites Afroasiatics? Alternatively, and more bluntly, were the ancient Israelites black? Bailey avoids this line of argumentation because he recognizes the problems inherent in any such enterprise. Still, the issue of ethnicity remains. By implicitly rejecting such a view, Bailey makes his arguments more defensible. This does not settle the question, however. The initial advocates of this hermeneutical strategy argued that the ancient Israelites were of mixed ethnicity. By avoiding the issue, Bailey only heightens the stature of this claim. It would be helpful to the overall enterprise if Bailey were to address the issue directly.

Third, can a thoroughly persuasive argument for an African presence in the Hebrew Bible be made on scholarship and evidence that often are debatable? Bailey largely avoids these historical arguments by confining his analysis to the literary world of the Hebrew Bible. Yet he uses history at crucial points to support his literary claims. Take, for example, Bailey's argument regarding the Queen of Sheba. He observes that scholarship is divided on the matter of whether Sheba existed as a nation in Africa or Arabia. His choice of Africa is based, primarily, on his suspicion of a Euro-American bias in biblical scholarship toward de-Africanization. Such a bias notwithstanding, Bailey would be more persuasive if he offered such an argument based on the unequivocal placement of Sheba in Africa, for example. Unfortunately, history is often not as clear as we would wish, and Bailey's argument must rest on probability, leaving it open to the possibility of being overturned by subsequent historical data.

Last, are literary representations in the Bible a full presentation of Israel's perception of Africa? Bailey would admit that the positive references to Africans in the Bible represent only an elite view of the continent. The perspectives canonized in the Bible represent how a literate, high-status Israelite saw the nations of Egypt, Cush, and Sheba. We are not privy to the more widespread view of these African nations held by the people of Israel. Needless to say, such a view is unavailable to modern interpreters of the biblical material. Without proof to the contrary, modern readers are left with an elite orientation toward Africa as contained in the poetry and narratives Bailey examines. Fortunately, Bailey provides us with a more nuanced reading in his next essay.

The complex and contextual nature of Bailey's work can be seen in his provocative essay "They're Nothing but Incestuous Bastards: The Polemical Use of Sex and Sexuality in Hebrew Canon Narratives."[10] In this work, he situates his argument as contextual from the start. "I do not approach this subject without bias," he says.[11] Bailey places himself among those who have been historically marginalized. He feels that his social location gives him a distinctive perspective on the narrative texts he examines. He is repulsed. Looking at the sexual imagery and innuendo that can be found in prophetic and narrative literature in the Hebrew Bible, Bailey indicts both the ancient authors and their modern apologists.

He begins the essay by looking briefly at sexual language in prophetic literature. He observes that within the prophetic corpus one can detect the gradual growth of sexual imagery. In addition, these images become more graphic. For example, Bailey points to Hosea 4:13b–14, which depicts harlotry, as an example of the early use of sexual imagery by the prophets. He then moves to later uses in Jeremiah and Nahum, which depict rape. As he points out, these images frequently are used in connection with divine judgment. For example, Hosea 2:3 says, "I will strip her naked and expose her as in the day she was born." Of course, the graphic nature of such images makes their message unequivocal. The implication of these types of statements, however, is to devalue their rhetorical subjects and objects. Using the rape of a woman as a metaphor for divine judgment may be an effective means of communicating the depth of divine anger, but by attributing such imagery to the deity, the prophets, perhaps unwittingly, appear to condone sexual violence against women. Whether directed at Israelites, Canaanites, Egyptians, or Philistines, Bailey joins a growing list of scholars who question the acceptability of such imagery to modern people of faith. Therefore, he challenges one of the aims of the historical-critical method, which is to situate a text within is own historical context. He labels the traditional handling of such texts as ineffective and unsympathetic, if not implicitly misogynistic. He says, "One of the effects is 'redeeming' the text from the horrors found within it because the reader can say, 'Well, that's just the way they thought about women then, but in our enlightened state, we don't think of them in this way.'"[12] To Bailey, these kinds of texts are simply and irrefutably oppressive. Since these texts frequently describe the abuse and devaluation of women, their continued existence in the canon, as well as their continued use in sermons, Bible studies, and educational materials, only serves to desensitize modern readers to unredeemable sexual violence.

Bailey admits "that finding such polemical works within the canon makes the struggle of exegesis more painful but all the more necessary for liberative efforts."[13] Instead of merely accepting a patriarchal reading and appropriation of these texts, Bailey constructs an alternative. His liberative and "subversive" reading of these texts entails an examination of the ideology or ideologies that lie behind these literary representations.[14] In effect, Bailey challenges the traditional notion of biblical authority found among American Protestants. His subversive reading of these texts complicates the general use of the Bible as a source for the construction of theological statements. *Sola scriptura,* the Protestant idea that Scripture alone is the primary and absolute norm of doctrine, cannot stand against more pressing social concerns such as human liberation. In this specific instance, the language of Scripture functions as an anti-norm for persons concerned with the affirmation of female humanity.

Bailey begins his examination of Hebrew narratives by looking at Abraham and Sarah. He calls one literary motif found in Genesis 12, 20, and 26 the "jeopardizing of the matriarch."[15] He says that Abraham speculates in these narratives that the foreigners with whom they come into contact are sexual deviants who would kill him to marry his wife. Bailey observes that the tradition history of these narratives indicates that the Elohist edited the prior work of the Yahwist, especially by correcting many of the ethical problems they raise. For example, Abraham is absolved of lying by the addition to the narrative that Sarah was Abraham's half sister. Detecting ancient efforts to rehabilitate Abraham's conduct illustrates for Bailey the strong "in-group/out-group" orientation that pervades these narratives. It is a bias that can lead only to the marginalization of those outsiders stigmatized by the text. In addition, Bailey challenges scholarship by pointing out that modern commentators rarely notice the questionable actions of the patriarch compared to the moral uprightness of the foreigners involved. He says, "[The] reader, especially the one holding the Israelites to be the 'in-group,' misses the ending and is fixated at the beginning."[16] Bailey goes on to remark that the only recorded monarch in antiquity who killed a foreigner to marry his wife is found in 2 Samuel 11, the story of David and Bathsheba. "This should cause us to wonder," he says, "whether we have in these jeopardizing-of-the-matriarch narratives Israel's attempt to foist onto foreigners its own foibles."[17]

The second narrative Bailey addresses has to do with the Moabites and the Ammonites. After the destruction of Sodom and Gomorrah, Lot is seduced by his daughters, who apparently believed that the entire human race had been decimated (Gen 19:29–38). Their offspring, the products of an incestuous encounter, are given names that proudly announce the circumstances of their birth. These bastards *(mamzerim)* are the progenitors of the Moabites and the Ammonites in ancient Israelite myth, which justifies their demonization by the community. Bailey argues that although this narrative has been attributed to the Yahwist, he believes that the hand of the Deuteronomistic redactor can be detected. Joining the seduction of Lot to texts such as Deuteronomy 23:2, 4, which excludes Moabites, Ammonites, and *mamzerim* from the assembly of the Lord, Bailey believes that the Genesis narrative forms the background for the rejection of these two nations. As he says, "The effect of both the narrative in Genesis 19 and the laws in Deuteronomy 23, therefore, is to label within the consciousness of the reader the view of these nations as nothing more than 'incestuous bastards.' "[18] Such a designation makes them fair game for oppression and exploitation.

The final narrative Bailey examines is found in Genesis 9:18–28, the end of the Noah story — a story that is "fraught with ambiguity as to what exactly happens," according to Bailey.[19] He does not approach the Hamite curse in the traditional manner of other scholars; he chooses to avoid the "knotty exegetical problems" in favor of examining the ideology behind the narrative.[20] Again, he questions the editorial hand at work in the story, challenging the commonly accepted idea that it was a production of the Yahwist. He says, "[All] of the terms in the narrative that open up the subject of sexual misconduct have their locus within the sexual prohibitions of the Holiness Code in Leviticus 18 and 20."[21] Thus, Bailey attributes at least the story's final revision to the Priestly hand.

Looking at the ideology that informs the text, Bailey points out that another Priestly passage, Leviticus 18:3, labels Egyptians and Canaanites as sexual deviants. This is important because still another Priestly document, the Table of Nations, attributes both nations to the lineage of Ham (Gen 10:6). Bailey argues that the story of Ham in Genesis 9 forms the background for the Israelite denunciation of the Egyptians and Canaanites as sexual deviants, since they are the descendants of a potential sexual deviant, Ham. Again, by recasting a curse against Canaan as occurring within the context of a suspicious sexual act committed by Ham, the biblical authors opened the door to exploitation and oppression through stigmatization. According to Bailey, the Priestly school wanted its readers to identify themselves with "Shem, the one who took the lead in covering up Noah, the one to whom Canaan is to be a slave, the one whose God, YHWH, is to be blessed."[22] In addition, Bailey detects an anti-African tone in the rhetoric of the Priestly writer. He notes that in other Hebrew Bible writings, Africans are venerated. Yet he concludes, "The Priestly school was not in favor of such veneration of Africans."[23]

At the conclusion of his analysis, Bailey reflects on the negative consequences many of these kinds of texts have had on marginalized groups. The worst consequence, according to him, may be an oppressed person's acceptance of such ideologically motivated literary motifs. He says, "I am most surprised how often we oppressed people find ourselves identifying with the insiders in these texts, even though our own stories might be closer to those of the outsiders."[24]

Bailey labels passages such as those examined in this essay, as well as those that marginalize others (such as homosexuals), as examples of "holy hatred."[25] Furthermore, interpretations of these texts that support the continuing marginalization and oppression of women, various ethnicities, homosexuals, and others are enduring acts of such hatred. Liberation requires that such a supremacist orientation in the Bible and such supremacist readings of the Bible be placed aside in favor of the more subversive reading advocated by Bailey.

As in "Beyond Identification," Bailey walks a fine line between literary analysis and historical reconstruction. By examining the in-group/out-group motif and the use of sexual imagery in it, Bailey does not need to prove the dehumanizing implications of the narratives he examines. He does not need to prove the existence of Abraham, nor does he have to prove that Abraham lied about his relationship to Sarah. He can stay at the level of the literary and avoid many of the pitfalls that would confront other more historical interpreters. He does assume, however, that literary rhetoric influences real life. Thus, he can talk about these narratives as a pretext for the oppression of others.

Bailey's questioning of *sola scriptura* is not new. As we saw in the last chapter, a growing number of African American scholars have begun to question an uncritical biblical authority. They look at the role the text plays in the life of the African American Christian community and see how its prominence both promotes and limits human liberation. Using liberation as a hermeneutical lens allows them to discriminate between texts, as Bailey has done in this essay. The first step in this process of critical engagement, it appears, is to see the Bible as the product of a particular cultural perspective advanced and canonized by social elites. At least, this appears to be the perspective of Hebrew Bible scholars who question the ideology at work behind the text. New Testament scholars have been less willing to attack the second testament as a product of an elitist and patriarchal social structure. Without question, African American New Testament scholars view Jesus as the model for human liberation. They tend to gloss over parts of the New Testament that portray him in a nonliberatory light. Thus, it may be fair to say that their Christian commitment unduly influences their engagement with certain passages in the Bible. Alternatively, one might say that a scholar's Christian cultural context serves as the lens through which she reads the biblical texts. *Sola scriptura* then protects Jesus and the gospel writers, making them normative for faith and practice, but it leaves others exposed and vulnerable. I will say more on this below.

In "Beyond Identification," Bailey attacked Euro-American biblical scholars for attempting to de-Africanize the sacred text. Here he attacks historical-critical scholarship again. Bailey calls biblical commentators to task for redeeming offensive biblical narratives such as those he examines and for desensitizing readers and hearers of these stories to "the extreme nature of the objectionable material."[26] Bailey is certainly correct in his assertion that scholars have a tendency to diminish the harsh realities of life in the ancient world. This tendency is passed on to preachers and Christian educators, who attempt to explain the texts in a manner that is more palatable to modern readers and hearers. One pervasive tendency can be found in the American effort to obscure slavery in the biblical texts, especially the New Testament, by translating words such as *doulos* — "slave" — as "servant." This revisionist tendency notwithstanding, Bailey must admit that life for the ancients was difficult. Furthermore, their social and ethno-religious values were not our own. Bailey's critique suggests that we can somehow ignore those portions of the biblical text that portray the stark underside of life or otherwise offend us. Of course, he attempts to use some of these texts for a liberatory purpose by offering a subversive reading of them. This is helpful, but it does not solve the central and disturbing historical issues. Scholars may not be dealing with these issues well, and Bailey attempts to offer an alternative, but they certainly cannot be ignored.

One of the real strengths of Bailey's interpretation of Scripture is his ability to put scholarship in conversation with a culturally specific context. This is a subtler but effective application of the Afrocentric paradigm. As an African American with sensitivities to race, gender, sexual orientation, and class, Bailey uses his context as a lens through which to interpret the Hebrew Bible. Although his reading may not initially strike the reader as Afrocentric in its traditional sense, it is at the core of his analysis nevertheless. Again, Bailey has moved beyond the arguments I examined in the last chapter. Very little of this essay is devoted to questions traditionally central to the African American hermeneutical enterprise — skin color, historical reconstruction, and defining race. Instead, Bailey chooses to use his context as a backdrop and standard against which to judge these biblical representations of sexuality.

Another strength of Bailey's argument is that it provides a voice for the marginalized. His subversive reading of the text brings in the voices of women and other supposed minorities who were excluded or stigmatized by these texts in the past. Bailey offers an alternative reading that places their concerns at the center of his analysis. Of course, this means taking on more traditional readings and applications of the Bible. Through source analysis, he complicates a simplistic understanding of biblical authority. Instead of pinning the authority of Scripture on God, which would make it sacred, Bailey locates its authority with various editors who represent and advocate particular ideological understandings, which would make Scripture less than divine. This approach permits Bailey to criticize any supremacist appropriation of these texts as unwarranted, being based in the ideology of the biblical author rather than in the divine voice that stands behind the texts. Bailey's focus on ideology revives, somewhat, the issue of authorial intention. The idea that one can determine what an author intended to communicate to his original audience lies behind Bailey's argument regarding ideology. For example, in his discussion of Genesis 9, Bailey imports other texts attributed to the Priestly school as a means of determining the intent behind recasting the narrative. A repeated criticism of the historical-critical method is that it attempts to recover something — authorial intent — that it cannot truly recover. If this is true of original meaning, would it not likewise be true when it comes to ideological motivation?

If we take ideology here in the poststructuralist sense, then Bailey understands ideology as a system of representations that point to the lived relation between human beings and the condition of their lives.[27] How different is this from a systematic analysis of the past looking specifically at human activity in time, space, and society?[28] In effect, ideological analysis is a form of historiography. The fact that it looks at literature, the representations that express the lived relation, does not disqualify its relationship to history. Thus, ideological analysis, if not equivalent, is analogous to authorial intention.

A fundamental strength of Bailey's ideological analysis is its demonstration of the diversity of perspectives found in the Bible. One of the benefits of historical criticism has been its concern with and appreciation of individual biblical authors. Such a concern for the individual voice can be found in Bailey's analysis as well. After a general statement regarding the high esteem Israelites placed on Africans in "Beyond Identification," Bailey teases out a dissenting voice in this essay that opposed African veneration. This demonstration of diversity within the canon reinvigorates the idea that the Bible speaks with more than one voice. Diversity in presentation allows for the possibility of the recognition of a degree of social tolerance in the ancient context, which could serve as the basis for a diverse and relatively tolerant society in the present.

Diversity brings us again to the canon issue. The arguments underlying the orthodox Protestant idea of *sola scriptura* are complex indeed. Bailey calls into question two of them, authority and sufficiency, and in turn invalidates the third, clarity. Specifically, he attacks the notions of scriptural authority, that is, the formal authority of Scripture as the primary datum of Christian thinking *(authoritas scripturae)* and its twofold divine authority *(authoritas divina duplex)*. With respect to the formal authority of Scripture, Bailey attacks the foundational character of the biblical text by complicating its certitude and infallibility. He undermines its intrinsic certitude by suggesting the absence of holiness in the narratives he examines, and consequently undermines their truth-value. That is, even if the literary representations found in the Bible are expressions of the lived experience of its authors, such instances of "holy hatred" do not express the true meaning of the biblical witness. Bailey undermines its extrinsic certitude by suggesting that the narratives he examines do not contain the profundity of knowledge necessary to validate this claim.

With certitude duly complicated, Bailey also complicates the claim of scriptural infallibility. By attributing the use of sexual imagery and innuendo to the editors of the biblical texts instead of God, he implies the absence of a divine origin to them. The second major component of formal scriptural authority is then questioned: inspiration. If God is not the sole author of Scripture, then the degree to which it is inspired must be measured against some other external authority. Bailey most likely would agree that God is the primary author of Scripture, but this acknowledgment is not equivalent to the more conservative concept of inspiration that prevails in many African American congregations. Thus, acceptance of Scripture as the normative authority in Christian faith and practice must be examined anew. Bailey claims that the narratives he examines constitute, in fact, an anti-norm for Christian life. With infallibility duly complicated, the twofold divine authority of the Scriptures, at least as traditionally understood, can be dismissed, both with respect to the text as a thing and its expression of the divine will. Of course, Bailey is not doing anything other critical biblical interpreters have not done already.[29] What is different about his analysis is the basis on which he does it.

It is generally agreed that the majority of African Americans hold a more conservative view of biblical authority. They see the Bible as the Word of God in its fullest traditional sense. Bailey appeals to the idea of the Word of God as well. However, he would not necessarily accept the idea that the written Word, the Bible, is a sufficient expression of the wisdom of God grounded in the authority of the Son (i.e., the eternal Word) and manifested in the ministry of Jesus Christ (i.e., the incarnate Word). Rather, he

68 *Blackening of the Bible*

would see the written Word as potentially containing the wisdom of God, and thus of limited sufficiency. It must be judged against the standards of the eternal Word, as displayed in the ministry of Jesus, and the witness of the internal Word, the work of the Spirit in the heart of the believer. The validity of the written or external Word contained in the Scriptures rests on the putative continuity between the unwritten preaching of the apostles and prophets, testified also to the believer by the internal Word of the Spirit and its textual manifestation. By using liberation as his unwritten and internal Word, Bailey is able to both discriminate between valid and invalid norms presented in the Bible and use the Bible as the Word of God. Liberation is what defines the difference in Bailey's approach, an orientation that places him squarely in the midst of Afrocentric scholarship.

Randall Bailey has done what Ron Liburd advocated in the last chapter. He has disavowed the idea that the "Bible is God's Word for all people in all ages and, therefore, has applicability for every human condition."[30] What he has demonstrated in "They're Nothing but Incestuous Bastards" is that the Bible contains texts of terror and human devaluation that cannot promote, on their face, the ideal of human liberation.

"Cracker, Your Breed Ain't Exegetical":[31] Vincent L. Wimbush and an Afrocentric Reading of the New Testament

Unlike the major figures I have examined thus far, Vincent Wimbush has not spent the majority of his career teaching at a historically black theological institution. Having taught at Union Theological Seminary in New York City, and now teaching at Claremont Graduate University, Wimbush has had, however, a major voice in the development of African American hermeneutics. He once described his teaching situation at Union, a nondenominational freestanding seminary outside the norm for doctoral programs, as "partly the result of the influence of a few very bright students here *of varied backgrounds*."[32] According to Wimbush, what made this situation compatible with his interpretive enterprise was that his students "[found] themselves located at the mouth of Harlem engaged in the academic study of the Bible [clamoring] for something other than the old obfuscations called exegesis."[33]

Vincent Wimbush's program of biblical interpretation aims to be broad and varied but also centered and cogent. Like Felder, Wimbush uses a number of technical terms repeatedly in his writings. Among them are *world, reading, modern, translation, maroon,* and *the story.* Defining these terms will assist us in understanding Wimbush better.

According to Wimbush, African Americans are quintessentially moderns. By modern, he means an individual or community with "an acute sense of separation" from the past.[34] For Europeans, modernity began in the seventeenth century.[35] The degree to which they have appropriated, or otherwise negotiated, their acute separation from the past speaks to their standing as moderns. Wimbush questions, however, the idea that Europeans and their descendants in North America experienced modernity in the same way that Africans did. The European sense of separation was not as acute as that of African Americans. They approached modernity with a sense of "angst." Those who had immigrated to the United States particularly had to negotiate "how much of the 'old world' and its 'medievalism' to leave behind."[36] In contrast, Africans experienced a radical break with the past that made it irretrievably past. What was left for African Americans was survival in a new social context.

> Survival for Africans meant learning to assemble cultural pieces from shattered social-cultural experiences, from rupture and disconnection. It meant developing a facility for taking what is left of shattered experiences and "making do," learning what it takes to survive on what is at hand, and, in spite of consistently brutal opposition that continues to this day, the struggle with the names [by which African Americans identify themselves] reflects only one aspect of the fierce ongoing battle, forging an identity for themselves — "a new name" — in the strange setting and under most difficult circumstances.[37]

Such a radical sense of modernity distinguishes African Americans from almost all others in the American social context. Modernity then becomes a central concept in Wimbush's construction of the African American engagement with the Bible.

Related to modernity is Wimbush's idea of African Americans as maroons. Derived from the Spanish *cimarron,* the word came to be identified in the sixteenth century with runaway slaves.[38] He uses this term most forcefully in his essay "Reading Darkness, Reading

Scriptures," the introduction to *African Americans and the Bible*, of which he is the editor. In it, he points to the desire for "flight" that many African Americans undertook. Experiencing modernity as a radical dislocation from the past, African Americans sought cultural and social resources that enabled them to envision a social context that empowered them to speak and interpret life on their own terms, in their own voices — a flight away from the dominant Eurocentric construction of reality they experienced daily. As Wimbush observes, this longing for flight may never be fully realized, but it exists to the extent that it contributes to the construction of an alternative social context that stands against the dominant and oppressive reality faced by the majority of African Americans.[39]

This idea of African Americans as maroons leads nicely to Wimbush's idea of "world." By this, he means a particular orientation or understanding of existence as negotiated within a historically conditioned social context. He calls it, among other things, an "existential stance."[40] African slaves brought to the plantations of North America were radically dislocated from their own worlds. In their new environments, they had to construct an understanding of their social context that brought meaning to their experiences and helped them survive their ordeals. In the case of Africans in what came to be the United States, one of the central tools in the construction of this existential stance was the Bible. As Wimbush understands it, the Bible should be seen foremost as a "language-world" whose cultural functioning far outdistances its use as a repository for doctrine and piety.[41] In the stories of the Bible, the slaves found the material for the understanding of their own radical social existence as well as critical attitudes toward oppression. In the merging of these two worlds, the slaves and their descendants discovered survival techniques, reinforcement of their self-worth, and a liberatory religious consciousness.[42] What I have called "merging," Wimbush calls "fusion," an idea that also has a technical meaning. He says, "Ultimately, only something approaching a fusion of 'worlds' can explain the phenomenon of the African American engagement with the Bible. 'Fusion' here suggests a shared stance from which all things that matter are viewed."[43] In short, the existential stance ("world") of African Americans was fused with the recorded existential stance of the Bible ("language-world") around a particular social location of oppression, along with its resistance and critique ("all things that matter").

The merging of the biblical world and the world of African Americans fostered certain reading practices or strategies that are historically discernable and retrievable. Thus, any examination of African American engagement with the Bible must take account of, among other things, these historic strategies conditioned by a peculiar North American social location. Wimbush identifies four characteristics of these reading practices. First, they are public or communal rather than individualistic. Second, they emerged out of "particular life-settings" and are "more or less manifested and preserved in different types of sources — e.g., songs, sermons, testimonies, addresses."[44] Third, they either quote directly or more often allude to specific biblical passages that function as a norm for African American faith and practice ("canon"). Fourth, they can be divided roughly into discernable historical occasions of utterance. Yet, as Wimbush cautions, "[It] is important for me to note that even as each type of reading represents a period in the history of African Americans, the types of readings are not strictly chronologically successive — no one reading completely disappears when another begins."[45] In sum, African American engagement with the Bible developed around a certain locus of interpretation that was conditioned on their experience of their own social location.

Modern academic efforts to retrieve and understand this existential stance and engagement with the biblical materials involve, by necessity, a certain degree of translation. By this, Wimbush means an "unearthing of the relevant influences upon the responses to the social and physical world which betray [existential stance]."[46] To understand the African American engagement with the Bible, one must also understand the "relevant influences" that contributed to the construction of their existential stance ("world") and the degree to which the Bible as a language-world participated in that construction as a cultural resource. This leads to the final technical term used by Wimbush, one also advocated by Thomas Hoyt, Jr., in chapter 2 of this book, the African American "story" as the *locus classicus* of their appropriation of Christianity.

Wimbush argues that, in a manner quite different from their Euro-American counterparts, African Americans appropriated the symbols, concepts, and language of Christianity to suit their own existential condition. Coming from an oral culture, and being denied for the most part the bourgeois capacity of literacy, African Americans engaged the broad stories of the Bible rather than the textual details. As Wimbush understands it, "What became important was the *telling* and *retelling,* the hearing and rehearing of biblical stories — stories of perseverance, of strength in weakness and under oppressive burdens, of hope in hopeless situations. To these stories African Americans related."[47] We could sum up the relationship among Wimbush's technical terms in this manner: This decidedly modern people, cut off from any relevant sense of their past, in their oppressed and often marooned state in what came to be the United States, constructed a world that fused with the biblical world around reading practices that emphasized the analogies between the social locations of persons in the Bible and their own. Furthermore, this world is accessible to the modern interpreter through translation, the unearthing of the relevant influences that contributed to their construction of this existential stance.

Having discussed Wimbush's use of technical terms, we now turn to five central themes that run throughout his work. The first is the function of the Bible in the African American experience as discerned through a history of readings. He identifies five historic reading strategies used by Africans in America in his essay "The Bible and African Americans: An Outline of an Interpretative History."[48] Each characterizes a certain instance in the African American experience in the United States. The first, suspicion and rejection, was the initial experience African slaves had with the sacred text. The strangeness of the American context, as well as the oral character of African culture, made many slaves suspicious of the white man's "Book Religion."[49] The absurdity of this bookish engagement with the divine was not the only African response to Christianity, however. Many also recognized the power the Bible held in their new environment. As the central icon of American cultural self-understanding, the "Bible functioned as a cultural image-reflector, as a road map to nation-building. It provided the Europeans justification to think of themselves as a 'biblical nation,' as God's people called to conquer and convert the New World to God's way as they interpreted it."[50] The perdurance of this biblicized cultural understanding occasioned the slaves' subsequent engagement with the Bible as a source of power.

Through the revival movements of the eighteenth century, slaves and former slaves began to engage the power of the Bible in their new environment. They latched on to the Protestant idea of the priesthood of all believers, the idea that each person was free to interpret the Bible as she saw fit, among other things. This second phase in the African American engagement with the Bible transformed it from a cultural icon accessible only to whites to a language-world that gave voice to their own experiences as strangers in a strange land. Through spirituals, sermons, and testimonies, Africans in America mined particularly the Hebrew Bible for stories, statements, and orientations that gave cosmic meaning to their daily struggles. Barred for the most part from reading the Bible, this period reflects "a hermeneutic characterized by a looseness, even playfulness, vis-à-vis the biblical texts themselves."[51] Having unleashed the power of the Bible for themselves, this period for Wimbush reflects the classic engagement of African Americans with the Bible.[52] He concludes, "They manipulated the religions they embraced until such religions became their own and began to reflect their views about themselves and the world to which they were brought."[53]

The third reading strategy, which began in the nineteenth century, built upon the African American's recognition of the Bible as a powerful cultural force in the United States. Called "prophetic apology" by Wimbush, this reading of the Bible sought to develop a hermeneutical principle through which the entirety of the biblical corpus could be read.[54] Drawing on the work of Peter Paris, Wimbush characterizes this hermeneutic as the universal kinship of human beings under the sovereignty of God.[55] It represents an attempt to hold America true to its self-understanding as a biblical nation. As he says of this period, "The clamor for African Americans was for the realization of the principles of inclusion, equality, and kinship that they understood the Bible to mandate."[56] Wimbush uses Reverdy Cassius Ransom, an African Methodist minister most active in the early part of the twentieth century, as a powerful example of this reading strategy among African Americans. Pointing out Ransom's relatively elite position compared to that of others in his community, Wimbush says,

> The New Testament provided Ransom with the ideological principle that he, as a member of an oppressed, marginalized group, could readily embrace, not only in order to name and characterize the racial situation in the United States but also to seek to transcend it, to find a grand perspective from which to relativize racial distinctions.[57]

Although many would identify this more consistent and systematic engagement with the Bible according to the hermeneutic of universal kinship as classic, Wimbush would not. He sees it rather as "an example of biblical interpretation done from a complicated and relative social and ideological position within [the African American community]."[58] This integrationist position, according to Wimbush, was most powerful among those who had the most to gain from inclusion in the dominant American social construction.

The fourth reading strategy Wimbush identifies is more sectarian. Characteristic of such groups as the Black Muslims, Black Jews, and others, this strategy exhibits a "tendency to develop esoteric knowledge or principles of interpretation" based on canonical and noncanonical ancient texts.[59] He says that these groups are more critical of the American presentation of itself as a biblical nation than are those who used the last reading strategy. "They tend to be less concerned about holding America to its responsibilities as a biblical nation because they generally do not believe any of America's claims about itself to be true."[60] Glossing over some of their uses of the Bible and other materials, Wimbush argues, "The syncretistic tendency of many of these groups implies a universalism that intends to transcend the limiting historical reality. In other words, through the esoteric books and esoteric knowledge about such books, a new, egalitarian, cosmopolitan community-world is envisioned."[61] Wimbush accepts what Copher called aberrant as a legitimate African American reading strategy that developed at the beginning of the twentieth century.

The final reading strategy Wimbush identifies is fundamentalism. A product of late twentieth-century global culture, Wimbush characterizes this type of reading as an attraction to white fundamentalist communities based on a search for identity. He characterizes the situation in this way:

> The search for identity, for belonging, for wholeness and understanding in this [modern] situation has propelled many of a religious bent toward a hardening and tightening, toward an effort to freeze in time that which is judged to be self-defining, good, and meaningful in a world perceived to be moving too fast, spinning out of control.[62]

Wimbush sees in this reading strategy a denial of an African American cultural perspective, characterized particularly in the second strategy, hermeneutical improvisation, as well as a disassociation from those African Americans who become fundamentalist with their own modernity.

This brings us to a second theme that pervades Wimbush's work: his disdain for fundamentalism. It receives different degrees of attention in his various works, but Wimbush clearly rejects the recent fundamentalist move among African Americans as a negative harbinger for African American culture. His most forceful attack against the trend can be found in " 'Rescue the

Perishing': The Importance of Biblical Scholarship in Black Christianity."[63] Here he identifies the problem among African Americans as one in which their religious institutions have failed to respond constructively to a more literate and inquisitive community. As he says,

> [It] is now evident in every local black parish as parishioners plead for more guidance in their reading of their Bibles, as astute comments are made and questions asked in response to sermons preached, as great interest is shown in the teaching claims of the electronic preachers, as befuddlement and intimidation are expressed in the face of the rise in number and complexity of books on religious subjects.[64]

Traditional African American approaches to the Bible, including the second reading strategy identified by Wimbush, accepted the Bible as the Word of God that addressed the present. "What did not speak to the present was ignored."[65] Such an appropriation of the Bible is no longer acceptable in a community that finds itself inundated by electronic media, by Euro-American and African American preachers using the airwaves as a vehicle for the dissemination of a "doctrinalist Christianity."[66]

In response, Wimbush argues for more serious engagement with the Bible and Christian doctrine among African Americans, but from their own historic-cultural perspective. In his view, African American Christianity has the vitality to speak to its community's most recent engagement with the Bible. Doctrinaire, or doctrinally oriented, readings of Scripture are not a necessary component of the future of African American Christendom. African Americans have always had their own distinct readings and appropriations of Scripture, readings borne out of their own historic engagement with the sacred text. What is potentially lost in this latest reading of the Bible is that peculiar African American existential stance toward the world that engages Scripture in a creative manner. Joining African American Christianity, a peculiarly modern phenomenon, with academic biblical scholarship, another modern phenomenon, appears to Wimbush to be the solution for the community's crisis. Simply harkening back to the African American religious experience is not sufficient to counteract this trend. He says:

> What is required is a move beyond apologies for "black experience," even beyond "black religious experience." The

former, even when defined in the most inclusive terms, always
seems to lag decades behind black folks' present experiences
and existential situation. The latter, setting and ethnic origin of participants notwithstanding, is no longer *of* black
people.[67]

Wimbush believes that intense historical investigation of the kind
performed by academic biblical scholars is the antidote to this disturbing trend. According to Wimbush, what biblical scholarship
can provide are the "interpretative elements" of the biblical witness, the basic diversity that characterized early Christianity, which
can challenge and topple the monolithic presentation of Christianity characteristic of fundamentalism.[68] "The fact that the New
Testament betrays a number of different ways of describing the experience of salvation gives us freedom also in describing our own,"
says Wimbush.[69]

The third theme found in Wimbush's work is related to his rejec-
tion of fundamentalism. As he understands the history of African
American readings of the Bible, the classic paradigm for engage-
ment with the Scriptures is one of playfulness and transformation.
African Americans appropriated the biblical stories as their own.
Through a manipulation of the biblical stories, they gave voice
to their own existential concerns. Such an orientation lies behind
Wimbush's call for a new hermeneutical project.

Instead of a singular reading of African American engagement
with the Bible, Wimbush offers a more self-critical and varied interaction between the biblical texts and African experiences in the
United States. The variety of African American readings of the
Bible serves as an illustration of the profound and complex impact
that sacred texts have on their users. Drawing upon the history
of readings outlined above, which he calls the "collective cultural
wisdom" of African Americans, Wimbush argues for a shift in
biblical investigation away from the texts as texts to human interactions with the texts as the foundation for the construction
of "world." Such a mode of interpretation would be controlled
by four interrelated principles. The first principle is an ongoing
consciousness raising among American Americans regarding the
impact the Bible has had in the development of their own cultural self-understanding, even if the full import of that impact is
not fully recognized. The second principle is the highlighting of
those biblical texts that speak to the development of this cultural
self-definition, "texts that seem to arrest the collective imagination

and strike a chord."[70] The third principle is the assessment of these texts in light of the history of readings of the Bible among African Americans found in various literary genres. The fourth principle is critical reflection on contemporary interpretations of the Bible in light of the witness of the collective cultural wisdom compiled by African Americans. This final critical posture is important to Wimbush because it privileges neither the history of readings nor the contemporary interpretation of biblical passages. Such a critical stance is fundamental to Wimbush's engagement with the Bible. He makes this clear when explaining the character and aims of religious literature:

> [Such] texts, precisely because of their empathy-producing qualities, should also inspire among readers again and again over time a certain suspicious posture, the cultivation of certain critical sensibilities and faculties — such faculties that will allow them to see themselves as chronologically and ideologically distant and different from both "the tyranny of the present" and the texts and text-worlds if only in order to return to these texts with a grasp of cultural and communal clarity of interpretive history.[71]

The success of this hermeneutical project rests on the scholarly community's ability to translate the African American experience with the Bible effectively and African Americans' ability to maintain a culturally specific engagement with the Bible based on a certain type of cultural imagination. As defined by Wimbush, this cultural imagination involved the following:

> It was freedom in the playfulness, whimsicalness, and release of the collective cultural imagination in the engagement of the Bible that was translated into psychic affirmation and power — the power to imagine the other, something other than the given of slavery and disenfranchisement, the power to imagine the "by and by," a future situation better than, if not altogether a reversal of, the status quo.[72]

Wimbush's hermeneutical program would not entail a "simple, unquestioning acceptance and valorization of 'traditional' interpretations."[73] It would function rather as an ongoing self-critique of a historically conditioned and culturalist reading of the Bible. It would be contextual not only in terms of its subject matter but also in terms of its claims and their appropriation. Yet, according to

Wimbush, it also would point to the possibility for communication across cultural, ethnic, and religious divides.

An expanded version of this third theme constitutes the fourth theme found in Wimbush's work. He proposes a radical reorientation of biblical scholarship using the African American experience as an exemplum. This clarion call for the reorientation of the discipline can be seen most forcefully in "Interrupting the Spin: What Might Happen If African Americans Were to Become the Starting Point for the Academic Study of the Bible."[74] Drawing on the work of Toni Morrison and the American Studies scholar Mary Helen Washington, Wimbush suggests that a new understanding of and orientation toward biblical studies can be gleaned from a serious examination of the African American interaction with the Bible.

His proposal, to place African American experience at the center of academic biblical studies, is not, in fact, a privileging of this experience above others, but a *"decentering* of the prevailing [Eurocentric] paradigm."[75] It opens up the possibility for different orientations to the practice of biblical scholarship. Attention to the African American experience would rescue the discipline of biblical scholarship from its present "mode of silence" and give it a voice in the existential issues that face not only African Americans but also human beings generally.[76]

In tandem with his more provocative proposal, Wimbush offers three related proposals on how biblical scholarship would change if his main proposal were adopted. First, there would be more consistent and intense critical focus on the present, instead of antiquarian preoccupation with the past. The present ideal espoused by the historical-critical method — to begin with the texts — would wither in light of the function of those same texts in the everyday lives of African Americans. As Wimbush says, "Those who view their present in terms of struggle, conflict, resistance, and pain are less likely to want to begin serious questioning and thinking in general, certainly not about meaning, anywhere but in the present."[77] Historical investigation of the Bible would then be oriented not toward disciplinary concerns and the endurance of a Eurocentric grand narrative — what he calls "the spin" — but toward the analogies, or absence thereof, between the historical-social locations of persons in the Bible and modern African Americans.

Second, there would be more consistent and intense critical focus on social-cultural formation and sacred texts. A focus on the African American engagement with the biblical text would force biblical scholars to confront the complex relationship between the language-world of the Bible and the existential stance or world constructed by this modern people of faith. Such a confrontation would disrupt the American academic biblical myth that the Bible is the "result of a long, seemingly natural quasi-historical process that leads from ancient cultures around the Mediterranean to the twentieth-century European-North American acculturative cooptation and authoritative interpretation of it."[78] Since African Americans engaged and appropriated the Bible on their own terms, at least in the initial stage of their engagement with the texts, their experience serves as a potent example of the complex interaction that occurs between texts and persons. As Wimbush says, "Sacred texts are as much determined by society and culture as society and culture are determined by (among other things, to be sure) sacred texts."[79] Instead of seeing the Bible as a suprahistorical and transcultural compendium of sacred texts, the Bible should be viewed as a socially and historically conditioned tool to be used repeatedly in ideological and historically situated struggles between human beings.

Third, there would be more consistent and intense critical focus on the Bible as a repository or "manifesto for marginal existence."[80] Wimbush admits that the Bible contains mixed existential stances toward the world. At points it supports patriarchy, xenophobia, heterosexism, and misogyny, among other things. He believes, however, that the "view and stance that are most consistently registered and found most compelling are those that are in solidarity with the powerless, the outsiders, the weak."[81] The history of biblical interpretation in the West has been to rationalize and domesticate such a manifesto rather than to appropriate and celebrate the disruptive character of the biblical existential stance toward the world, that is, the dominant society and its construction of reality. African Americans, an enduring modern example of such a stance, force biblical scholars to reexamine the nature of the Bible's witness and its interaction with its readers and interpreters.

The "radical orientation" Wimbush identifies in his third proposal leads to the fifth and final theme found in his writings. Implicit in Wimbush's interpretive agenda is a biblical theology. To compare his thought with that of Randall Bailey, Wimbush's notion of "radical orientation," in that it seeks to empower the powerless and affirm the marginalized, is analogous to Bailey's subversive or liberatory reading. Both approaches have as their primary aim the existential transformation of those who adopt them. In reading

Bailey, however, one is not confronted with such a well-developed biblical theology as Wimbush espouses.

To continue the comparison, Bailey's liberatory interpretation of Scripture, particularly the Hebrew Bible, is open-ended and critical. It rests on a larger corpus of literature, a problem that in itself calls for a careful and critical stance toward the biblical materials. Bailey is in agreement with the Bible at certain points and in disagreement with it at others. Wimbush, in contrast, is more like Felder in his approach to the biblical materials. Distinctive, and sometimes contradictory, biblical orientations and statements are subsumed under an overriding ethic of transformation. Furthermore, Wimbush is strongly christocentric in his orientation to the biblical materials. Like Felder, Wimbush views Jesus Christ, the liberator and redeemer of humanity, as the paradigmatic figure for his understanding of and engagement with the biblical materials. Even this centering of the African American experience, as reconstructed and interpreted by Wimbush, is an attempt to foreground this collective human experience with the suffering, death, and resurrection of Christ in the background. In effect, Jesus Christ is the central paradigm in Wimbush's biblical theology and interpretive schema.

One wonders at times whether African American New Testament scholars pride themselves on the construction of grand orientations or stances toward the Bible as such, or whether African American Hebrew Bible scholars are silenced or humbled by the sheer number of books (and variations of material) that constitute their research focus. It appears easier for New Testament scholars to find and proclaim ethical norms that involve activity than it is for Hebrew Bible scholars, an insight that may prove more prophetic than I now realize. Because of the overriding literary and theological presence of Jesus Christ in the New Testament, these scholars are able to subsume contradictory Scriptures under the rubric of the ministry of Jesus, or ascribe them to an authority other than Christ. Such a hermeneutical "out" often is not available to scholars of the Hebrew Bible. In short, New Testament scholars find it easier to construct grand biblical theological visions than do their Old Testament African American counterparts.

This brings us to some lingering questions that accompany Wimbush's Afrocentric reading of the Bible. First, is his biblical theology too christocentric to be fair to all the biblical materials as academically understood and reconstructed? Wimbush's biblical theology is grounded in the canonically represented ministry of

Jesus. It does not take into serious account the vast variety of materials that constitute the Bible, nor does it pay serious attention to the wide variety of other witnesses that were not canonized. It consequently overlooks those passages in the Hebrew Bible that call into question, or at the very least complicate, the dominant existential orientation he imposes upon the corpus. Wimbush addresses such detractions from his program when he says, "There have also been arguments proffered to convince readers that the legacy of the Bible is decidedly more mixed than the argument for the radical orientation suggests and that any claims about radical orientations ought to be tempered."[82] He goes on to say,

> What these arguments fail to reflect is understanding of the critical difference between, on the one hand, the necessary mirroring of the societies and cultures on the part of biblical characters and communities as they interact with the societies and cultures of which they are a part, and, on the other hand, the different baseline orientation being modeled by biblical characters and communities.[83]

He says the relationship between the biblical characters and communities and their larger cultural contexts was more often synergistic than bipolar. And although one would find it difficult to disagree in principle with Wimbush's characterization of the biblical materials, determining the "baseline orientation" of these characters and communities is not as simple as he represents. When biblical materials (i.e., characters and communities) fall short of the ideal of radical orientation as understood by Wimbush, are we supposed to fault the synergistic relationship or the characters and communities? As one biblical maxim reads, "Thus you will know them by their fruits" (Matt 7:20). The only trustworthy radical orientation to be discerned from the biblical materials is the one that is practiced by its characters and communities. As Bailey's analysis demonstrates quite vividly, actors and authors of the Bible can act in ways diametrically opposed to Wimbush's radical orientation. Are we simply to dismiss such actions as misunderstandings of the baseline orientation, or should we conclude that a diverse understanding and appropriation of the divine call was present from the beginning?

Wimbush is most certainly correct when he asserts that how the discussion is framed makes all the difference.[84] In addition, his claim for a radical orientation may still win at the end of the day. However, it cannot succeed, in my estimation, as long as Wimbush suggests that his hermeneutic of radical orientation is discovered inductively through reading the wide range of biblical materials themselves. Clearly, Wimbush has determined and highlighted a strongly christocentric liberatory center to his enterprise, one that seeks to bind the materials together in a meaningful fashion for modern marginalized readers of the text. In many respects, he has broached again the issue of canon.

Wimbush's proposals raise a second lingering question: Is his hermeneutical enterprise, with its emphasis on the history of African American engagement with the Bible and privileging of the second reading strategy as he defines it, really an engagement with the present situation of African Americans, or is it, in truth, a veiled call for traditionalism in African American engagement with and appropriation of the Bible? When Wimbush says that his interpretive project "reflects the challenge to return to and privilege traditional African and African American traditions and sensibilities," is that not equivalent to his saying that African Americans should go back to the past, the tradition, rather than attempt to understand, exegete, and confront the current conditions they face?[85] Of course, in Wimbush's schema the tradition would serve as a point of interaction with the present. Still, one is suspicious that, more often than not, the tradition will determine the trajectory of modern appropriation of the Bible by the community rather than the other way around or dialogically. In essence, Wimbush still wants to begin with the texts — although he would reject this approach using the same criticism he leveled against the historical-critical enterprise — but in his case these "texts" are the record of African American engagement with the Bible rather than the Bible itself. One wonders whether Wimbush's rejection of doctrinalist Christianity and its attempt to Europeanize African American Christianity does not unduly influence his orientation in these matters. By identifying the second reading strategy, with its playfulness and lack of concern for doctrine, as the classic African American engagement with the Bible, Wimbush is launching a frontal attack on any type of engagement with the Bible that looks for fundamentals or absolutes in the sacred text, as he makes clear in his critique of the third African American reading strategy. According to Wimbush, "the Bible actually does not resolve problems, it only raises them again and again in story or different forms of speech."[86] This means that the determination of biblical fundamentals, even when such an absolute entails the sovereignty of God and the universal kinship of humanity, are in effect constructions of historically and socially conditioned engagements with the Bible ("world"). These need to be translated, in the technical sense, and critiqued alongside other historical engagements with the Bible to determine the degree to which they express the radical orientation Wimbush detects. Clearly, more discussion needs to be conducted on this matter.

The final lingering question that confronts the reader of Wimbush's proposals is more personal in nature: Is his contextual orientation to the biblical materials too grand a project? Wimbush offers more than just a reading of the biblical materials from a historically conditioned social location; he proposes to reorient radically the entire field of biblical studies. He says, "Anyone can read darkness."[87] By this, he means reading from a particular existential orientation, one that sounds suspiciously similar to the radical orientation Wimbush says the biblical materials possess. The idea that anyone can read the Bible from the traditional African American social location and derive the same "dark" meaning from the texts is to posit a fundamental, although implicit, universalism of human experience that threatens to replace Eurocentric biblical engagement with its no less arrogant Afrocentric counterpart.

The problem with the Eurocentric paradigm, as traditionally challenged by African Americans and others, is that it claims to be all-encompassing, accounting for the entirety of human interaction with the Bible in light of its European appropriation. By suggesting that all persons can read "darkly," although it would open up the possibility of more voices being included in the conversation, Wimbush appears to be saying that the Afrocentric, or darker, paradigm sufficiently attains the universality that was missing in the Eurocentric model. In a sense, we are back to Felder's claim that the Bible is the product of persons of African descent with a particular message for other persons of African descent. To substitute Wimbush's terms, the Bible is the product of "dark" persons with a baseline radical orientation that speaks to other "dark" persons confronting somewhat analogous circumstances, and so can be read only "darkly" if it is to be read properly at all. Such universalist tendencies, which appear more often in New Testament scholars, threaten to undermine the central benefit of the recognition of social location as a tool for biblical investigation, the idea that individuals and communities bring distinctive and historically conditioned values and perceptions to their engagement with the biblical texts. Can Wimbush's notion of "darkness" sufficiently account for the variety of social locations found among biblical readers, including those whose location challenges the radical orientation he detects? It remains to be seen.

Clearly, a great deal of Wimbush's rhetoric is self-referential. His playfulness with language, evident throughout his writings, may reflect his privileging of the second reading strategy he identifies. One wonders if his hermeneutical project is not an effort to make his own professional experience in the academic field of biblical studies central to the radical reorientation he proposes. Having experienced the marginalization of his engagement with the Bible in the past, Wimbush boldly proposes to replace the dominant guild orientation with one that would honor his mode of interpretation: "I assume that I am not the only one to face such a problem," he says.[88] Of course, speaking from one's social location or context is central to this mode of biblical interpretation, and efforts to universalize such a perspective are to be expected, but this approach still raises issues of accountability. Wimbush says that his Afrocentric paradigm serves as only one example of the decentering of modern biblical scholarship. This may be true. Still, any effort to speak from one's distinctive social context as a starting point for a more universal program of biblical engagement must be viewed with a degree of suspicion as a potential limiting of the range of possible engagements with the Bible.

The Blackening of the Bible and Its Meaning for Biblical Scholarship

This may be an appropriate point at which to assess the significance of the hermeneutical approaches examined thus far — to schematize them for the sake of clarity. Let us begin with the issue of the acceptance of an African presence in the biblical materials. Copher and Felder build the majority of their analyses around the identification of an African or Afroasiatic presence in the Bible. Bailey, in contrast, accepts an African presence in the Bible but does not go on to argue for an Afroasiatic ethnicity for the Israelites and their descendants. All three begin with the biblical texts as a means of engaging the conversation. Wimbush does not use the Bible as the starting point for his examination but rather uses the function of or engagement with the Bible among African Americans. In this way, he avoids the issue of an African presence in the

Bible, as well as the issue of skin color, which haunts the work of Felder and Copher. It is not clear from Wimbush's work whether an African presence in the Bible plays a significant role at all in his mode of interpretation.

The second issue to be considered is that of the mode of engagement with the Bible. Bailey takes a decidedly literary approach to his interpretation. Although it could be classified as a historical-critical approach in the classical sense, Bailey spends little energy attempting to reconstruct the original historical context of the biblical passages he examines. In stark contrast, Copher, Felder, and Wimbush take a decidedly historical orientation to the biblical texts. Copher and Felder concentrate their energies on reconstructing the original historical contexts of the biblical passages. Wimbush focuses on the history of engagement with the Bible ("readings").

This second issue for consideration leads to a third: the starting point for their respective hermeneutical approaches. Copher, Felder, and Bailey assume a more traditional starting point for textual inquiry — the texts themselves. Copher and Felder use their historical reconstructions to speak to modern African Americans and their social plight. Bailey takes a more nuanced approach by looking at the texts as literature, seeking to understand them on their own terms, and then applying his liberatory hermeneutic to address modern social concerns. Wimbush stands apart from this more conventional orientation by beginning his investigation with the tradition of African American engagement with the Bible ("the historic 'readings' of the text").[89] Certainly, Copher, Felder, and Bailey more reflect the norm for biblical scholarship, while Wimbush embraces a more contemporary, almost reception history orientation looking at the history of African American appropriations.

The fourth issue for consideration is the function of Afrocentricity in the approaches of the various scholars. Copher and Felder are decidedly historical in their establishment of Afrocentricity, making it dependent on the identification of particular ethnic groups in the Bible. The value of Copher and Felder's hermeneutical engagement with the Scriptures rests in the ability of modern African Americans to read themselves in the biblical witnesses and thus derive existential strength from their long and proud history as reflected even in the sacred text. Bailey's Afrocentricity does not necessitate the presence of Africans in the biblical materials, although he does accept their presence. His liberatory orientation challenges the biblical literature in light of an extratextual standard that is nevertheless echoed at the core of the biblical witness. Bailey's Afrocentricity is found in his mode of engagement with the text. It is not dependent upon the historical presence of Africans in the Bible, just as it is not dependent on a baseline radical orientation to be discovered in it. Wimbush stands somewhere in the middle. Using African American engagement with the Bible as his starting point, he detects a radical orientation in the existential stance that African Americans constructed from their reading and appropriation of at least some of the biblical materials. What validates this engagement with the Bible, however, is the presence of such a radical orientation in the Bible itself. Thus, Wimbush's hermeneutical program is just as dependent on the veracity of his historical reconstruction as are those of Copher and Felder.

This raises a fifth issue for consideration: the degree to which these authors connect the biblical materials to the everyday lives of African Americans. Wimbush is the most explicit in his connection between the Bible and modern African American existence. By focusing on the complex interactions between African Americans and this particular sacred text, he easily establishes a context in which modern African American engagement with the Bible can occur. Bailey, functioning as both an advocate for a particular liberatory voice behind the biblical texts and a critic of instances wherein the biblical materials fail to heed that voice, offers a more complex mode of engagement with the Bible. While he clearly seeks the liberatory, although sometimes subversive, reading of biblical materials as a means of engaging modern African American concerns, Bailey's approach is not as explicit as that of Wimbush.

On this issue, Felder and Copher must be divided. Although both projects contain more implicit connections to the modern African American experience — connections that must be determined on the basis of a racialized reconstruction of antiquity — Copher's program does not appear to be as grand as the one proposed by Felder. In this case, Felder's insistence on a certain racialized understanding of the biblical authors transforms the entire biblical corpus into a message by black folks to black folks, as well as others. It is only when one accepts Felder's understanding of the biblical context that one can make connections between the Bible and modern African American life.

The sixth issue to be considered is each author's relationship to an overarching biblical theology, that is, the degree to which each scholar can identify and articulate one central concept, vision, orientation, or hermeneutic with respect to the biblical materials. Felder and Wimbush offer strong biblical theological orientations to the reader. Bailey's orientation is weak. For Copher, such a position is difficult to determine. Because of Bailey's orientation toward the liberatory potential inherent in the biblical texts, his central orientation lies somewhat outside the biblical materials themselves. This mode of engagement, however, allows Bailey to affirm and challenge texts while simultaneously allowing them to speak with their own voices. Felder, in contrast, points to the biblical mandates for (social) justice as the central unifying concept behind his reading of the Bible. Justice in historical reconstruction, as well as justice in modern social interactions, especially those within the fictive kinship relationship that constitutes the church, characterizes Felder's understanding and appropriation of the Bible. Likewise, Wimbush points to a radical orientation among biblical characters and communities as his fundamental and pervasive unifying concept. The validity of this biblical orientation is confirmed for him in the historic appropriation of this same existential stance by African Americans, at least at the initial stage of their engagement with the Bible.

The final issue for consideration in this schematization of African American scholars is their understandings of canon. Again, although Copher appears to take a more traditional approach to the understanding of canon, his views are not sufficiently known (at least by this author) to come to any concrete conclusions. As we saw in the last chapter, other scholars have already questioned Felder's decidedly traditional understanding of the scriptural principle, that is, the idea that Scripture should function as the primary datum on which Christian theological claims are built.[90] Thus, there is no need to address it again here other than to affirm their reading of Felder based on the materials examined. Bailey situates his canonical voice not in the biblical materials as they presently stand, but in the Word of God that stands behind these historically and ideologically conditioned literary representations. His understanding of canon is, consequently, more complicated and nuanced than Felder's. Wimbush's program, in contrast, appears to take the more traditional Protestant approach of appealing to a canon within the canon. By this, I mean the theological approach that emphasizes some biblical concepts more heavily than others, thereby establishing a group of Scriptures that function with more authority than others. What is distinctive about Wimbush's canon is that it is not found in the Bible per se; rather, it is found in the history of African American engagement with the Bible. The cultural self-formation informing his hermeneutical project, as well as the third characteristic of the African American history of readings according to a clear hermeneutical principle, makes his theologically constructed *principium cognoscendi* abundantly clear, without which no consist radical orientation could be discernable at all. His notion of radical orientation is just one reflection of his understanding of canon. By accepting his canon in a mediated form, Wimbush is able to sidestep the sticky issue of addressing the various materials in the Bible on their own terms. Furthermore, he does not need to justify the validity of his canon through detailed biblical analysis, a mode of engagement that might disprove his canonical claims. He only has to point to a particular African American appropriation of an existential stance to prove his point.

Having situated these scholars' various approaches in light of larger disciplinary and theological concerns, let us now move on to another mode of African American biblical interpretation. Unlike the previous approaches discussed, this mode of engagement with the Bible factors in gender as well as ethnicity.

Chapter 4

The Womanization of Blackness

Usually referring to outrageous, audacious, courageous, or willful behavior.... [Womanism means wanting] to know more and in greater depth than is considered "good" for one.[1]

In Search of Our Mothers' Gardens: The Relationship of Womanist Interpretation to the Larger Afrocentric Enterprise

Many, even among African Americans, may not be familiar with womanist engagements with the biblical texts. In the last chapter, I looked at the development of Afrocentric interpretation in light of its relationship to corrective historiography. I observed that African American biblical scholars, such as Bailey and Wimbush, employed the Afrocentric paradigm in a manner that made it less dependent on the historical-critical paradigm of beginning with the texts and their historical reconstruction as a basis for constructing hermeneutical and theological claims. With varying aims at stake, these authors made Afrocentricity a culture-specific engagement with and appropriation of the biblical materials. In this chapter, I examine another aspect of the Afrocentric paradigm, the inclusion of gender, as well as ethnicity, in one's approach to the Bible. For those unfamiliar with the outlines of the womanist orientation to reading the Bible, I offer the following overview.

Claiming Their Voices in the Struggle

Defining a womanist appears simple enough. She is a black feminist or feminist of color.[2] The implications of this form of self-understanding, however, are enormous. Womanist biblical interpretation involves focusing on the African American woman's

experience as a point of departure. It begins with an analysis of
the multiple forms of oppression, such as racism, sexism, classism,
and heterosexism, that historically have affected and stigmatized
African American women in their domestic, religious, and political lives. (By political, I mean their broader social engagements as
citizens in a legally constructed and determined social order.)

Womanists have cultivated their own collective hermeneutical
voice. Dissatisfied with feminist interpretation as well as mainstream African American biblical interpretation, womanist scholars
of the Bible, although still a rare find in the guild, have vocalized their distinctive although related hermeneutical agenda. From
feminists they have constructed an engagement that focuses on the
interplay between the biblical text and the biblical interpreter. Like
other Afrocentric interpreters, they recognize that one's reading
and appropriation of the Bible is influenced by historically conditioned social, political, religious, and cultural experiences that
demand as much attention as does the Bible itself. Womanists, feminists, and Afrocentrists join in the rejection of a value-free mode
of interpretation. Womanists cannot disregard issues of ethnicity,
gender, and class in biblical interpretation because they constitute
the very structures that determine their social location from the
beginning.[3]

Claiming their theological voices has come with a price. Feminism, a predominantly Euro-American female enterprise, focuses
on divesting the biblical texts and their interpretations from the
patriarchal structures that call for women's submission and subordination. In the past it tended to avoid the related issues of race
and class that face African American women daily. In time, African
American sympathizers felt that feminism was part of the problem
itself. As bell hooks explains,

> Racism abounds in the writings of white feminism, reinforc-
> ing white supremacy and negating the possibility that women
> will bind politically across ethnic and racial boundaries. Past
> feminist refusal to draw attention to and attack racial hier-
> archy suppressed the link between race and class. Yet class
> structure in American society has been shaped by the racial
> politics of white supremacy.[4]

In a similar manner, African American liberation theologians
and biblical interpreters, a predominantly male group, have railed
and continue to rail consistently against Euro-American structures
of racial oppression and their supporting religious ideologies, yet

they impose and perpetuate patriarchy in their community. The decision to break away from their male counterparts was not an easy one, as poet Gwendolyn Brooks makes clear: "Black women, like all women, certainly want, and are entitled to, equal pay and privileges. But black women have a second 'twoness.' Today's black men, at last flamingly assertive and proud, need their black women beside them, not organizing against them."[5]

African American women cofounded civil rights organizations, led protests, and risked their very lives for the community's freedom, only to be relegated to second-class partners in the struggle — their existential concerns being subsumed under the black man's desire to realize his own freedom. Eventually, as Kelly Brown Douglas once said, "Many of the African-American women involved in this struggle ... discovered that the civil rights/Black Power movement was as sexist as the women's movement was racist."[6] Out of this crucible, the womanist voice was born.

Acknowledging an undeniable solidarity with feminists and male African American liberationists, womanists distinguish themselves with an interpretive paradigm that is "broad in the concrete."[7] Focusing initially on their particular existential issues, womanists also make connections with and seek to address the existential concerns of African American men (racism), Euro-American women (sexism), and the poor (classism) — a multidimensional problem that necessitates a multidimensional approach. The singular concern of the womanist enterprise is the full liberation of African American women from these multiple oppressive structures that influence their daily lives; this liberation would lead to the liberation of the entirety of humanity. "Wholeness" is a central conceptual paradigm employed by womanists to expand their analyses of their own social locations to address broader human existential concerns.

As has become apparent, the hermeneutical approach that forms womanist interpretation is foremost contextual. It begins with the social location of black women. It decisively addresses a world comprised of multiple forms of oppression that work simultaneously to marginalize them as well as others. Womanist scholars extract the values and traditions inherited from African American women — a remote and often overlooked area of the repository of human knowledge passed on to us — as a source for theological reflection. Autobiographies, songs, slave narratives, speeches, and sermons form the primary and canonical sources for the

womanist hermeneutical enterprise. With this repository, womanists approach the biblical texts with a critical posture. They seek
not only to unmask the historical context of the Bible, but also to
name the specific agendas, cultural biases, ideological motivations,
and political influences that brought forth the texts in their final
form. In a similar manner, they analyze the history of interpretation that accompanies the inheritance of these texts by the modern
reader. The task of unmasking any ideological subjugation inherent
in the biblical texts, as well as in their interpretation, is performed
in service to a holistic liberatory stance that rests on the womanist
canon of sources. Womanist interpreters discriminate between biblical texts that affirm their liberatory posture and those that seek
only to perpetuate their subjugation and marginalization. Howard
Thurman's grandmother, an ex-slave, serves as a good example of
this form of biblical interpretation:

> "During the days of slavery," she said, "the master's minister
> would occasionally hold services for the slaves. Alas the white
> minister used as his text something from Paul. 'Slaves be obe-
> dient to them that are your masters...as unto Christ.' Then
> he would go on to show how, if we were good and happy
> slaves, Christ would bless us. I promised my Maker that if I
> ever learned to read and if freedom ever came, I would not
> read that part of the Bible."[8]

This internal critique of the Bible by an ex-slave — weighing the
relevance and usage of the materials in light of a liberatory hermeneutical paradigm — forms part of a tradition or repository that
womanists seek to exploit intentionally.

In conclusion, womanist biblical interpretation seeks to engage
and unmask the multiple forms of oppression that determine the
parameters of their daily lives. Going beyond the critique of patriarchy found in feminist biblical scholarship, as well as the critique
of racism found in male African American biblical scholarship,
womanists recognize that attacking singular forms of oppression
is not sufficient to counteract the multifaceted subjugation they
experience as women of African descent living in America. By
unmasking a variety of oppressive structures, including their in-
terrelationships, womanists seek to understand and address the
experiences of all marginalized groups as they "[writhe] silently
under a mighty wrong."[9]

With Her Eyes Wide Open: Renita J. Weems and a Womanist Reading of the Old Testament

Like a majority of contemporary African American scholars, Renita Weems does not teach at a historically black seminary. She teaches at Vanderbilt University Divinity School, a nonsectarian, decidedly ecumenical theological institution situated in a university context with historic ties to the Methodist Episcopal Church, South. As the first African American woman to receive a Ph.D. in Hebrew Bible studies from an American university, Weems has been instrumental in the emergence of womanist biblical interpretation.

Weems employs reader-response criticism in her engagement with the biblical text in a manner reminiscent of *Rezeptions-ästhetik*. By this, I mean that she is concerned primarily with the ways in which texts are received, either by individual readers or by readers belonging to specific groups. The focus is "the extent to which a text circumscribes or directs a particular response, which aspects of a text may be considered inherent and objective, and which are reader-constructed and thus subjective."[10] *Rezeptionsästhetik,* a form of reader-response criticism developed by German theorist and critic Hans Robert Jauss, argues that a "reader approaches any text with a historically informed 'horizon of expectations,' which consists of a reader's knowledge and assumptions about the text and literature in general."[11] In essence, Weems's mode of textual engagement seeks to unmask the complex network of relationships that influences African American women's reception of the Bible as an enduring cultural resource used by both the centrists and the marginalized.

This objective comes across forcefully in Weems's article "Womanist Reflections on Biblical Hermeneutics," in which she offers a critique of the historical-critical paradigm in light of the still emerging insights of reader-response criticism.[12] She challenges the popular assumption that individual existential concerns cannot reflect the entirety of human existence as such. For example, when Felder distinguishes between the status of women in the church and their wider political status, and likewise concludes that Galatians 3:28 is "a call for the emancipation of women within the life of the *Church* (not necessarily society in general)," he is attempting to separate the domestic from the political.[13] He is adopting the same mind-set as those who separate the "public" from the "private." On this basis, women have been relegated to the domestic/private sphere.[14] Even Felder's symbolization of the church as a family suggests that the church, as a domestic realm, can tolerate women in leadership positions while their leadership in the wider social realm is problematic and potentially unbiblical. In response to an almost impermeable public/private differentiation, Weems responds, "[The] personal is political."[15] Any attempt by historical critics, even African American ones, to deny any sort of subjective orientation to their reconstructions of history and readings of texts constitutes outright fraud. As Weems sees it, "[All] interpretive strategies are advocacy positions," to the degree that they have as one of their primary aims the ideological seduction of their intended audience.[16] For Eurocentric male biblical scholars, such an advocacy position seeks to "rationalize and defend their own bourgeois social, economic, political and militaristic orientation."[17] For many of their African American counterparts, advocacy means privileging race to the detriment of sex and class. This is a problem that circumscribes and limits the human potential of women.

The voices of African American women in biblical studies adds to the project of human liberation by naming and addressing the multiple forms of oppression that they experience — oppression that is interconnected and falsely legitimated by the larger society.[18] In other words, the contextual character of this mode of textual investigation is always in the foreground. Weems illuminates how womanist concerns are of a different order than those addressed by feminist biblical interpreters. She explains, "Victimized by multiple categories of oppression (e.g., race, gender, class) and having experienced these victimizations oftentimes simultaneously, women of color bring to biblical academic discourse a broader, and more subtle, understanding of systems of oppression."[19] As a result, Weems evokes the concept of "wholeness," a characteristic of this approach that marks it as distinct from other forms of textual investigation

Wholeness, the recognition that a womanist biblical scholar must confront "all rationalizations for domination and exploitation both within the Bible and in scholarship," is grounded in the recognition of the sociality of all human existence as such.[20] This idea, somewhat analogous to Charles Hartshorne's claim that "all life whatsoever has social structure," illumines the womanists' recognition of the organic and interconnected nature of all systems of oppression.[21] The most fascinating analytical move womanists are able to make involves their ability to address the enormity of these social issues by drawing on the experience of each African American woman. Weems makes such a move in her essay. She evokes her own experience as the epistemic underpinning for her more theoretical assertions.[22]

Weems addresses the Bible directly as an American cultural icon, as well as the research focus for womanist biblical interpretation. Calling the Bible "a thoroughly political document," she makes a claim more common for Hebrew Bible scholars than for their New Testament counterparts: "What we discover in the canon, therefore, is a complete skein of ideological domination that evolved over a long period of time undergirded and rationalized by an equally complex theological structure that evolved over an equally long period of time."[23]

Weems's idea that the Bible is a repository of supremacist ideology is complicated, but not contradicted, by her admission that patriarchy is not a social structure of biblical design. As she understands it, "The Bible is a compilation of materials that accrued over a thousand-year period; and while it is capable of providing important illumination as to how patriarchy spread and flourished within a certain geographic region, it does not provide any information about the origins of patriarchy."[24] Simply, the canon is a repository of ideological domination that has influenced, and continues to influence, the construction and maintenance of systems of existential marginalization, although it cannot be said to be the actual source of that ideology itself. The Bible is only one aspect of the womanist existential dilemma.

The degree to which the Bible supports and perpetuates oppression must be an aspect of womanist analysis nevertheless. Weems uses the Israelite concept of election as just one illustration. Drawing on the insights of other biblical approaches, she argues that the core of biblical authority resides in its ideology:

> For what functions as the cornerstone of the Bible's authority is not only its claim to a divine guided history (which historical criticism challenges), nor is it simply its claim to a patriarchal value-system which is sanctioned by a patriarchal deity (which feminist theology rightly criticizes). Rather, the Bible's renown is grounded in large part in the claim of Israel's (and later the church's) election.[25]

The idea that the Israelites were chosen undergirds much of the rhetoric one encounters in the Hebrew Bible, as it also influences the literary depictions that portray interactions between this privileged group and their unprivileged counterparts. The impact this ideology of election had on the ancient Israelites and subsequent readers, including the church, which adopted its own version of election, must be analyzed in order for modern readers to resist the ideological seductiveness of this exclusivist biblical concept. Such a critical posture toward a widely accepted biblical-theological construction demonstrates, quite vividly, the womanist concern for ideologies of domination, however they may be portrayed or justified. As a counterexample, Weems points to the prophetic book of Amos as one intrabiblical critique of the Israelite ideology of election.

The differences between Weems's mode of engagement with the biblical materials and those examined thus far are numerous. First, unlike other modes of Afrocentric engagement that take a critical posture toward Eurocentric representations of history, but present historiography itself as benign, Weems approaches the entire enterprise with a critical posture. She recognizes that history is as much a narrative intended for a particular audience with a certain ideological orientation ("history for") as it is about the assemblage of available data ("history of"). Second, Weems is not only critical of Eurocentric male biblical scholars but also self-critical to the degree that her interpretive communities include Afrocentric and feminist biblical scholars of whom she is also critical. The self-referentiality of womanist biblical criticism, according to Weems, allows it to maintain its "prophetic edge."[26] Unlike feminists and Afrocentrists, womanists maintain that the multiple influences of oppression that affect the lives of African American women cannot be unmasked through a single method or approach. They can be confronted effectively only through a multilateral orientation that includes continuing self-critique. Third, Weems employs a womanist canon to engage the Bible, one that derives from a long tradition of historically conditioned female interactions with the Bible as a cultural and ideological tool. This authority is actually extrabiblical but is grounded in a history of reception. This hermeneutical stance trusts in the history of African American women's appropriations (or lack thereof) of the biblical materials as existentially valid and authoritative. Unlike Wimbush, Weems does not advocate the critical engagement of the reception history itself. Criticism lies with the modern interpreter and her immediate circumstances. The repository of womanist tradition appears sacrosanct. One might suspect that selectivity arises when it comes to the inclusion of African American women's voices in the canon, but Weems does not address this issue. Finally, Weems is the first author examined thus far whose hermeneutical enterprise involves an explicit recognition of the socially ordered character of existence as such. Her recognition that even the structures of oppression that influence African American women's lives are organic suggests that life, even at its most basic level, is an interconnected or socially ordered system. In this way, Weems expands the Afrocentric paradigm to include not only issues of gender but also broader philosophical and theological concerns. Her method of interpretation embraces philosophical theology — "the sustained, deliberate, and therefore specialized reflection whereby the primary expression of religion is subjected to critical analysis and interpretation" — in a way that other liberatory hermeneutical approaches have not.[27]

A more developed discussion of Weems's hermeneutical approach is found in "Reading *Her Way* through the Struggle: African American Women and the Bible."[28] In this essay, she examines how women read the Bible to discover the rationale by which African American women can continue to regard the Bible as meaningful.[29] What is most interesting about her analysis is the central thematic chord she strikes repeatedly. According to Weems, the history of African American women's engagement with the Bible is one marked by ambivalence. This hermeneutical insight marks an important departure from other analyses of African American appropriations of the biblical text.

Weems begins by drawing on the insights of feminist literary criticism and African American scholarship to argue for the importance of social location to the reading encounter. Responding to a query once raised by Jonathan Culler — "Suppose the informed reader of a work of literature is a woman. Might this not make a difference?" — Weems says that it does.[30] Like Wimbush, she believes that the interaction between the reader and the text is complex. She argues that the values of the reader when confronted by the values of the text determines the text's ability to arouse, manipulate, and seduce the reader to its ideological perspective.

Of course, a reader's values are historically conditioned. Meaning then has as much to do with the various social influences that act upon her as she engages the text as it does with the values embedded in the text itself. Weems points implicitly to Howard Thurman's grandmother as an example of how African American women have engaged the Bible in the past. This leads to her assertion that "African American women have not attempted to negotiate fully the socio-literary universe of the Bible as paradigmatic of a truly liberationist and liberated hermeneutic."[31] As a consequence, Weems justifies her appeal to the womanist canon as a standard that African American women apply when reading and interpreting the Bible. This orientation then pervades the rest of her analysis. She proceeds in two parts. The first consists of a brief examination of the social location of African Americans within the context of American history. The second consists of an examination of selected biblical texts to illustrate how African American women attempt to engage them.

Weems admits in an accompanying footnote that some may challenge her analysis, arguing that her language "tends to obscure the enormous differences among African American women."[32] She responds by appealing to the contextual nature of the womanist enterprise itself. She admits that her perspective is somewhat limited. She says, "I am referring to myself (and a small sample of women with whom I am personally familiar)," but counters that her aim "is simply to call attention to the special circumstances of a segment of readers who previously have been overlooked in biblical and theological studies and to reclaim their presence in American religious history."[33]

In the first part of her examination, she reflects on the effect that illiteracy had on the subsequent reading practices of African Americans. Like Wimbush, she believes that the original mode of African American biblical engagement was marked by a great deal of hermeneutical freedom. African Americans, because they were barred from reading during slavery, were "without allegiance to any official text, translation, or interpretation."[34] Their primary mode of engagement with the Bible was through "word of mouth."[35] Through public readings, sermons, stories, songs, prayers, and other means, Africans in America appropriated and "studied" the Bible through the facilities of listening and memory.[36] Weems concludes that this mode of engagement created an aura around the Bible, as it did around the act of reading itself. She says, "African Americans to this day continue to view reading as an act with mystery, power, and danger."[37]

Illiteracy permitted African American slaves the latitude to appropriate the Bible — and to transform it — to suit their own existential interests. At this point, Weems diverges from Wimbush's reconstruction of the earliest period of African American engagement with the Bible. She suggests that while some slaves may have appropriated the Bible, even if it was according to their own hermeneutic, others resisted the Bible, or at least certain parts of it. She implies that these different forms of engagement were grounded in the different experiences of male and female slaves. Again, Thurman's grandmother is an illustration. Weems argues that the innate sense of dignity of female slaves was offended by certain biblical statements. Thurman's grandmother resisted and rejected certain readings of the Bible based on her own theological construction of the deity she worshiped ("a God worth believing in"). Still, she knew that offensive statements resided in the canonical text. Consequently, African American female slaves adopted an ambivalent posture toward the sacred text. As Weems explains,

> African American women's earliest exposure to the Bible was characterized by their history as a community of enslaved women of color trying to find meaning and hope for their (communal) existence from a text that was held out as congenial to them as long as they remained slaves, but censorious of them should they seek to become free human beings.[38]

To further clarify her argument, Weems offers two conceptual aids. First, biblical interpretation is not simply a matter of reading a text. "Accuracy" in biblical interpretation also is influenced by the social location of the reader and the extent to which her reading is legitimated and enforced by the dominant culture.[39] Second, the experience of marginalization gives African American women the right to resist both the Bible and the dominant culture when they attempt, either separately or in concert, to negate the "innate sense of identity" and survival instincts of the reader.[40]

Weems concurs with Wimbush regarding the cultural importance of the Bible in the United States. Because of its iconic standing, it is not a text that simply can be ignored. Moreover, since most African American women are raised in an evangelical Protestant environment, the Bible has been presented to them "as *the* medium for experiencing and knowing the will of the Christian God."[41] Such rhetoric only serves to complicate further African American women's engagement with the text. The Bible has been a tool used by the dominating and the dominated in their struggles against each other. As Weems sees it, the interpretations that each group constructs grow out of markedly different social locations. The insight that interpretation derives from context may permit women the ability to overcome their ambivalence through interpretations that advocate a mode of existence to which they can aspire, but it also threatens their engagement because of supremacist interpretations that are legitimated by the dominant culture. In short, the cultural status of the Bible in the United States only further feeds the ambivalence of African American women.

Weems examines the social convention of reading. She argues that "proper" reading conventions are largely a construction of the dominant class and its interests: "[What] is considered the appropriate way to read or interpret literature is dependent upon what the dominant reading conventions are at any given time within a culture."[42] Now Weems has moved beyond the initial aural engagement of African American women with the Bible, assuming it appears to be a literate engagement with the text. Somewhat surprisingly, her argument hovers around the phenomenon of multiple reading strategies flourishing simultaneously in the American Protestant context. Demonstrating the assertion that the dominant reading convention is not absolute, American Protestantism displays a tendency toward fragmentation. By highlighting this tendency, Weems opens up the possibility for different reading strategies between African American men and women. Her argument is complicated somewhat by the lack of a clear distinction between a "reading convention" and a "reading." That is, Weems does not spend a great amount of effort differentiating between readings, reading strategies, and reading conventions. As I see it, a reading convention, the manner in which one approaches and attempts to understand a text, governs, for the most part, a reading. As the example of American Protestantism illustrates, reading conventions do not exert absolute control over the reader's engagement with and appropriation of a given text, but they are important nonetheless.

Reading conventions become pivotally important when individuals attempt to adjudicate between legitimate and illegitimate readings. Because these conventions are generated by the dominant class and its interests, only certain approaches to and appropriations of a text are deemed legitimate by society (e.g., taught in its schools), while others are rejected. According to Weems, the historical-critical method, a specialized reflection of a now dominant reading convention, indicates one approach legitimated by the broader culture. It is one way of saying that "one must be prepared to abandon oneself completely to the world" of the literature that one is reading. Such a convention, according to Weems, complicates the reading process for an African American woman.

She is told by the dominant society, through this convention, that to read properly she must "renounce her experience of reality, suspend her understanding of life, and waive her right to her own values."[43] Dubbed "allowing the text to speak for itself," this convention for textual engagement threatens to negate the importance and relevance of the African American female as a social agent and reader. Weems concludes,

> [The] negative result, especially as it has become evident in the way this [reading convention] has been used by those in power, has been to undermine marginalized reading communities by insisting that their questions and experiences are superfluous... and their interpretations illegitimate, because of their failure to remain objective.[44]

Adopting the perspective of the literature, when it comes to the Bible, means adopting a male, elite, supremacist outlook: "[The] African American female reader of the Bible has, like other women, been taught to suspend her female identity long enough to see the world through the eyes and ears of the male narrator." This reality is further complicated by the role that interpretive communities play in the appropriation of such a male reading perspective. For example, African American women have been influenced to identify with the male narrator of the Bible not simply as a man but as "a certain kind of man."[45] The degree to which an African American female, as a member of a number of different and simultaneously active reading communities, identifies with more than one community at any given time decidedly influences her ability to adopt the biblical narrator's perspective. Using Ruth as an example, Weems illustrates how community influence and the dominant reading convention of the time can work in concert to influence women to adopt an androcentric narrative or "manly" perspective. To read Ruth's story is to see the world through a man's eyes, since the story's narrator was undoubtedly a man. Interestingly, with African American women, this man is often an oppressed one.[46] Weems suggests that even this appropriation of the Bible does harm to and marginalizes African American women: "The African American female reader, in essence, finds herself permanently reading as an outsider as long as she is unwilling and incapable to deal creatively in partitioning out her double identity as woman and African American."[47]

Because the Bible was not written with African American women as its intended audience, it projects their femaleness as a problem. Thus, these women must be ambivalent and critical about its usage and acceptance — what Weems calls their "aural hermeneutic."[48] This critical posture functions as sensitivity toward all forms of

social and literary oppression. Weems asserts the womanist response
to any sort of biblical oppression:

> She could elect either to reject totally the Bible on account
> of its androcentric bias, to elevate portions of the Bible that
> in her estimation are central for understanding God's liber-
> ating activity and allow those passages to become the norm
> by which all other passages are judged, or to supplant the
> biblical account of salvation history altogether with extra-
> biblical accounts that help provide a fuller, more egalitarian
> reconstruction of the biblical history.[49]

Notice that Weems does not name acceptance as one of the possible
responses. Later, she dismisses momentarily the idea that African
American female academics would reject the Bible totally. She says,
"I believe, at this juncture in their history, African American female
theological scholars want to stand, for as long as they can, with
their constituency within the Christian and biblical traditions."[50]

Seeking to name someplace as affirming, Weems points to the
African American female interpretive community as the most self-
expressive locus of identification for African American women.
As one historically conditioned and culturally specific reading
community, the African American female interpretive community
complicates Wimbush's conceptualization of the overall reading
community by arguing that women's interests are, at times, divergent from those of men. Weems makes this clear when she quotes
Mary Helen Washington:

> If there is a single distinguishing feature of the literature of
> Black women — and this accounts for their lack of recogni-
> tion — it is this: their writing is about Black women; it takes
> the trouble to record the thoughts, words, feelings, and deeds
> of Black women, experiences that make the realities of be-
> ing Black in America look very different from what men have
> written.[51]

In short, African American women have effectively two available
strategies: discriminate in usage or supplant.

Weems begins the second part of her essay by revisiting the
cultural importance of the Bible and highlighting its ideological
situatedness. As the product and legitimizing agent of the victors,
the Bible offers scant hope to African American female readers,
who are among the vanquished. The Bible has not muffled the

marginalized voice entirely. As she sees it, "While the conspicu-
ous ethos of the Bible is the viewpoints of those in history whose
claims won out, close scrutiny of the Bible will yield in some cases
sketchy hints of counterclaims of rival groups."[52]

Instead of reading the Bible from the perspective of its canonized
narrator, which leads inevitably to reinforcement of the dominant
class's interests, Weems proposes that "[marginalized] readers in
general, and African American women in particular...use whatever means necessary to recover the voice of the oppressed within
biblical texts."[53] Recovering the voice of the marginalized in the
Bible allows the African American woman the ability to use the
Bible in an existentially self-affirming manner.

Employing the work of Sheilah Briggs, Weems demonstrates
how the voice of a marginalized individual can be recovered.
She focuses her attention on Philemon, a Pauline epistle with a
controversial history of interpretation. Instead of engaging this
complicated history of interpretation, Weems simply highlights
Onesimus as the marginalized voice in the text. The shared social location of the author and the recipient is clear to Weems.
Paul's privileged social status is reflected in his advocacy of Onesimus's case. Weems then asserts that Paul had a restrictive vision of
the kingdom of God. As she reads him, Paul's vision of kingdom
existence is confined to "a vindicated community of religiously oppressed men."[54] This may explain his popularity among African
American male (patriarchal) readers. Peering through Paul, Weems
"hears" the voice of Onesimus, a runaway slave, who thought a
precarious freedom to be superior even to Christianized slavery.
She concludes that there were those like Onesimus among the early
Christians who "understood their humanity and their religiosity
differently" from Paul, the dominant (and dominating) voice of
the text.

After a brief discussion of the exodus account, Weems turns her
attention to the story of Hagar, the Egyptian slave of Abraham
and Sarah (Gen 16:1–16; 21:1–21). She highlights the unmis-
takable analogy between Hagar's experience and that of many
African American women. Recounting the power struggle that
ensued between Hagar and Sarah, Weems bemoans that many African American women throughout history have struggled under
similar circumstances. Hagar's story may not offer many positive
strategies for African American women and their survival, but it
does underscore why ambivalence has occupied a central place

in their approach to the Bible, other feminists, and other Afro-centrists. Weems concludes with this insight: "The voice of the oppressed in the end is not the predominant voice. In fact, theirs is a voice that could be viewed as random aberrant outbursts in a world otherwise rigidly held together by its patriarchal attitudes and androcentric perspective."[55] Nevertheless, if the Bible is to remain meaningful to African American women, then the voices of the marginalized must be recovered, nurtured, and claimed in spite of their embeddedness in a document that otherwise continues to marginalize them.

It may now be good to consider the central themes that run throughout Weems's work. It is clear from this discussion that her closest conversation partners among the scholars we have examined thus far are Wimbush and Bailey. Because of his own engagement with a form of reader-response criticism, Wimbush appears even closer to Weems's position. As one can see, she complicates the paradigm Wimbush proposed. Weems's reading of the African American response to its first engagement with the Bible challenges Wimbush's strong suggestion that the African American community appropriated the Bible uniformly. It further undermines Wimbush's claim that African Americans detected a "radical orientation" at the core of the biblical witness, a cornerstone of his biblical theology. When she points to African American women's ambivalence regarding the biblical texts, her analysis operates as a potential foil to all universalist claims regarding the appropriation of biblical texts.

Another way in which Weems distinguishes herself is the absence in her work of any discussion regarding the African or black presence in the Bible. Of course, one finds the same tendency in others' work. She focuses rather on the African American presence in front of the Bible. We can see then a decided shift away from arguments about the Bible itself to arguments about the persons who engage it. As with Bailey, the move away from issues of skin color (and now issues of ethnicity) in the biblical literature allows for the construction and maintenance of a more defensible Afrocentric hermeneutical approach.

The third theme that characterizes Weems's engagement with the text is her view of the Bible as a complicated literary document that can influence positively its historically conditioned readers. Although she understands the Bible to be a repository of the ideological orientation of the dominators, she argues for its potential meaningfulness to marginalized people nevertheless. Her under-standing of scriptural authority, more radical in orientation than Bailey's, undermines the evangelical Protestant enterprise entirely. If ambivalence and resistance are to characterize womanist engage-ment with the biblical text, then the degree to which they can be used as the norm for Christian faith and practice is severely jeop-ardized. Weems acknowledges that women have found, and will continue to find, values in the Bible that affirm their own. In itself, this is not a problem. The difficulty lies in the Bible's cultural status as sacred text. To put it another way, her central concern with the Bible is not that it functions as an influential text in American cul-ture but that the dominant culture has determined that the Bible *ought* to function as an influential text in our society, governing how individuals experience and understand their everyday lives. If the Bible were consistently liberating and affirming of "the least of these," then such a status might not be a concern. But it does not. Its use, then, as a trustworthy guide to Christian faith and practice is complex and relative at best.

As we saw with Bailey, it is possible to question aspects of the doctrine of *sola scriptura* without discarding it altogether. Weems, a well-known preacher with a national reputation, does see re-demptive value in the biblical materials. Still, she has a complicated relationship with the text, one mediated through her experience as an African American woman and her exposure to the historical-critical method. In her challenge to biblical normativity resides a vigorous dialogical engagement among experience, doctrine, and scholarship. The degree to which any viable notion of *sola scrip-tura* can continue to function alongside such a thoroughgoing critique may rest on the results of a similar contextual approach.

Weems's approach provides an undeniable voice to the mar-ginalized. Whether through recovery or resistance, the voices of the oppressed are foregrounded in her hermeneutic. She is Afro-centric in that she speaks from an explicitly African American female perspective. Beginning with her experience of multiple forms of oppression, she addresses the existential concerns of Afri-can descendants in America, giving depth and complexity to that experience through her engendered social location. The woman-ist concern for wholeness also allows Weems to speak to concerns other than those facing African American women specifically. Her stance thus allows her to address traditional Afrocentric concerns as well as to reinvigorate the universal scope that Afrocentrism has always sought to maintain.

What marks a stark contrast between Weems and the others is her singular conceptualization of the biblical message. The Bible is the ideological product of ancient social victors seeking to justify their own oppression, and the tool of contemporary social victors seeking to do the same. The idea of diversity within the canon, which Wimbush believes will rescue African Americans from the monolithic error of fundamentalism, and the idea of divergent stances among the victors, demonstrated by Bailey's analysis, are not to be found in Weems, at least not in the same fashion. She advocates the recovery of the voices of the marginalized in the Bible and believes that sometimes they come to the fore (i.e., to the level of the text), but for the most part Weems maintains that the clear and consistent voice of the Bible speaks in favor of the few dominating the many. One wonders whether this singular orientation to Scripture will prove difficult to maintain in the future, or even if it will be helpful to the further expansion of womanism. It remains to be seen.

Will womanist scholars, like Weems, be able to argue persuasively their fundamental Christian commitment, given such a critical posture toward the canon? This may prove the most important question for womanists to answer. African American Christians traditionally have held rather conservative views regarding what can and cannot be said of the Bible. The womanist unmasking of the ways in which the Bible creates and maintains oppression may not appeal to the larger, male-dominated, African American reading community. Weems does not propose, for example, the sort of christocentric focus that one finds in Wimbush. Although womanist theology does have a christological component, it is not apparent here. Womanists may have to engage in an intense internal debate to define and communicate their Christian, especially Protestant, commitment.

Another issue is the sufficiency of the womanist canon to authorize their critique of the canon as well as their theological constructions. Appealing to an "innate sense of dignity," like appealing to the internal Word, is difficult to maintain in a discipline so reliant on so-called objective criteria for its conclusions. Recovering the voices of Onesimus, Hagar, and other marginalized individuals based on often little more than intuition is difficult to legitimate. If Weems is correct in her suggestion that the historical-critical method is a specialized derivative of a reading convention that advocates self-denial and is maintained by dominant class interests, then womanist interpretation may need to wait for a more advanced epoch in human understanding. Copher, Felder, Bailey, and Wimbush, as well as others, employ this reading convention to some degree in their hermeneutical endeavors. It does not appear that this reading convention, even if modified, will be replaced soon.

Another lingering question that should be raised with respect to Weems's scholarship is this: Is the wall between the personal and the public as permeable as she intimates? By saying that the personal is political, Weems suggests that they are equivalent. In order to clarify the relationship between the two, if any, Weems or another womanist needs to define or refine the boundary.

The final lingering question that Weems raises for the reader has to do with the future of Afrocentric hermeneutics. As indicated above, Afrocentric hermeneutics in the style of Weems and Wimbush appears to have left behind most attempts at historical reconstruction, especially in the case of identifying an African presence in the text, and appears to have bypassed a focus on the literary representations of Africans as well. We will see later how this trend manifests itself.

A Quest for Wholeness: Clarice J. Martin and a Womanist Reading of the New Testament

Clarice J. Martin, who formerly taught at Colgate Rochester Divinity School as well as other theological institutions, currently teaches in the department of humanities at Colgate University. A New Testament scholar, she has been a consistent voice for womanist interpretation in the guild of biblical studies.

Martin begins her essay "Womanist Interpretations of the New Testament: The Quest for Holistic and Inclusive Translation and Interpretation" on familiar ground.[56] In her description of the effects of multiple forms of oppression on African American women, she includes language as one of those forms. She argues that linguistic oppression, as with other forms of oppression, has a detrimental effect on how African American women experience the sacred. She says, "Experiences of oppression, like all human experience, affect the way in which women and men code and decode sacred and secular reality."[57]

In her focus on language, Martin maintains that African American women, like African Americans generally, must "imagine" themselves as represented in popular secular and sacred imagery. They must imagine themselves as "represented in so-called generic representations of all humanity in biblical traditions that are [punctuated] by the almost exclusive usage of male-gendered pronouns."[58] Soon, Martin moves to her central focus: the translation of the term *doulos*.

Martin begins by engaging the debate surrounding how *doulos* should be translated: either as "slave" or "servant." The tendency among many in the United States is to render *doulos* as "servant" because of the cultural sensitivities around slavery that have arisen in the post–Civil War era. After looking at several scholarly analyses of the term, Martin concludes that *doulos* should be translated as "slave" in most New Testament texts. She says, "In the final analysis, every single occurrence of *doulos* in the New Testament must be examined within its particular literary and sociohistorical context to determine the author's intention in the use of the term, including any nuance which should be assigned to it."[59] Martin does recognize, however, the volatile potential in such a program of translation.

Describing the social context of the Greco-Roman world, Martin amplifies the social status of the slave for the modern reader. She even observes that Jesus is described as "taking the form of a [*doulos*]" in the famous Philippians hymn, and that slavery becomes paradigmatic for early Christian understandings of discipleship (Phil 2:7).[60] She concludes that instead of rejecting the proper translation of the term, scholars should carefully and empathetically explain the complexities of slavery in the ancient world in order to assist modern readers in understanding its central importance to early Christianity.

Recognizing the importance of retrieving the voices of the marginalized, Martin highlights the complexity of the existential issues that confront more than just African American women. The Bible, according to Martin, has within it texts that are pervasively androcentric and oppressive for women, as well as for children, slaves, foreigners, and others. She says, "Not all of the suppressed voices in androcentric texts can be intoned in a feminine key."[61] Martin seems to suggest by this statement that patriarchy, as defined traditionally by feminists, is not sufficient to unmask and confront the multiple forms of oppression present in society.

In fact, her examination of patriarchy clarifies that this is her understanding. As she points out, "Patriarchal oppression and degradation includes and transcends the category of gender."[62] This oppression pervades not only the Bible but also biblical interpretation, including translation. Using Onesimus as an illustration,

Martin argues that any translation of *doulos* as something other than "slave" would obfuscate the precarious nature of slavery in early Christianity. Translating *doulos* as "servant" amounts to a retreat into euphemism. This is unacceptable to Martin, who says, "[Euphemistic] translation risks 'masking' socioeconomic or political verities that are of fundamental significance in assessing historical and symbolic meaning."[63] Moreover, such a translation would make it difficult for nonspecialized readers to identify, unmask, and confront the oppressive authority structures embedded in the Bible. In short, it would amount to a reinforcement of patriarchy in euphemistic guise.

Of course, one concern behind the translation of *doulos* is how African Americans will respond to pervasive slave imagery in the New Testament. At this point, Martin summarily surveys the history of the arguments surrounding slavery in the United States. She observes that arguments on behalf of slavery appealed to the Bible as an authority without equivocation. She then notes that African American slaves resisted such an interpretation of the Bible. Believing that something liberatory may have been operative in the earliest Christian engagement with slavery, Martin calls on womanist scholars to probe the Bible, as well as other Christian traditions, "to determine whether anything in those traditions suggests that there were impulses at work in the earliest Christian communities which either ameliorated slavery and (or) advocated its abolition altogether."[64] In essence, Martin argues that the concern of African Americans regarding slavery as represented in the New Testament is valid. She also argues, however, that rather than euphemistically translating *doulos* as "servant," womanist scholars should find ways to redeem the term for modern African American readers. In her view, "A womanist biblical hermeneutic must clarify whether the *doulos* texts, potential 'texts of terror' for black people, can in any way portend new possibilities for our understanding of what actually constitutes the radicality of the good news of the gospel."[65]

Martin takes up a similar issue in her essay "The *Haustafeln* (Household Codes) in African American Biblical Interpretation: 'Free Slaves' and 'Subordinate Women.' "[66] She says in her introduction that almost no other texts in the New Testament have had such a "malefic" effect on African Americans as the household codes (Col 3:18–4:1; Eph 5:21–6:9; 1 Pet 2:18–3:7).[67] She examines these codes in four ways. First, she gives a brief assessment of contemporary scholarship on the *Haustafeln*. Second, she looks at the household codes in the context of the slave debates in the United States. Third, she looks at the codes with respect to women. Finally, she raises hermeneutical issues confronting the African American community and its use of the *Haustafeln*.

Martin begins by arguing that the texts, generally attributed to Paul, are, in effect, deuteropauline and that 1 Peter is a pseudonymous writing.[68] The relevance of this stance can be found in the debates surrounding the composition of these letters and their relative datings. If Colossians and Ephesians are deuteropauline, then their attribution to Paul notwithstanding, they cannot be classified among the earliest New Testament documents. The "late" dating of these materials then allows Martin to argue that they were not part of the earliest Christian proclamation and thus cannot be taken as a definitive statement of the Christian witness regarding human social interaction.

Recent scholarship has engaged the household management texts by looking at them in their Greco-Roman context. In the first century, the *paterfamilias,* the head of the familial unit, held power over all other members of the household as subordinates. Martin points out that the household codes are really addressed to the weaker members of the social order, giving them advice on their relationships to the dominant male figure. In this sense, the *Haustafeln* represent the perspective of those who would impose this hierarchical structure. Quoting E. A. Judge, Martin says, "What we hear in the *Haustafeln* is 'the voice of the propertied class.' "[69]

Recognizing the fundamental inequality in such an arrangement, Martin reviews three interpretations of the regulations that seek to make sense of their placement in the letters as well as in the larger first-century context. The first argues that the early Christian community, as a minority group, drew on the models of the larger culture. These regulations were Christianized in the process. As ethical mandates, these texts are based on the idea of the "inner equality" of all persons in Christ. This is what Gerd Theissen and others call "love patriarchalism."[70] According to this interpretation, hierarchical relationships of male dominance are to be considered normative, although they must be regulated according to the ethics of agape.

The second has been called "a form of apologia for the Christian faith."[71] According to this reading, the church adopted the *Haustafeln* as a way to deflect criticism from the fledgling movement. By adopting generally accepted societal norms, the New

Testament authors were communicating the idea that Christianity was not a threat to the dominant social order. Similar to this interpretation is the third. Advanced primarily by Elisabeth Schüssler Fiorenza, this argument says that Christianity began as a "discipleship of equals" based on a "praxis of inclusive wholeness."[72] In this early community, women and slaves were permitted to enjoy an equal status with free male citizens. Such a practice of equality threatened to disrupt the highly status-conscious Greco-Roman social order. To protect the emerging movement, the authors of these texts adopted the prevailing social order for the church. Again, this was done to communicate to the larger culture that Christianity was not a threat. In effect, there were only two reasons that the *Haustafeln* were adopted: either as a true representation of Christian social values or as an effort to protect the church from extinction.

Martin then addresses the function of the household codes in the slave debates in the United States. She points out that Charles Hodge and other proslavery advocates used the household regulations in the construction of their arguments. African Americans, in contrast, rejected such a literalist interpretation of the Bible. Martin maintains, " '[Free] slaves' and not 'submissive slaves' was the ringing cry of African Americans in these centuries."[73]

Drawing on the work of James Evans, Martin argues that African Americans approached the *Haustafeln* with a rather sophisticated and astute hermeneutic: "They accepted Paul's statement within *its own sociohistorical context*."[74] She augments this claim by referring to three additional claims. First, the slave regulations did not represent the central thrust of the gospel. Second, slavery was not the primary focus of the letters in which the *Haustafeln* are located. Third, Paul was not Christ and thus was not a completely trustworthy and consistent representative of the truth of the gospel. The curious aspect of Martin's claim has to do with the level of historical sophistication required for slaves to render these kinds of hermeneutical judgments. Of course, slaves could have concluded that "that was then" and "this is now," but Martin is arguing for much more than that. As a largely illiterate population, slaves would have had difficulty arriving at such a conclusion regarding a text with which they had only limited literary access. Even with widespread access to the Bible today, many in the African American community would not arrive at such a critical posture.

This fact is evident in Martin's analogous discourse on women, the heart of her essay. She points out, "[The] notion of females' "inner equality" with males was — and is — viewed as compatible with women's hierarchical subordination, marginality, and inequitable treatment in the domestic, ecclesiastical, and socio-political spheres."[75] She characterizes this interpretive orientation as perpetuating a state of domination. By this, she means "a situation wherein persons assume the right to control individuals or groups that may differ from [them] in race, national origin, class, religion, or sex."[76] In other words, patriarchy, as well as other forms of domination, arises from an inability to negotiate difference.

After briefly examining scholarship on the appropriation of the regulations regarding wives, Martin points out that these texts have been used to dictate not only the nature of marital relationships but the relationships between men and women generally. The continuing marginalization of women suggests that many in the African American community do not engage Scripture with the same level of sophistication as Martin attributes to the slaves prior to the Civil War. Pointing to the same reasons for the rejection of the slave regulations, Martin appears puzzled regarding the continuing strength of such an androcentric interpretation in the African American community. She says,

> Why is the African American interpretive tradition marked by a forceful critique and rejection of a literalist interpretation of the slave regulations in the *Haustafeln*, but not marked by an equally passionate critique and rejection of a literalist interpretation regarding the subordination of women to men in the *Haustafeln*?[77]

Such a question raises concerns about the widespread level of hermeneutical sophistication among African Americans. While it might be true that certain literate African Americans critiqued the household regulations in the manner suggested by Martin, it does not appear evident that such a critical posture was taken across the board.

Martin points to two factors that may negatively influence African Americans' engagement with the *Haustafeln*. First, although African Americans have gravitated toward liberatory texts in the Bible, such as the exodus story, the Bible does not explicitly and consistently model "the liberation of women from patriarchy, androcentrism, and misogyny."[78] Second, although African Americans have been sensitive and critical to the issues of race

and slavery, many of them embrace uncritically a form of socialization that maintains "the patriarchal model of male control
and supremacy that typifies the Eurocentric, Western, Protestant
tradition in general."[79]

What Martin proposes in response to the pervasive and continuing androcentrism of the African American Christian community
is a critical reengagement with Scripture, a "profoundly integrative praxis," that will move women from the margins of African
American religious life to the center.[80] She acknowledges that the
problem with the biblical materials is one of thoroughgoing androcentrism. Even "the early Christian movement is presented through
a patriarchally tinged filter," she says.[81] What is needed are paradigms and strategies for reading the Bible that encourage males
and females to assume an advocacy stance for liberation. Moreover, Martin believes that increased numbers of women in the
ordained ministry and the academy will help to bring to reality this "resocialized vision" of the African American believing
community.[82]

One finds in Martin's work many of the themes we have already
identified with Weems and other womanist interpreters. She is sensitive to the effects of oppression on African American women.
The two essays point to her concern for historical problems that
have faced African American women in particular. Her complimen-
tary concern for wholeness is evident in the way she approaches
the materials. Her engagement appears somewhat traditional when
compared to that of Weems, but this may be due to a difference in
testamental emphasis. Weems begins with a deeply contextual orientation. She attempts to address as fully as possible the context of
African American women before raising broader concerns. Martin
always keeps the broader concerns in view. This approach may give
the reader the impression of timidity at times. Still, Martin puts a
great deal of effort into engaging broader concerns from the outset.

Martin addresses the issue of canon, as have other scholars we
have examined. Like her other New Testament colleagues, Martin
is highly critical of scholarship but not as critical of the New Testament itself. In this way, her analysis is more traditional than that
of Weems. For example, by classifying the *Haustafeln* as late en-
tries to the New Testament, by labeling them deuteropauline and
pseudonymous, Martin is able to create a degree of critical distance between the earliest Christian proclamation and these texts.
This distance grants her the opportunity to critique the texts as
outside the central thrust of the Christian message. Martin never

takes an explicit stand on which of the two reasons for inclusion of the *Haustafeln* she accepts. Implicitly, however, she appears
to adopt the second argument: New Testament authors adopted
the household codes as a means of deflecting negative criticism
of the emerging movement. The reasoning behind this conclusion
is simple: If the *Haustafeln* were an expression of the true self-
understanding of the early Christian communities, Martin would
need to critique not only these "secondary" texts but the core of
the Christian vision of social existence as well. In short, Martin's
engagement with and appropriation of the canon strikes the reader
as more "Christian" than that of Weems. Although she concedes
that the New Testament is filtered through the lens of patriarchy,
she does not appear to think that Christianity is patriarchal as
such. Thus, she protects the "core" of the Christian message from
critique.

Missing from Martin's writing is the "innate sense of dignity"
found in womanist sources; one finds this orientation clearly in
Weems. As a normative source for womanist hermeneutics, at least
according to the presentation in Weems, dignity should be at the
heart of any womanist discuss. The absence of such a conceptual
orientation in Martin appears curious. Martin primarily engages
biblical scholarship as a means of constructing and executing her
arguments. She does appeal to African American women's voices
(e.g., Jarena Lee, Julia Foote, and others) but not in the same way
that Weems does. If an "innate sense of dignity" does operate in
Martin's hermeneutical approach, it is not readily apparent.

Another argument missing from Martin is Weems's bold statement regarding the permeability, or complete absence, of the
personal and the political. Of course, Martin argues for the liberation of African American women in society and the church,
but one does not find in her approach such a radical theoretical
stance. Finally, what one also loses in Martin's writing is the aes-
thetic eloquence that characterizes Weems's approach. Both writers
are Afrocentric in that they address the concerns of African American women in particular and the African American community in
general. Martin, however, engages the broader scholarly conversation in a more explicit manner than does Weems. In short, what
one encounters in Martin's approach is another way of conducting
womanist interpretation. More optimistic of the central message
of the gospel as one of liberation, Martin presents an approach to
biblical interpretation that may gain wider currency in the African
American community than that of Weems.

Sowing Other Seeds in Their Mothers' Gardens

Of course, Weems and Martin are not the only two womanist interpreters in the field. Other voices can be included as well, voices that highlight some of the central tendencies and tensions we have already outlined. We will look at two of these voices to illustrate this point.

Constructing Bridges to Wholeness: Wilma Ann Bailey

Wilma Bailey, who teaches at Christian Theological Seminary in Indianapolis, analyzes the Hebrew Bible laments and the African American spirituals in her essay "The Sorrow Songs: Laments from Ancient Israel and the African American Diaspora."[83] This work amounts to an elaborate analogy between the laments and the spirituals. It is difficult to determine whether Bailey is arguing that there is some deep connection between the two in terms of literary influence, or whether both are just expressions of a pervasive human desire to express pain through poetry. One is more inclined to accept the latter understanding based on Bailey's own statements. For example, she says, "Blacks and Jews created a similar way of responding to the experiences that traumatized their communities."[84] She goes on to say that both spirituals and laments "functioned as a catharsis, a mnemonic device, and an affirmation of the intrinsic hopefulness that nurtures life in the most difficult of situations."[85]

Bailey acknowledges that African Americans not only identified with the biblical Israelites but adopted imagery from the Hebrew Bible as well. Yet she concedes that the laments were not frequently part of the biblical literature presented to slaves, who engaged the Bible primarily through oral presentation. In fact, drawing on the work of John Lovell, Jr., she says, "[The] Bible of the spirituals is a 'thin' Bible with some names and events recurring quite often, others mentioned but rarely, and still others of alleged importance never mentioned."[86]

Pointing to the differences between the laments and spirituals, Bailey observes that African American slaves never understood God to be responsible for their enslavement. Likewise, they did not see it as a punishment for their own sinfulness. One finds both themes in the Hebrew Bible laments. However, both literary forms express a strong belief in God's ability to transform the existential situation of African Americans. Complicating matters, Bailey suggests that the absence of blaming God in the spirituals may have something to do with the not-quite-Christianized status of slaves prior to the Civil War. Quoting former slave Charles Bell, she writes:

> Many [slaves] believed there were several gods, some of whom were good, and others evil, and they prayed as much to the latter as to the former...There [was], in general, very little sense of religious obligation, or duty amongst the slaves on the cotton plantations; and Christianity cannot [have been], with propriety, called the religion of these people.[87]

Bailey posits that the spirituals that either blamed God or expressed non-Christian sentiments were later excised from the collection, acts committed by Euro-American collectors as well as African American ones. Bailey lifts up the slave spirituals as abiding expressions of grief and lament similar to those found in the Hebrew Bible. Like that of Martin, her analysis strikes the reader as generalized. Bailey's womanist focus is implicit in the topic she addresses and the wholeness her engagement seeks to foster. As her conclusion attests, "The grieving could not come to an end until they were free to live as whole human beings."[88]

Telling and Engaging the Whole Story of Liberation: Cheryl A. Kirk-Duggan

Cheryl A. Kirk-Duggan, who teaches at the Graduate Theological Union, although primarily an ethicist, also engages in womanist biblical interpretation. Her essay "Let My People Go! Threads of Exodus in African American Narratives" exemplifies an approach more akin to that of Weems.[89] She challenges the unreflective way in which the exodus narrative has been used by African Americans, including African American theologians, in their quest for liberation. She points out, "The exodus story is a complex, powerful story of deliverance, freedom, enslavement, and genocide as well as a story of powerful women, without whom the protagonist, Moses, could not have survived."[90]

Kirk-Duggan maintains that the current appropriation of the exodus story in African American liberation theology is one in which a divine preference is displayed for the persecuted and the disempowered.[91] This insight, however, is not readily apparent in African American churches. The reason for its absence has to do with the critical stance that theologians have taken, even in ecclesial matters. She says that the advent of black theology cre-ated a rift between the church and its scholarly community. Black theologians speak more to their white colleagues in the academy than they do to those in the pulpit and pews. Likewise, black church leaders have tended to embrace the Euro-American evan-gelical community for its religious insights, a situation Wimbush bemoaned.

Kirk-Duggan says, "When Black theology shifted away from the church, removing prophetic self-criticism from the church and re-moving a praxis context from the discipline, both institutions lost, and the language of liberation became opaque, fostering alienation between Black church leaders and Black theologians."[92] This im-passe, according to Kirk-Duggan, cannot continue if both entities are to survive and flourish. She advocates a multilateral approach: critical use of the biblical texts, scholarly analysis, and attention to diverse voices in the African American community, including the wealthy and middle class.[93]

The exodus story is a complex one. It does not conform to the easy "oppression-liberation" model employed by many Afri-can American theologians. Kirk-Duggan says that such a selective understanding of the exodus only obfuscates the glaring problems the narrative raises: "[Many] womanist scholars question the move to use the biblical exodus experience as a normative model for validating God's liberative acts for all oppressed peoples of the world."[94] This is because upon close examination the narrative does not display the type of epistemological privilege that Afri-can American theologians generally attribute to it. In the particular case of women, Kirk-Duggan says, "While the book of Exodus begins with paying attention to women, it manages to distort and displace their power, finding them acceptable when they play within the boundaries and dangerous when they blur boundaries or step outside."[95]

The exodus might be liberatory for certain types of men, but it only perpetuates oppression for women, non-Israelites, and others. Echoing Weems's criticism of election, she demonstrates that liber-ation is not for everyone. Kirk-Duggan makes this clear when she says, "So often, it is much easier to deal with the concept of a cho-sen people and to cheerfully disregard matters of manifest destiny, demonization based upon the Egyptians' race, and the vast com-plexities of how class and diversity plays out within the book of Exodus."[96] In other words, the exodus narrative is not the story of liberation for women, Canaanites, unsuspecting Egyptians, and others whose only crime was the historical accident of "being in the wrong place at the wrong time."

After demonstrating the complex nature of the exodus account and the way that many in the African American community have appropriated it uncritically, Kirk-Duggan turns to African American sources that assist in understanding the complexity of the concept of liberation. Her first selection is Lorraine Hansberry. Using *A Raisin in the Sun* as a conversation partner, Kirk-Duggan demonstrates how Hansberry recognized the complexity of any exodus-type move. The characters in *A Raisin in the Sun* struggle with the possibility of liberation within the complexity of their lives in inner-city Chicago. As Kirk-Duggan points out quite deftly, no liberation is innocent. Her second selection is the female group Sweet Honey in the Rock. She points out how their music speaks of women's concerns regarding liberation. She says,

> The songs, named for women and focusing on women, grow out of a freedom to self-express profoundly and provocatively: about friendships and struggles, about loneliness and bruises; about babies and singing; about the freedom to take names and air complaints; and about the freedom to dare the world to change.[97]

Kirk-Duggan's final conversation partner is the African American homiletical tradition. After a poignant and telling account of the aims of African American preaching, she addresses the frequency of the use of the exodus narrative in contemporary sermons. According to Kirk-Duggan, after consulting a dozen volumes of sermons, she was able to find "[fewer] than ten sermons...based on the exegesis of the book of Exodus."[98] Most of these, it appears, were written by scholars, who were not consistent in their engagement with the material. For example, Dwight Clinton Jones's sermon "The Lord Is on Our Side" argues, "God is on the side of all oppressed, but not against the rich."[99]

Kirk-Duggan acknowledges that the exodus story has a long and proud history in the African American community. It has been a traditional text employed by African Americans to denounce Euro-American hegemony, privilege, and supremacy. However, she demonstrates quite convincingly that the way in which African American theologians approach the exodus narrative does not reflect its contemporary usage in African American preaching. Nevertheless, the problems with the exodus narrative persist. As Kirk-Duggan points out, "[These] sermons reflect a tendency to read the liberative themes in the book of Exodus without reckoning with the cost to innocent Egyptians, persons also presumably created by God, and the later cost to the indigenous persons already occupying the land."[100]

One can see in Kirk-Duggan's essay similarities to Weems. She approaches the Bible as a complicated document with often contradictory messages for its readers. Even while acknowledging the historical importance of the exodus narrative to African Americans in the United States, she calls for a fresh investigation of it to ensure that its appropriation is liberatory for all human beings. She criticizes both African American scholars and religious leaders for their selective engagement with the text, and employs womanist resources to demonstrate the complexity of the matter.

Although this examination of womanist biblical interpretation appears to have isolated it from the larger Afrocentric hermeneutical enterprise, it appeared necessary to address adequately the specific concerns of womanists, concerns that often differ from those of their male counterparts. Womanist biblical interpreters have added a great deal to the sophistication of the African American engagement with the Bible. We will now focus on the most recent examples of Afrocentric engagement with Scripture.

Chapter 5

A Dark Enterprise Redolent with Political Implications

Jesus Christ is crucial to black Christianity because darkness was his experience, and we know something about darkness.[1]

Reading Darkly in the Twenty-first Century

In previous chapters, we examined a variety of modes of engagement used by African American scholars in their interpretations of Scripture. They have taken seriously the idea that the individual reading the text is as important to the interpretive process as the text itself. Social location plays a pivotal role in the reading process, and the various interpretations arising from it say as much about the Bible's ability to complicate, inspire, and liberate in a modern context as they do about the historical context in which these Scriptures were produced.

In the last chapter, we saw that the inclusion and recognition of gender added to the complexity of Afrocentric biblical readings. Womanist scholars have challenged approaches to biblical interpretation that see gender as almost irrelevant. They have called into question historical reconstructions of African American readings of the Bible that fail to acknowledge differences between how females and males engage the text. These insights are just beginning to seep through into the mainstream of Afrocentric interpretation.

In this chapter, we will see how the most recent voices in the enterprise of African American biblical interpretation are reshaping the notion of Afrocentricity as a construct for hermeneutics. Likewise, we will examine how this new generation of biblical scholars addresses the concern of liberation for the community. We will see that changing the notion of Afrocentricity brings about changes in how these scholars read and appropriate the biblical message.

120

Challenging the Discipline Again: Brian K. Blount and a Cultural Interpretation of the New Testament

Brian Blount teaches at Princeton Theological Seminary, a place more frequently known for conservatism than radicalism in its theological approach. His distinctive contribution to our discussion comes as another challenge to the predominant practices of biblical interpretation in the academic guild. Blount makes this clear when he says, "The entire program of ideological biblical interpretation [i.e., the predominant practices of academic interpretation] will be challenged."[2] Blount's challenge to the discipline finds its theoretical basis in what he calls a sociolinguistic approach to biblical interpretation.

It begins with a simple idea: Different people read texts and experience reality differently. This, in itself, is not a problem for Blount. It becomes an issue only when certain interpretations become dominant or totalizing. At this point, what amounts to a singular interpretation becomes what Blount labels an ideology. By this, he means that the reader attempts to read a text as if the differences in readings and experiences did not exist.

Although nearly all modern biblical interpreters acknowledge the interested character of their readings, Blount charges that the old, supposedly disinterested paradigm still remains active in the guild as a whole. His criticism is succinct and biting:

> A researcher cannot determine that he or she interprets out of a particular context, acknowledge the probable influence of that context on the interpretative process, and then methodologically set it aside as if he or she can work independently of it to draw an unaffected meaning from the text.[3]

Since scholars are influenced by their social contexts, the meanings they derive from the traditional historical and literary modes of textual investigation say as much about them as they do about the texts they read. In order to account for the interpreter's social context as a central and determinative component of the interpretive process, Blount employs the functional approach of M. A. K. Halliday with modifications.

According to Halliday's approach and Blount's analysis of the enterprise of academic interpretation, the deficiency with the scholarly approach is that it emphasizes what he calls the "grammatical-textual" and "conceptual-ideational" aspects of the interpretive process without acknowledging the "interpersonal" aspect.[4] Scholars then miss the full meaning potential of a text. In contrast, liberationist interpreters, who emphasize the interpersonal, miss the importance of the context in which a text was produced. Each ends up potentially mirroring his or her own concerns.

Blount suggests that reading from either the scholar's perspective (grammatical-textual/conceptual-ideational) or the liberationist perspective (interpersonal) is illegitimate, because neither position accounts for a "full" reading of a text. By full, he appears to mean an interpretation that accounts for all major aspects of the communicative act of reading. Blount argues that all interpreters implicitly include this interpersonal aspect in their interpretation. Blount even begins his book *Cultural Interpretation: Reorienting New Testament Criticism* with the words: "It is now commonplace to hear biblical scholars admit that textual inquiry is influenced by the contextual presuppositions of the researcher."[5] Part of his program, therefore, is to make this contextual aspect more explicit. The real legitimation for Blount's theoretical approach may be the acknowledgment that different individuals and groups engage the Bible for different reasons, with different agendas, which lead to different readings, and that none of these are innocent. This recognition throughout the guild should soften scholars' resistance to admitting their own biases. This is nothing new. What has changed is the proposed solution. What Blount seeks is at least a minimal "accommodation" on both sides, an ability to recognize what the other is doing and possibly benefit from it.[6] Such an approach may be especially important for the marginalized. He says, "Unfortunately, the New Testament has been more often a minefield than a gold mine for scholars, students, and believers interested in themes of liberation and empowerment of the disenfranchised."[7]

Blount makes an impassioned argument for the explicit inclusion of the interpersonal aspect of the communicative process in academic biblical interpretation. By interpersonal, he means the reading environment in which the text is experienced. This involves the background of the reader as an important component in determining what a given text can potentially mean. Language is social, and meaning is as dependent upon the social environment in which something is read as it is on the grammatical construction of the text or the author's intent and historical social context. Pointing to what is called the "context of situation," Blount argues that "who is taking part" in the reading act is as important as "what is taking place" and "what part the language is playing," if not more.[8]

Language is not acquired or understood in isolation. Every individual develops language skills based on her experiences, including education, social contacts, reading habits, and so forth. The context of the reader, then, influences heavily how she approaches and reads a particular text, even the Bible. On this basis, Blount challenges the practices of biblical scholars:

> What we look for then, is not so much the antiseptic acknowledgement by scholars that they are influenced by their contexts; this already occurs. What also needs to take place is the recognition that context is a necessary interpretative ingredient that should be consciously explored and promoted so that not only the contextual influences and strategies of mainline scholars are accepted as legitimate contextual byproducts of the investigative enterprise, but also that the contextual perspectives of marginalized communities be recognized as appropriate interpersonal determinants of and challenges to text interpretation.[9]

As Blount's quotation suggests, biblical scholarship promotes one mode of engagement, called "mainline" here, but discourages (and even rejects) other modes of engagement, called "marginalized." This accusation is based on two presuppositions critical to Blount's proposed hermeneutic. The first takes us back to our statement that different people read and experience reality differently. Blount, using Halliday, accounts for these differences based on language acquisition. Language is the tool through which human beings are socialized into their cultures. It transmits values, beliefs, and worldview. It is what Wimbush would identify as "existential stance," one's historically and culturally conditioned orientation to existence as such.

Since individuals acquire language differently, no two individuals will share precisely the same language, which means they will not share the same existential stance. Of course, each individual's language cannot be truly unique. Otherwise, true socialization, which requires some degree of shared meaning, could not occur. The distinctiveness of one individual's existential stance lies in the combination of experiences appropriated, the loci for language acquisition. For example, the existential stance or language of an African American raised in relative prosperity would most likely be distinct from that of an African American raised in affluence or in abject poverty. Distinct, because as African Americans they share, in theory, being African American as a socialized experience. Other forms of socialization exert influence as well — relative class status in our example — and these contribute to the distinctiveness of an individual's language. To be sure, Blount's argument could become quite complex upon reflection. This becomes clear when he argues that linguistic distinctiveness can be posited on various levels: degree of urbanization, regional location, class status, gender, race, sexual orientation, and so forth.[10] Nevertheless, what is truly important for Blount's project is the degree to which individuals share language, the cornerstone of socialization as such.

Groups that share a particular language, even though there will be some variation within the group, often understand and promote their collective existential stance as "reality," an objective analysis and appropriation of experience. This tendency leads to Blount's second presupposition. Since language reflects socialized experience, the potential exists for one form of language to dominate others based on the relative status of the group using it. In other words, "a collective perspective that has been embraced by those who maintain political and numerical superiority [can easily become] the 'official' one."[11] Language, in short, is a reflection of power.

In science, as well as other disciplines, the language often is standardized. Certain "rules" exist for how the subject area should be approached and how it can be communicated legitimately (the idea of a discipline itself). Blount argues that this standardized language does not reflect objective engagement with the subject matter; rather, it reflects the ability of one group to dominate the linguistic potential of the discourse, forcing either assimilation or rejection on others.[12] Using the work of Enrique Dussel, Blount labels the linguistic dominance exercised by one group an "ideology."

In the case of biblical studies, historical and literary forms of investigation have become part of an ideology. As Blount argues, "Meaning that is derived from beyond the boundaries of the historical-critical/literary arena of inquiry, where conversation consciously invites interpersonal rather than allegedly exclusive textual and ideological concerns, is considered suspect."[13] Because the field of biblical studies excludes other forms of explicitly interpersonal engagement, Blount argues that individuals seeking to enter this field must either learn the language of academics or have their readings dismissed as irrelevant. They can learn the language, but he says that they must deny their own experiences and social locations in the process. In short, they must assimilate the language of the dominating class.

Blount believes it is possible to create a nonideological inter-pretation of Scripture, one that affirms the interpersonal insights of those outside the dominating class. It involves, first, accepting the insights of the marginalized as legitimate; then analyzing real-ity from the marginalized perspective; and, finally, integrating this marginalized perspective into that of the dominating class to cre-ate "a new, vibrant, and more inclusive whole."[14] In this sense, the marginalized are a revelation to the centrists, a challenge to their erroneous and absolutized readings of Scripture.

Addressing the particular concern that haunts scholars when it comes to the acceptance of multiple readings, Blount argues that a text cannot mean just anything anyone wants it to mean. Meaning in a text is limited by those "grammatical-textual" and "conceptual-ideational" aspects mentioned above. Thus, he only wants to include the interpersonal explicitly, not do away with the historical-critical altogether. He illustrates this aim through his analysis of the work of one of the most influential New Testament scholars of the twentieth century.

Rudolf Bultmann, a German scholar who has cast a wide shadow over even the most recent of biblical interpretations, be-lieved in the idea of a universal or absolute meaning. Blount demonstrates that Bultmann's program of demythologization was thoroughly contextual.[15] Translating the text into the language of the modern individual was its goal. Its controls were the original meaning of the text, as determined historically, and the com-monness of human experience, as understood by existentialist philosophy.

At this point, Blount offers a helpful distinction promulgated by Bultmann's interpretive program. He says, "The correct read-ing is a static possession that is supposedly scientifically loyal to the textual and ideational language of a text. The true reading is fluid because it is achieved interpersonally, through a dialecti-cal engagement between the existential situation of the reader and the language of the text."[16] In order to arrive at a true reading of a text, one must inject something of the interpersonal into the process. Bultmann identifies this interpersonal aspect as an indi-vidual's preunderstanding and "life-relation." Without access to the interpersonal, one can never really understand the message of Scripture. Bultmann sought to translate the conceptual truths be-hind the mythic language of the New Testament, but in order to accomplish this goal, he had to draw on his experience as a human being in relation to history and the subject matter presented in the text.

Blount has no qualms with this approach as a legitimate mode of textual engagement. The problem arises when Bultmann claims that his perspective is a universal one. Blount says, "Bultmann's method absolutizes 'modern humanity,' which is in reality humanity in the perspective of the post-World War I period, and then makes that existential foundation the ground on which all critical interpretation should be based."[17] In other words, Bultmann gave a true reading of the New Testament based on his particular social location, one that spoke to the historical conditions that confronted Europeans in the period immediately following World War I. Although Bultmann believed his demythologizing program offered a universal and suprahistorical means of textual engagement, Blount joins Bultmann's critics in maintaining that it does not.

Having demonstrated the contextual character of one of the last century's best-known New Testament historical critics, Blount turns to other contextualized readings of the Bible. These readings have been dismissed by mainstream scholarship as inappropriate because of their ahistorical and contextual character. For our purposes, we will focus on Blount's discussions of the Negro spirituals and black preaching.

As described by Blount, the spiritual is a product of the language acquired by African slaves in their attempt to find meaningfulness in their existential circumstance. He argues that the slaves acquired the biblical language as a result of their horrendous condition for the purpose of bringing that experience, as well as their hope for liberation, to articulation. Blount says, "Their key intent [was] not so much to understand the Bible as it [was] to understand their historical circumstance."[18] In their appropriation of biblical stories and images, the slaves demonstrated their understanding of what they took to be analogous experiences. Furthermore, because their engagement with the Bible was primarily oral, the normal literary controls that would accompany the act of reading were absent. In effect, the slaves used the biblical language to forge a new identity. As Blount maintains, "The language of the biblical texts fashioned who and what they were, it gave shape to their hopes and aspirations, and in the end it helped them push beyond the symbolic boundaries placed on their reality by the slave system."[19]

The language of the slave spirituals, according to Blount, was an interpretation of their social circumstances in three significant ways. First, they convey a language of hope in the possibility of existential liberation. Second, they are an affirmation of human dignity in the face of social structures that sought to deny it. Third, the spirituals are concerned with physical justice and freedom. Although the songs make no effort to be accurate to the biblical details, Blount makes it clear that the

> slaves actualized the text by refracting their oral understanding through the lens of their sociohistorical circumstance. In this way their lives gave meaning to the text, an interpretation that provided the strength to endure their circumstances and the impetus to act for change.... The song became the instrument of their resistance, a defiant cry echoing in hope and comfort, even as its coded images summoned a thunderous call for change and confrontation.[20]

In Blount's discussion of preaching, we return to the problem of language again. As he makes clear, "Simply because the congregation and the preacher share a theoretical knowledge of a language such as English, there is no guarantee that the congregation will hear exactly what the minister intends to say."[21] Blount offers two examples of how language disparities are alleviated in the African American setting.

The first is the black experience itself. According to Blount, the black experience has three characteristics. The first is a notion of the unity of life involving the sacred and the secular. As he argues, African Americans make no clear distinction between the two. The second characteristic is an undying and perplexing patriotism or loyalty to the core values of the American ideal. The American "dream" as enshrined in the Declaration of Independence and the Constitution have been, and continue to be, beliefs for which African Americans live and die. The third characteristic is a critical awareness of racial issues. African Americans are keenly sensitive to the ways in which the dominant class has subverted, perverted, and deferred the promises this nation has made to all of its citizens; especially those of color. Out of this experience, a certain language has emerged. Blount thus points to the black experience as one of the crucibles by which shared meaning can be conveyed.

The second example offered by Blount, according to my reading, is that of the structure of the black sermon itself. The traditional structure of the black sermon provides the parameters within which a shared homiletical language is developed. According to Blount, black sermons have two overriding characteristics. First, they are christocentric.[22] They somehow always find room for the inclusion of the story of the suffering, death, and resurrection of Jesus. Second, they have a high degree of "prophetic awareness."[23] By this, Blount means that the sermons are borne out of the inequities that traditionally have characterized African American existence in the United States. He says, "Present-day struggles serve as the lens through which the preacher interprets the biblical text. In turn, the biblical interpretation helps the parishioners interpret and survive their own present circumstance."[24]

What is interesting in Blount's assessment of the African American preaching tradition is his desire to distinguish between the Negro church and the black church. Joining other critics of what they believe to be an accommodationist form of Christianity, Blount consigns the Negro church to the pre–civil rights era. The prophetic awareness that he says characterizes black preaching is a product of the black church, the African American Christian entity that is self-conscious and strident in its criticism of the larger social and political context. This is where Blount's argument becomes somewhat confusing. He posits three time periods: the time of the slave spirituals, the time of the Negro church, and the time of the black church. Each was (and is) characterized by its own hermeneutical approach. In the first and third periods, the approach was and is liberatory. In the second, it was accommodating. He says,

> The preunderstanding of [the Negro church's] leaders was similar to Bultmann's; they believed that social injustices were a societal evil too powerful to be stamped out by human endeavor. They thus turned away from any hope of systemic societal change, and sought instead a hope for individual peace and salvation in the world beyond this one.[25]

The historical circumstances of each period notwithstanding, Blount's assessment of the period of the Negro church, roughly the time from Reconstruction to the civil rights movement, appears superficial. It largely ignores the strides made by African Americans toward what became the civil rights movement, and also paints the liberatory agenda of the black church with too broad a brush. For example, Blount conveniently overlooks the fact that not one African American denomination officially supported the civil rights movement. Moreover, he disregards the years of painstaking work that went into the famous *Brown v. Board of Education* case. To classify roughly what amounts to one hundred years of African

American church history, as exemplified in its preaching, as accommodationist, and by implication inconsequential to the cause of liberation, appears to be unwarranted. As a biblical scholar and thus a student of history, Blount should be among the first to recognize that one hundred years may not be a sufficient time frame by which to characterize the African American quest for freedom. What Blount labels accommodation, I see as a period of regrouping and resurgence.

In all, Blount maintains that preacher and parishioner in the African American setting are able to share meaning through language that draws on the interpersonal (i.e., the black experience) and the ideational (i.e., if one takes the centrality of the Jesus story to be ideational). In the preaching event, African American ministers interpret the biblical text in a largely interpersonal manner. Blount maintains that the preponderant hermeneutical lens through which the Scriptures are read is liberation.

The importance of Blount's proposal lies in his appeal to the polysemic nature of language and its potential application to the African American reading experience. As he says, polysemy "implies that textual meaning cannot be defined completely; no one meaning of a word or an entire text is the correct, *complete* meaning."[26] Whether the interpretation comes from a biblical scholar, such as Bultmann, or from African Americans, as in the spirituals and sermons, none of them can claim to be absolute. They are complementary parts of a never-to-be-completed whole. Blount makes this clear when he says, "The task, thus, is not to choose for correctness between the interpretations of a Bultmann or [of African American spirituals and sermons], but to open oneself to the light each can shed on the text by such diverse interpretations and realize that they can broaden the horizon of meaning."[27] Since meaning is partially influenced by social context — the interpersonal — then one can never arrive at a final and enduring interpretation. Almost all interpretations are valid based on the contextual nature of every interpretive method as such.[28]

We can only say that almost all interpretations are valid because Blount recognizes that certain restraints are imposed on the text's meaning potential by the historical situatedness of the language itself. The historical-critical method, which Blount never dismisses entirely, has been concerned traditionally with the original meaning of the words a biblical author used. The historical context of the language used in the Bible does not provide the interpreter the possibility of attributing to the text "a meaning for which there is no historical precedent."[29]

Blount's intention has been to develop "a single method that would comprehensively convey the meaning of a text," one that would accommodate the interpersonal readings of African Americans, liberationists, and others.[30] He realizes that traditional approaches to the biblical text used by scholars have not been helpful in the development of a liberatory reading of the Bible. More important, Blount recognizes that alternative readings offered in the past by African American Bible scholars and theologians have been largely dismissed by the guild as being too contextual in orientation. Blount's proposal thus seeks to make room for such marginalized interpretations. The greatest strength of his approach is his relentless assertion that all interpretation is contextual. He argues this most pointedly when he says,

> We have found that black, liberation, and other kinds of micro-interpersonally oriented text interpretations cannot be dismissed because all research must deal with the fact that micro-interpersonal factors determine how the text is interpreted. Traditional, historical-critical research is determined by the same kinds of internal and external sociolinguistic factors that influence intentional micro-interpersonal interpretations.[31]

Without the interpersonal, an interpretation would fail to be compelling to its potential audience. African American biblical interpretation, like its Euro-American and other counterparts, seeks to divulge what is potentially compelling about a particular Scripture.

Let us situate Blount's proposal in relation to the other scholars we have examined. Blount, like Weems, Wimbush, and a few other scholars we have examined thus far, begins his analysis by considering the individual reading the text. Labeling it an explicitly interpersonal mode of engagement, Blount argues that scholarship must accept and celebrate the insight that all readings are interested readings. As he demonstrates through his analysis of Bultmann and other European and Euro-American biblical scholars, all interpretation is fueled by interpersonal insights and concerns. The particular context of the scholar, whether she is African American, Asian, or Latina, weighs heavily upon what she finds compelling in a particular biblical passage. According to Blount, the varieties of interpretations that arise from such contextually driven readings promote a "fuller" or more meaningful engagement with the Bible.

It would be safe to say that we have experienced a decided shift in the development of African American biblical interpretation away from the identification of an African presence in the Bible to the historically and culturally situated engagements of African Americans with the Bible. We have seen in Randall Bailey and Weems a concern for how modern African Americans appropriate or resist certain biblical claims and ideas. In Martin's work, we saw something similar. Although she appears more concerned to place African American interpretation in conversation with the larger enterprise of biblical scholarship, Martin argues for the importance of the womanist voice as a necessary ingredient in legitimate biblical scholarship. Wilma Bailey and Kirk-Duggan drew analogies between pertinent biblical texts and African American cultural resources. In the case of Kirk-Duggan, such resources included more modern, ecclesially oriented engagements with the exodus narrative. All of these scholars argue, to one degree or another, for the importance of the inclusion of this perspective in the ongoing work of the academic guild.

In the work of New Testament scholars, we have encountered more systematic proposals for reorienting the way biblical studies are carried out in the academy. Felder was arguably the first to challenge the predominant orientation of the discipline by calling into question the assumptions and biases inherent in the historical-critical enterprise. His Afrocentric reading of the biblical history challenged the implicit model of the biblical narrative pointing to a Christianized Europe. Having complicated the normative reading of the biblical history, Felder places the biblical message within the context of the aspirations of the marginalized for liberation. In a similar manner, Wimbush calls for a reorientation of the discipline by "interrupting the spin" placed on Scripture by Eurocentric scholarship.[32] Unlike Felder, Wimbush does not argue for the centrality of African American experience based on the presence of Africans in the Bible. Instead, Wimbush argues that Scripture reads differently if viewed through the eyes of the dominated. He believes that the true existential stance of the Bible can be recovered and appropriated only when read darkly.[33] Blount, like Wimbush, wants to reorient the discipline, at least of New Testament studies, by taking seriously the context of the person reading the Bible. His proposal, however, does not call for a wholesale replacement of the Eurocentric model. He appears resigned to the idea that scholarship will not reorient itself that dramatically. Rather, Blount calls for the explicit recognition that all interpretation arises from context, and that this context (i.e., the interpersonal) influences greatly the way one reads and consequently interprets the biblical text. Thus, Blount's proposal asks for accommodation and inclusion unlike the more singularly oriented proposals offered by Felder and Wimbush.

Blount's theoretical approach to the task of interpretation involves the acquisition of language. As Blount proposes, language is acquired from experience, and the variety of experiences an individual undergoes influences the distinctive character of his language. Logically pursued, the distinctive character of an individual's language acquisition becomes apparent. Blount's proposal borders on subverting his main premise when it comes to interpretation: Language is indicative of shared experience and meaning. He argues, "No two speakers have the same language, because no two speakers have the same experiences of language."[34] One can easily see how this position can become contradictory without qualification. If anything, this is the most problematic aspect of Blount's theoretical approach.

There is nothing distinctively African American about Blount's theoretical approach to interpretation. In *Cultural Interpretation* and many of his other works, he deals with African American readers, as well as others (e.g., *campesinos* in Nicaragua). In *Then the Whisper Put on Flesh,* for example, Blount theoretically constructs an African American New Testament ethics based on information gleaned from the slave narratives.[35] Following the lead of Wimbush, Blount argues for the displacement of the Eurocentric paradigm in favor of this marginalized perspective. He argues that African Americans will never fully understand their approach to reading the New Testament without recourse to these primary materials of their collective experience. He says, "The perspective from which most African Americans peruse the New Testament texts, if they peruse them at all, occurs from a brutal, sharply drawn angle of oppression."[36] What is surprising to the reader, however, is just how little of the actual slave narratives are incorporated into Blount's project.

Although Blount will argue that liberation "is the lens that slaves and ex-slaves used to bring focus and clarity to their thoughts about their world," *Then the Whisper Put on Flesh* is more of an engagement with traditional or Eurocentric scholarship reconfigured in a liberatory mode. Yet there are still other problems. For example, in his early discussion of the slave narratives, Blount says, "[The] narratives sketch a reciprocity between males and females that is not represented in the surrounding Southern culture."[37] This would suggest that African American slaves saw equality as a fundamental tenet of human social interaction. Later, Blount admits that this vision was obscured within the slave community's own practices. He says, "While seeking liberation, male slaves also, for example, treated women in a highly patriarchal, nonliberating, manner."[38] Such ambiguity makes it difficult to determine with any accuracy the exact contours of slave "theology" and its relationship to ethics and/or practice.

Attempting to categorize Blount's mode of engagement with the biblical materials is not always easy. Randall Bailey, Copher, and Felder began with a particular biblical text and used it as the basis for developing an African American hermeneutic. Wimbush, Martin, Wilma Bailey, and Kirk-Duggan engaged the Bible by commencing with the historic forms of African American engagement with the Bible. Blount uses a piece of this approach. Through his discussions of African American spirituals, sermons, and slave narratives, he constructs a hermeneutic that attempts to remain true to a certain historic form of Bible reading. In contrast, Weems began with the experience of the contemporary African American female reader using the historic resources when and where necessary. What is intriguing is the degree to which Blount wants to use a bit of this approach as well. By focusing on language acquisition, Blount is able to straddle the two modes of engagement. When a contemporary African American reads the Bible, he reads it in relation to his linguistic insight, something derived from the larger well of African American experience. In this way, a contemporary reading becomes a historically conditioned and accountable reading as well. Yet, given the diverse ways by which individuals acquire language, a contemporary African American, although she may number the slave narratives among her experiences, also numbers others. To this extent, every reading is a contemporary reading, because the language of the slave narratives has been added to and modified with other acquired experiences.

The idea of Afrocentricity also has been complicated by Blount's approach. Revisiting our discussion in chapter 3, Blount's proposal shares a great deal in common with Wimbush. What is missing is the latter's idea of radical orientation. Because Blount seeks accommodation rather than radical disciplinary change, his call for a liberatory hermeneutic is not as pointed as that of Wimbush. This is seen clearly in *Then the Whisper Put on Flesh*, in which Blount's Afrocentric voice is muted by his vision of inclusion. One sees something similar in Martin's womanist approach. Her unrelenting engagement with mainstream biblical scholarship makes it difficult to detect clearly her liberatory voice. Wilma Bailey also could be placed in this vein, although she makes every effort to control the materials — instead of them controlling her. Kirk-Duggan and Weems present strong womanist arguments for their readings of Scripture.

What is common among all these approaches is their desire to address the history of oppression that has plagued African Americans since their introduction to the United States. They perceive the nature of this oppression somewhat differently, however. Womanists speak of multiple and interconnected forms of oppression. As they configure their existential context, issues of race cannot be separated from those of gender, class, language, and others. In this manner, their Afrocentric engagement with the Bible functions as one contextualized approach that has the ability to connect and dialogue with various other experiences of oppression, whether African American or otherwise. Others are more singular in their approaches. African American male interpreters tend to subsume the various forms of oppression experienced by members of the community under the decidedly important historical category of race. Bailey, as an exception, is more nuanced in his approach.

Blount's proposal marks somewhat of a shift in the construction of Afrocentricity. Although he argues on behalf of African Americans and their experiences with scriptural interpretation, this concern is placed repeatedly in the context of a multilateral understanding of how the Bible is read. African American readings are placed alongside those of others. One might think that this approach, in light of the womanist critique, would compel Blount to complicate his understanding of oppression. This would be wrong. Instead of taking into account multiple forms of oppression, Blount is more singular in his orientation. The overarching concern for him is race. Admittedly, he does address other concerns in his works, but these occupy a subsidiary position with respect to that of ethnicity. Afrocentrism as a conceptual tool, however, has been changed in the process. Instead of the approach advocated by Felder and others, either Afrocentrism has become an implicit component of African American engagement with Scripture, or it has become one approach among others in an unquestionably pluralistic society.

Emerging Afrocentric Voices in the Discipline

This decided change in the understanding of Afrocentrism can be seen as well in the most recent work of other African American biblical scholars. Randall Bailey, in one of the most recent collections of edited essays on African American biblical interpretation, has outlined this change well. He says that in its most recent application, Afrocentrism "refers to scholarship whose questions grow out of the experiences of people of African descent."[39] *Yet with a Steady Beat,* a book also edited by Bailey, addresses issues of pluralism, class, folk tradition, and exegesis with a view toward the contemporary African American social situation. By looking at a few of these essays, we can see with greater depth the changing appropriation and application of Afrocentrism among emerging African American biblical scholars.

Injustice Made Legal: Harold V. Bennett

Harold V. Bennett teaches at Morehouse College in Atlanta, Georgia. His essay "Triennial Tithes and the Underdog" is an abbreviated form of his book *Injustice Made Legal: Deuteronomic Law and the Plight of Widows, Strangers, and Orphans in Ancient Israel.*[40] Using social science and critical theory, Bennett attempts to reconstruct and challenge the Deuteronomic pattern of public relief that affected the socially marginalized in ancient biblical society. The pressing concern behind his investigation is the practice of public relief in contemporary African American churches.

Bennett begins his analysis by looking at the relevant biblical legislation, Deuteronomy 14:22–29 and 26:12–15. He argues that this biblically justified form of public relief relegated persons already experiencing marginalization to an even more vulnerable status.[41] In the process, Bennett must take on a history of scholarly interpretation that has argued otherwise. He says, "These commentators advocate the position that these laws spawned a public relief system that rectified economic disproportion and ameliorated the quality of life for this category of defenseless persons."[42]

In contrast to past scholarship, Bennett employs a social-scientific framework that assists him in the development of "possibilities" regarding the functioning of the biblical community.[43] Furthermore, Bennett turns to critical theory as a conceptual paradigm within social science to address specifically the issues raised in this discourse. According to him, three ideas about law arise from this approach: (1) the idea that law reflects the special interests of subgroups within human communities, (2) the idea that law focuses on individuals who are selected for the most part because of social characteristics they cannot control, and (3) the idea that the critic should focus upon the effects of legal injunctions upon all members of a society, especially those who are most vulnerable. In short, this approach seeks to unmask and analyze the ways in which particular social groups use legally sanctioned means to create and maintain dominance over other groups. Bennett makes this clear when he points to the effects of urbanization on Israelite society:

> Concomitant with political and economic centralization and with urbanization in ancient Israel, the socioeconomic infrastructure was conducive to the emergence of an elite ruling class whose bases of social standing and economic affluence were not completely dependent upon land ownership.[44]

Dominance in the community, then, was a central concern for an elite subgroup. This group sought to advance its own interests over against those non-elites from whom they extracted, presumably, some sort of social, moral, or economic capital.

The legislation from Deuteronomy centralized the distribution of public aid. Bennett argues that the "site for the distribution of produce and meat was a great distance from the local villages or cities where these individuals lived."[45] Consequently, this arrangement put these already vulnerable individuals at risk. If they traveled to the official cultic site to receive their dole from the representatives of the Lord, they put themselves at risk of harm or homelessness. Although many have argued that this legislation was humane to the poor, Bennett says, "[This] regulation prescribed a solution that appears to be indifferent to their circumstances."[46] Moreover, the centralization of public relief only served to advance the interests of religious officials: "[Centralizing] the presentation and distribution of produce positioned priests and prophets to advance their religio-politico-economic ideas and to diversify the sources from which they could draw material sustenance."[47]

In addition to centralized public assistance, the Deuteronomic legislation provides for local assistance for the marginalized through the advocacy of periodic assistance from other members of the citizenry.

Bennett dismisses the possibility of such assistance as fiction. In his reconstruction of ancient Israelite society, the peasantry could not have produced enough to feed themselves, pay their various debts, and assist the poor. As he sees it, "Regulations that imply that the peasantry would share their small amounts of meat and produce with the *almanah, ger,* and *yatom* provoked these socially disadvantaged persons to exercise their imaginative abilities and create fiction."[48]

In the end, Bennett argues that social service organizations have a responsibility to "ameliorate the circumstances of this category of people."[49] He goes on to say, "The Black Church, therefore, should guarantee that their programs contribute to the humanization of marginalized groups."[50] His analysis of ancient Israelite practices of public relief provides him with insight into the mind-set that still pervades such efforts.

Much of what Bennett seeks to do in his revisionist analysis of Deuteronomy is worthy of recognition. The problems that arise have more to do with his approach and ability to apply it consistently throughout the argument than with the rhetorical force of the essay. First, Bennett is working with theoretical models of ancient human societies based on insights garnered from modern liberal democratic ones. This is why he can say only that his approach provides "possibilities" for the practices that prevailed in ancient Israel.[51] He acknowledges the otherwise inaccessible nature of that society, and so his suspicions regarding the philanthropic intent behind the scriptural legislation are assumptive rather than demonstrated. Second, Bennett appears to be working with an implicit classical Marxist paradigm. That is, he posits that urbanization brought about a centralization of material resources that only served to alienate further those living on the margins of the social order. In addition, this reorganization of public relief benefited the elite at the expense of those whom it was supposed to assist. This sort of win-lose scenario, although initially appealing, is far too ideologically driven to account for data that barely exists. Finally, Bennett builds his critique of centralization on premises that are not always adequately demonstrated by the text. His first premise, that these marginalized groups were without male protection, appears to be argued forcefully in his book. And he may be correct in his assertion. The second premise, that the site for the distribution of public aid was a great distance from the places these people lived, is highly questionable. Of course, some people would have been farther away from the site than others, but it would be difficult to believe that all marginalized persons lived a great distance from the centralized site. In sum, Bennett's revisionist reading of the Deuteronomic legislation suffers from a lack of credible evidence, as well as from a theoretical approach that assumes the worst of the elite.

Bennett's proposal revives the African American critique of economic discrimination in a Marxist mode. Since far too many African Americans live in poverty, it appears reasonable to view them as analogous to the marginalized groups outlined in Deuteronomy. Although there are numerous differences between the two groups, the idea that social justice should pervade a biblically oriented society is at the heart of Bennett's critique. What is interesting is the degree to which Bennett's reading contradicts that advanced by Felder and others. According to Felder, as Israelite society developed, it became increasingly philanthropic, extending social justice to all members of the community.[52] Bennett calls this notion into question. In fact, he argues that the benevolent rhetoric of Israelite society masked exploitative and alienating practices. We have encountered this hermeneutic of suspicion before in other authors, and Bennett's proposal follows in that vein, but it also demonstrates a complicating of the Bible's trustworthiness to provide models of social justice to its readers.

The Dodecalogue, Ideology, and Religious Control: Herbert R. Marbury

Herbert Robinson Marbury teaches at Clark Atlanta University in Atlanta, Georgia. His essay "Regulating Bodies and Boundaries: A Reading of the Dodecalogue (Deut 27:14–26)" involves the reconstruction of the historical circumstances of the dodecalogue and an ideological critique of its function in the ancient community. Marbury argues that Deuteronomy 27:14–26 serves the political and ideological interests of the Second Temple priesthood. His more contemporary concern, however, is the rhetoric employed by religious officials in the soliciting of funds and moral authority.

Marbury begins his analysis by examining the current state of scholarship on Deuteronomistic history. He argues against the traditional understanding of the historical context of the material. For Marbury, Deuteronomy 27:14–26 functions best in the context of the early Second Temple period. He argues that the "prevailing arguments and ideological discourses" function best when viewed as a "historical ritual" employed by the priesthood to garner and maintain control of the populace.[53]

Prior examinations of this text in Deuteronomy have placed it among presettlement materials. Looking specifically at the work of Gerhard von Rad, Marbury argues that he "envisions the *Sitz im Leben* to be a grand assembly congregating around the shrine at Shechem where religious functionaries officiate in a cultic ceremony."[54] Marbury disagrees with von Rad's form critical assessment of the context. He argues, "[The] very nature of this ritual, when read as a legal corpus, presupposes a centralized power structure, and not the loosely organized segmentary structure of pre-settlement Israel."[55] He believes that although the original curses probably were pronounced by tribal or clan leaders, they did not receive the full rhetorical import they attain in Deuteronomy until a much later date.

In dating the corpus, Marbury follows the work of A. D. H. Mayes, who dates this section of Deuteronomy, as well as others, to a later period than that portrayed in the text. Mayes bases his dating on four criteria. Marbury then outlines these criteria and his general agreement with Mayes that Deuteronomy 27 evidences a later redaction. He further adds his own insight. Looking at the thematic groupings in the text, Marbury says, "Each of these shifts appears to signify a redactor's 'cutting and pasting' of legal compendia."[56]

Marbury then turns to an ideological critique of the material. In doing so, he makes a couple of assumptions. First, he assumes that the text is the product of an ideologically charged social world. Second, he assumes that the ideology of the author/redactor is reproduced in and recoverable from the text.[57] Focusing on the modes of production prevalent at the time in the province, Marbury maintains, "Israel functioned under a foreign tributary system where its revenue was funneled off to Persia to support the empire."[58]

According to Marbury, the immigrants who returned to Israel under the Persians had not only the funds but also the political authority to take control of the province. Cyrus had instituted a policy of increased religious freedom for subordinate populations in the empire, and this policy allowed the descendants of the population deported in the Babylonian exile to regain their political and religious superiority over those who were not deported. As Marbury understands it, "By allowing elite groups of the Jewish society to return to their homeland, which few or none of them had ever seen, the king [of Persia] created a bond of personal loyalty between the Achaemenid rulers and this new Jewish group, whom the Achaemenids could count on to help them govern the province."[59] Of course, a struggle for power ensued between the returning immigrants and the indigenous populace. Marbury believes that this is precisely the social context in which passages such as Deuteronomy 27:14–26 became meaningful and employed.

The primary means the new immigrants used to gain control of the province was to create a religious scribal order working in tandem with the Zadokite priesthood. The Levites, functioning in this new scribal capacity, exerted power over the populace by "reinscribing certain legal and moral codes."[60] The Zadokite priests, without the competition of the monarchy, became the beneficiaries of taxes and tribute, as well as being the majority landholders in the province. Closely aligned with the Persian monarchy, the Levites and Zadokites sought to impose the imperial will upon the residents. Problems arose, however, under the reign of Xerxes.

Xerxes faced a number of localized revolts during the beginning of his reign. To restore order throughout the empire, he instituted a policy of economic depletion that shifted "the bulk of the tax burden to non-Persians."[61] Moreover, Xerxes stopped supporting local temples like the one in Judah. This change in policy diminished the monetary resources and power of the priests and Levites, whose rituals and other activities suffered in the process.

Marbury believes that priestly control eroded throughout the province and that religious pluralism erupted in the process. This new social environment challenged the hegemony of the religious elite. Marbury says, "This new pluralism likely decreased the number of devotees to the cult and *further* diminished the priesthood's economic resources."[62] In response, the Levites and priests turned to ancient legislative rituals. These ancestral rituals assisted in the reestablishment of their control. Marbury makes this clear when he says, "[This] literature reflected the struggle by the priesthood to maintain its position and to seek out new sources of revenue in [the] face of a reversal in imperial policy and the emerging religious pluralism."[63]

According to Marbury, the rhetoric of the passage displays a desire on the part of the religious authorities to bind the populace to themselves. The curse, a powerful rhetorical tool in ancient societies, is employed as a means of shaming the populace into obedience. Marbury asserts that the voice of the people is overshadowed in the text by the requirement that they assent wholeheartedly. Seeking to hear them, one can perceive their stance, suggests Marbury, by positing their resistance to the legislation: "Their voices seep through the cracks of the very rhetorical structures which suppress them."[64]

Marbury's use of ideological criticism in his analysis of Deuteronomy 27:14–26 is instructive in many ways. It attempts to resolve a critical redaction question as to when the material was added to the larger work. It provides a reasonable setting for the material based on posited circumstances confronting the populace and religious authorities. In addition, it marks a new direction in Deuteronomic studies, one that does not merely support the dominant voice found in the text but critiques it in light of its own concerns and their effects on a potentially marginalized class of people.

Like Bennett, Marbury relies on theoretical models to reveal aspects of an otherwise irretrievable ancient community. He mixes a traditional historical-critical approach with more recent literary critical approaches to text. Like Randall Bailey and Weems, Marbury seeks to retrieve the voice of the marginalized in, but more often behind, the text. What is problematic with Marbury's approach is similar to that identified in Bennett's reading of Deuteronomy: It assumes a win-lose scenario.

As read by Marbury, Deuteronomy 27 functions as a rhetorical tool to advance the interests of the religious elite in the province. He appears to discount entirely the complicity of at least a segment of the populace in the legislation advocated by the Levites and the priesthood. A more nuanced approach to the task of ideological criticism would necessitate the concession that the economic and religious interests of the religious establishment were not the only beneficiaries of such curses. In truth, the only real power the rhetoric had was the assent of the populace to its authority. In other writings, Marbury displays this type of nuanced approach.

What is implicit in Marbury's critique of Deuteronomy 27 is a concern for the methods employed by modern religious officials to raise funds. He appears to question the rhetoric used by many pastors in the African American community. Asking congregants to contribute substantial portions of their income — or worse, go into debt — for projects of questionable religious value worries Marbury. He believes that the key to the authority of these pastors may lie in the rhetoric employed to advance their aims. Like Randall Bailey and Bennett, Marbury looks carefully and suspiciously at the rhetoric employed in the Hebrew Bible to unmask potential oppression.

Ethnicity, Identity, and Christian Community:
Brad R. Braxton

Brad Ronnell Braxton teaches at Wake Forest Divinity School in Winston-Salem, North Carolina. His essay "The Role of Ethnicity in the Social Location of 1 Corinthians 7:17–24" is an abbreviated version of his published dissertation, *The Tyranny of Resolution: 1 Corinthians 7:17–24.*[65] Braxton argues that ethnicity is an often overlooked component of social location in various scholarly treatments of Pauline literature. He believes that if ethnicity were included in a social analysis, Paul's ecclesial struggles would be more lucid to modern readers. Further, Braxton is concerned with the role ethnicity plays in modern Christian notions of identity.

Braxton uses 1 Corinthians 7:17–24, a text better known for its discussion of slavery, as the focus of his analysis. Using cultural anthropology and sociology, Braxton enters the murky waters of ethnic classification. He rejects older methods of classification and opts for self-identification as an appropriate methodological technique. He argues, "[There] must be a shift from an infatuation with 'objective' reports from readers distant in time and space from those being investigated to an attentive investigation to what these (ancient) groups are *saying* about themselves."[66] To this end, he adopts six insights from Koen Goudriaan, a Dutch cultural anthropologist. This leads to one of his most helpful insights: "It is possible for groups to share the *same culture* yet understand themselves to belong to totally different *ethnic* groups."[67]

According to Braxton, Paul's symbolic world is in "upheaval" in the passage.[68] He "is attempting to avoid the restructuring of the community boundaries he has inscribed by means of his kerygma."[69] In other words, Paul argues against the reintroduction of external social values into his young and divided community. Braxton contends that ethnicity in this passage is raised in the discussion of circumcision.

The potential for upward mobility and the hindrance of "double identity" occupy a great deal of Braxton's discussion of epispasm (the attempt to reverse circumcision) in the next section of his essay.[70] He acknowledges that there was most likely a great deal of pressure on hellenized Jews to conform to the prevailing social practices of their Greek and Roman neighbors. Being a Jew in a Greco-Roman context fostered a double identity that might compel an individual to renounce all physical manifestations of his ethnic allegiance. Braxton points out, however, that such a physical disassociation might not indicate a complete denial of Jewish ethnicity.[71] On the contrary, it may be a strategic step to foster upward mobility. There are several examples of similar acts by ethnic minorities in antiquity.[72] At any rate, Braxton identifies the Pauline statement in 1 Corinthians 7:18 as referring to an ethnic identity marker.

On the other side of the coin, Braxton identifies the one who might seek circumcision as a proselyte, or at least a semi-proselyte. He argues that such an individual may have considered circumcision a way to make his ethnic conversion complete. Braxton says, "It is possible that such semi-proselytes were considered Jewish and not only by others but, more importantly, by themselves."[73] Such an individual, although now a member of the church, might have still considered circumcision as a form of ethnic identification.

Braxton argues that Paul considered membership in the church to be more important than any one ethnic identity marker. As he says, "The *ekklesia* is comprised of Jews and Gentiles, but the sum of the *ekklesia* is greater than its parts."[74] Thus, Paul rejects any sort of understanding of Christian social existence that allows for the maintenance of ethnic allegiances. Allegiance to their Christian identity is the only loyalty the Corinthians should maintain.

Braxton believes that "Paul underestimated the role of ethnicity in configuring social existence."[75] He labels Paul "naïve" for attempting to transcend ethnic boundaries in his ministry and congregations.[76] Although he agrees with Paul that church membership should have comprised an important aspect of the members' overall identity, Braxton argues, "[It] was not an exhaustive identity marker."[77] He goes on to disagree with those in the African American community who reject, for instance, the celebration of Kwanzaa on a basis analogous to Paul's in 1 Corinthians; he sees this rejection as underestimating the importance of ethnicity.

He ends his essay with an impassioned plea on behalf of ethnic identification:

> As a proud member of the *African American Christian* tradition — a tradition that has unashamedly mingled the ethnic and the religious to the point that it is nearly impossible to distinguish the ethnic from the religious — my response might be to Paul, "For me and my house, ethnic heritage is not a deterrent to 'keeping the commandments of God' but rather the very context through which those commandments are kept." I am an African American. I am a Christian. I am an *African*

American Christian. To single out and prioritize the parts that
make up my whole may substantially and negatively alter
that whole.[78]

In short, Braxton complicates any attempt to read Paul's statements
regarding circumcision in 1 Corinthians 7 as a simple appeal to a
unity that transcends ethnicity. On the contrary, as interpreted by
Braxton, Paul's appeal asks individuals to deny a central aspect of
their psychological and social constructions.

Braxton's analysis of ethnicity in Paul offers a fresh perspective to such debates among African American scholars. Instead of
seeking to identify black-skinned people in the Bible, Braxton uses
ethnic identity as a lens through which to critique implicit appeals
to homogeneity found there. I agree for the most part with his approach to ethnic identification, although I cannot say that reliance
on self-identification necessarily gives us a better picture of ethnic groups in antiquity. Ethnic identity is especially problematic in
1 Corinthians 7:18, where Paul merely suggests that there may be
some in the congregation who identify themselves along such ethnic lines. A better argument regarding ethnicity could be made, I
believe, by examining Galatians. Indeed, Braxton takes up the issue
in his book *No Longer Slaves: Galatians and African American
Experience.*[79]

The thorny issue Braxton avoids in this essay is the connection
between ethnicity and religion in antiquity. Scholars frequently use
the generic designation "Gentile," or the more specific "Greek,"
to identify all non-Jewish ethnic groups in the first century.[80] Yet
such a designation masks the ethnic diversity that pervaded the
Roman Empire. More important, it obscures the implicit connection between an ethnic group and its gods. To identify with an
ethnic group in antiquity often meant worshiping its god or gods.
Thus, to be Roman not only meant appropriating such things as
language, history, law, and so on. It also meant, at least for the
majority, worshiping Rome's gods. In truth, what Braxton is examining is not so much ethnic identification as ethno-religious
identification.

Christianity, especially in its Pauline manifestation, is distinctive in that it was able to appeal to persons outside its obvious
ethno-religious audience, Jews. Like Judaism, Christianity required
singular allegiance to its deity. In a world where one could retain one's core ethno-religious identity while also participating
in the ethno-religious identities of others, Christianity must have

appeared odd. It was, in many ways, a religion without an ethnicity. The Sarapis cult, for example, appealed to many, but even in its hellenized manifestation, he was an Egyptian deity. Although he proclaimed a Jewish messiah, Paul was able to strip his presentation of Christianity of those specific ethnic markers that purportedly characterized the gospel preached by James, the brother of Jesus. Paul's attempt to go beyond traditional ethnoreligious allegiances marked a strategic advance for Christian evangelization. To request singular obedience without a concomitant demand to adhere to specific ethnic practices made it easier for Greeks, Romans, Phoenicians, Numidians, Egyptians, and others to join the movement.

According to Braxton, what Paul is asking the Corinthians to do is deny allegiance to any sort of ethnicity. This interpretation marks an interesting reversal of other readings of Paul's rhetoric for unity.[81] What appears to concern Braxton in this essay is the rhetoric of Christian unity, especially in its modern manifestation. He is suspicious of conservative calls for unity around posited Christian identity. This so-called identity, more often than not, is implicitly Eurocentric. It asks African Americans and others to deny their ethnic allegiances for a false notion of Christian social existence. At the root, such appeals are hegemonic.

Braxton, like Randall Bailey and others, calls into question models of Christian unity that mute the voices and concerns of persons of African descent. In concert with Wimbush, Braxton reflects a strain of African American scholarship that fears the encroachment of fundamentalist theology in the community. His troubling of this particular New Testament call for unity marks a change, however, in the traditional mode of African American engagement with texts outlining Christian social existence. African Americans customarily have believed in the universal kinship of humanity. The question raised now is whether this universal kinship in its ecclesial manifestation is rooted in diversity or homogeneity. The retention of one's ethnic heritage, according to Braxton, is a necessary component of modern Christian discipleship. I am sure Braxton and others will pursue this provocative issue further in the near future.

Baptism and Liberation: Demetrius K. Williams

Demetrius K. Williams teaches at Tulane University in New Orleans, Louisiana. His essay "The Bible and Models of Liberation in the African American Experience" follows in the vein of the majority of his scholarly works. In fact, this essay on Galatians 3:28 appears to be a condensed version of an argument made in his book *An End to This Strife: The Politics of Gender in African American Churches.*[82] Williams argues that Galatians 3:28 offers a better model of liberation for African Americans than do its Hebrew Bible–based predecessors. Of particular concern for him is the development of an inclusive vision of liberation.

He begins with the work of Theophus Smith, who examines the various conceptual paradigms that have informed previous African American readings of Scripture, including exodus, wilderness, promised land, captivity, and exile, to name a few.[83] After working through these models, Williams contends, "[In] many ways these classical biblical models and configurations have not presented fully liberative paradigms." He uses the exodus as his prime example. He disputes the idea that it can still be used as a liberation model, at least without qualification. The dismantling of the exodus model does not trouble him, however. He says, "This is not unusual with the appropriation of biblical paradigms: they are useful for certain social and historical moments, but new information and situations entail a reevaluation of their use and function."[84]

The central concern of Williams's critique of past models of African American liberation is the nefarious absence of calls for the liberation of women. They are still expected to be subordinate (and excluded from ecclesiastical leadership) by the very men who take their own equality with Euro-Americans seriously. Williams adopts a fundamentally womanist position by arguing that what is needed is a biblical model of liberation that acknowledges and confronts multiple forms of oppression in the African American community.

This move from Hebrew Bible conceptions of liberation to potential New Testament ones is christocentric insofar as womanists view Christ as "a prime example of the notion of human *being,* who [exhibits] the principles of freedom and equality in his life and work: for all are created in the image of God."[85] Thus, any liberatory paradigm adopted by modern African Americans should conform to the ideal of human freedom embodied in the image of Jesus. This image informs even Paul's statement in Galatians. Williams makes this clear when he says,

> Since African Americans' political-religious protest rhetoric, interpretive traditions, and churches were organized and

founded upon the biblical principles of equality (which are expressed in Gal 3:28), in order to be true to the traditional struggles for nonclassism and nonracism (i.e., the protest posture against class and race discrimination), they must also combat sexism in the religious institutions and in the interpretive traditions.[86]

In short, he argues that Galatians 3:28 must be interpreted and appropriated in light of the central image of Christ, an image that calls for the obliteration of all forms of oppression in light of the kerygma. Williams goes on to say, "[Any] discourse or practice that is not guided by this model is to be deemed incompatible with African American aspirations for freedom and equality in the present and for the future."[87]

Turning to Paul's argument in Galatians, Williams surveys contemporary scholarly understandings of the text. With the majority of scholars, he believes Galatians 3:26–28 to be a pre-Pauline baptismal formula adopted by the apostle in order to explain his stance on justification. Furthermore, Williams concedes that Paul's use of the formula does not betray any real interest in sexual equality.[88] He explains,

[Paul's] teaching on justification by faith in Romans, Galatians, and Philippians was formulated to articulate and support his vision that Jew and Greek are equal and have equal access to the covenant promises (for Gentiles without recourse to the Jewish identity symbol of circumcision and the observance of certain parts of the law).[89]

Ethnic equality, not gender equality, is at the core of Paul's use of the baptismal formula.

Williams then engages the history of African American interpretation of the Scripture. He says that African Americans were forced to reconstruct Paul along the lines of a theological paradigm that denied the validity of Pauline statements that supported slavery.[90] As it developed, the African American interpretive tradition used Paul's statements, including Galatians 3:28, to argue for a nonracist (ethnic equality) and nonclassist (social equality) society. Williams argues that now the last part of the tripartite formula must be addressed:

For it was out of the crucible of racial injustice and class oppression that the interpretive tradition arose to institutionalize a nonracist and nonclassist appropriation of the

Christian faith. What the African American religious tradition has never done is to apply this very same principle to a consistent analysis of sexism.[91]

He realizes, however, that there are problems. Against some scholars in the African American community, including Felder, who argued that Paul does not advocate radical gender equality, Williams says, "[Even] if the position of Paul on various issues is unascertainable or unacceptable, his position alone does not determine a particular reading, hearing, or appropriation (regardless of authorial intent)."[92] This radical statement, although it contradicts the canons of historical-critical interpretation, is obviously at the heart of many contextualized readings of Scripture.

Williams does not argue for an uncritical appropriation of Galatians 3:28 among African Americans. He recognizes, for example, that unity in antiquity rarely meant equality. Paul most likely supported some view of equality that recognized the equal capacity of all human beings to perform as moral agents, if he supported equality at all. Furthermore, Williams acknowledges that to some the "phrase 'no longer...but all are one'" leads logically "to the loss of cultural/ethnic identity and uniqueness."[93] In the same way as Braxton's analysis of 1 Corinthians, many modern African Americans are unwilling to sacrifice their ethnic distinctiveness for the sake of Christian unity. More disturbing, many African Americans are afraid that calls for equality based on Galatians 3:28 will open the door for gays and lesbians, who also are arguing for their equal status in the Christian community, to press for their own inclusion. To them, Williams replies,

> [Within] the African American interpretive tradition, [Gal 3:28] was not used to argue that cultural and ethnic distinctiveness should be removed but that such distinctiveness should not be used as a basis for the oppression of another human being. This principle must also apply to [gays and lesbians], despite the uneasiness with it.[94]

Turning to the potential inherent in the text, Williams argues that Galatians 3:28 offers African Americans a new liberatory paradigm that does not carry the baggage of past biblical appropriations. First, it includes an acknowledgment of multiple forms of oppression, especially sexism. Against Felder and others, who would limit women's equality to the religious sphere, Williams says, "In its political-religious usage the element 'in Christ' has never limited it to the religious realm."[95] Second, it is inclusive of the concerns of women and is complementary to their present struggles. Williams argues that since Galatians 3:28 is not found in a narrative context, it is amenable to being incorporated into various arguments against oppression based on ethnicity, gender, and class. Third, it provides a counterbalance to more sexist biblical statements. Against hierarchical notions of gender, Williams believes that this text argues for a horizontally leveled Christian community. He says, "The activity of the Spirit in the Christian communities, empowering all indiscriminately (for the Spirit democratizes: Acts 2:17–21; cf. Joel 2:28–32), is evidence of this new order."[96] Finally, Williams believes that Galatians 3:28 allows for African American self-critical reflection. He thinks this theoethical paradigm will challenge male-dominated church structures to "consider liberation in holistic categories."[97]

Like Braxton, Williams has identified another problem with a modern appropriation of Paul. Braxton argued that Paul sought to subsume ethnic identity under the category of Christian identity. Williams acknowledges this potential in Paul's rhetoric but counterbalances it by contending that African Americans have never appropriated Paul in such a manner. He is clearly more concerned about Paul's limited capacity to include gender equality as a tenet of the gospel. Despite the potential of the rhetoric in Galatians 3:26–28, Williams says that Paul never intended to use the baptismal formula for more than his argument regarding ethnic equality in justification. Nevertheless, he finds in this pre-Pauline baptismal formula the potential for challenging sexist thinking and practices in the African American community.

Williams clearly has heard and incorporated the womanist critique into his scholarship. He is the first author we have encountered to reflect his engagement to such a degree. Unlike Blount, Bennett, and Braxton, as well as other male scholars, Williams has appropriated the perspective that what African Americans encounter is not oppression but oppressions. Approaching the African American community's problems from the vantage point of multiple and interconnected forms of oppression gives Williams an advantage over his colleagues. As with Randall Bailey's notion of holy hatred, Williams presses the liberatory potential available when one reads against the grain. Although many may disagree with his use of Galatians 3:28 as a theo-ethical paradigm for liberation, especially because of his disavowal of historical-critical restraints, Williams's approach marks a clear path in Afrocentric interpretation.

A Liberatory Interpretation?

What is shared by Blount and the other scholars examined in this chapter is an abiding historical orientation. Of course, they use other methods as well. Blount adopts Halliday's linguistic model. Bennett and Marbury use social-scientific models.[98] Braxton uses cultural anthropology in addition to the social sciences. Still, each demonstrates a decided historical interest. Moreover, each scholar displays a desire to engage traditional Eurocentric scholarship.

Unlike some of their predecessors, these more recent voices in the construction of Afrocentric biblical interpretation view their work as responsive to the ongoing work of the larger discipline. For example, Blount's work in *Cultural Interpretation* sought to situate African American hermeneutics in the context of other forms of biblical interpretation. He argues, like Bultmann, that African American interpretations of the Bible arise out of a particular historical context. Likewise, in *Then the Whisper Put on Flesh,* Blount spends the majority of his argument attempting to locate the ethics of the slave narratives within the context of scholarly reconstructions of the ethical orientations of the New Testament works. Bennett, Marbury, Braxton, and Williams employ the same disciplinary conversation in their own readings of the Bible.

Another interesting feature of these more recent engagements with the Bible is their acknowledgement of pluralism. Often implicitly, these forms of Afrocentric biblical interpretation arise out of a contemporary context of religious and social pluralism. Blount is most explicit in his recognition of pluralism as the environment in which modern biblical scholars read and interpret the Bible. Pluralism compels the practitioners of contextualized interpretation to accept the meaning potential inherent in various modes of biblical engagement.

Like Randall Bailey, the majority of the practitioners of Afrocentric interpretation surveyed in this chapter construct subversive readings of Scripture. Bennett questions the practices behind ancient Israelite philanthropy. Marbury questions the use of rhetoric in Deuteronomy for the purposes of Second Temple Judaism. Braxton questions Paul's call for ecclesial unity. Williams questions the African American church's commitment to the liberation of women. Each proposes some sort of model for the ongoing liberation and well-being of the community. All advocate caution in the ways that readers engage biblical texts. Williams, for example, finds theo-ethical potential in Galatians 3:28, although he acknowledges that Paul would not have advocated his position. In sum, with the exception of Blount, each of the emerging voices in Afrocentric biblical hermeneutics finds much that is non-liberatory in the Bible as well as the current practice of biblical interpretation.

All of the scholars in this chapter pursue some sort of political agenda in their interpretation of the Bible.[99] Whether it is a more humane system of public relief or the acceptance of ethnicity as a core component of one's Christian identity, these scholars have political commitments that compel them to question the various messages the Bible provides to modern readers in a pluralistic environment. In the process, these scholars complicate the idea of the Bible as a manifesto for marginalized existence (Wimbush). Blount argues for the inclusion of marginalized or interpersonal readings into the larger enterprise of biblical studies. He does not seek to exclude or de-center the predominant Eurocentric interpretation of the text. For him, liberation is wholehearted inclusion. For Williams, liberation cannot be reached in its entirety until those seeking liberation acknowledge their own oppressive interpretations of Scripture and develop new models for holistic liberation. In concert with womanist interpreters, Williams searches for biblical resources that can assist in the process. Like Braxton, liberation for Williams involves the acceptance of human diversity, particularly in terms of ethnicity and gender. Bennett and Marbury attack social institutions that seek to hide oppression under the guise of the divine will. For them, liberation means an ongoing critique of social structures.

The most unsettling aspect of these scholars' engagement with the Bible, at least for the majority, is their orientation to Scripture. They appear to reject the idea that Scripture is both authoritative and normative for Christian social existence. Afrocentric biblical scholars have questioned frequently the degree to which the Bible's statements and orientations are to be accepted as normative. These scholars reflect a furtherance of that suspicion. Unlike Wimbush and Blount, more recent Afrocentric biblical scholars appear to value the Bible as an authoritative document, but they reserve the right to reject its normative declarations as well as attempts to force conformity to a subsequent hermeneutical lens. This may present a problem for the larger body of African Americans who have been raised to believe that the Bible is an expression of God's will, even with respect to the ordering of society.

Chapter 6

Can the Eclipse Continue?

[The] things that you're liable to read in the Bible, it ain't
necessarily so.[1]

Accounting for the Eclipse:
The Fundamentals

The phrase "African American biblical hermeneutics" is misleading to many. They quickly form the impression that the subject
matter is how modern African Americans, primarily in churches,
approach and engage Scripture. Of course, this would be one way
to frame the subject matter. What we have encountered in our
analysis, however, is much different.

African American biblical interpretation is an academic enterprise consisting of a set of proposals for how to approach and
engage the Bible. It often explicitly, but sometimes implicitly, uses
historical African American resources in its attempt to construct
meaning from the biblical texts for the potential benefit of the
modern community. In the scholarship of Randall Bailey, Wimbush, Weems, Martin, Blount, and others, one can see how cultural
resources are tapped for the purpose of developing a distinctive
African American reading and voice on Scripture.

Even in its initial phase, in which corrective historiography
was central to the enterprise, scholars such as Copher and Felder were tapping into a long history of African American suspicion
regarding Euro-American interpretation. By challenging the historical narratives constructed by European and Euro-American biblical
scholars, these authors were able to provide a counterproposal to
a narrative that saw the lands and history of the Bible to be almost
extensions of Europe. Likewise, scholars such as Wimbush and
Blount have proposed fundamental changes in the discipline of biblical studies itself. Perceiving biblical studies, as practiced at least in

North America, to be captive to a pervasive Eurocentrism, these scholars have provided an exodus to those courageous enough to challenge the dominant disciplinary orientation. Promoting not only a recognition or mere acknowledgement of context's role in interpretation, they have encouraged the appropriation of a contextual orientation as a necessary ingredient in any attempt at interpretation that seeks legitimacy. Finally, more contemporary scholars have begun to explore the contours of liberation as a social phenomenon within and outside the community. Not always agreeing with current community practices, or with each other for that matter, they seek to expand the enterprise into one that has an influence on the lives of African Americans generally.

In my opinion, a great deal of African American biblical hermeneutics is a reaction or response to the perceived advancement of evangelical Christianity and fundamentalism in the African American community. Wimbush says this quite explicitly in his essay "Rescue the Perishing."[2] Of course, such an apparently reductionist statement is open to a considerable amount of challenge from those desiring to account for others factors that have affected the development of African American interpretation. For example, many associate the rise of this mode of interpretation with the spread of various liberation theologies, but especially black theology. African American hermeneutics, then, serves as a form of biblical engagement that promotes the larger liberatory enterprise. All of this is true. I contend, however, that the development and spread of various liberation theologies coincides with the development and spread of fundamentalisms as reactions to modernity. Although they may be opposite or antagonistic responses, they are related nonetheless. As moderns, African Americans have experienced an acute separation from their past and thus from their posited collective identity. Fundamentalism is one way to construct such an identity. Black theology is another. In this sense then, African American hermeneutics is a reaction or response to the spread of conservative Christianity in the community.

Others would point to the recognition and challenge put to biblical scholarship by persons who, until recently, were excluded from the guild. African American biblical scholars have begun to challenge the pervasive Eurocentrism they perceive as operative in the discipline. African American hermeneutics then is a counterproposal to a form of scholarship enamored with its European roots. It is the fruit of a critical mass of scholars "come of age," willing to challenge the discipline on something it took virtually for granted. And this is true. I contend, however, that embedded in this critique is a realization on the part of African American scholars that biblical scholarship has to this point enabled the spread of conservative evangelicalism by unwittingly providing scholarship that, when filtered, is used for evangelical advancement, and by demonstrating widespread disinterest in the social consequences of biblical interpretation. Through a certain form of benign neglect, biblical scholarship allows for the proliferation of scriptural readings that maintain an uncritical and potentially dangerous Eurocentric bias. For example, the vast majority of biblical scholars would agree that social location plays an influential role in how one approaches and interprets a given biblical text. In other words, they have disavowed the idea of disinterestedness in interpretation. Yet disinterestedness is a conceptual category still operative in the way that many, especially evangelicals, appropriate and apply biblical scholarship. Evangelicals give the impression that their interpretations of Scripture are objective (disinterested) and thus meet the fundamental criterion for truth. Scholars who are aware of the complexity of interpretation may dismiss such appropriations in private, but they do little or nothing to address them publicly. African American hermeneutics, then, challenges such neglect by taking seriously the ways in which biblical interpretation shapes community. That such communities may only continue the marginalization of so-called minorities is of paramount concern to scholars who believe in and are committed to liberation. In this sense, the attack on Eurocentrism in biblical studies is also an attack on conservative evangelicalism within the African American community, a movement that advocates uncritically the submission of women, the exclusion of homosexuals, and a rigid familial paradigm, among other things. Presented as objective (biblical) truths, these interpretations threaten to undermine the project of liberation, especially with regard to the fulfillment of individual human potential.

Still others may point to a perceived abandonment of the traditions accompanying African American Christianity as a basis for the advent of African American biblical interpretation. Many of the scholars discussed here use traditional African American resources in their interpretative enterprises. This becomes then a way to "remind" African Americans of the rich history that accompanies their Christian orientation, a history related to but not synonymous with that of their Euro-American Christian counterparts.[3] Again, there is a great deal of truth to this position.

I still contend, however, that the need for reclaiming African American historical resources has been sparked by the promise inherent in conservative evangelical and fundamentalist Christianity. As African Americans continue to integrate into American society in this post–civil rights era, they have become increasingly conscious of the ways in which their lives have differed from others, particularly in the religious arena. Influenced by their Euro-American counterparts in educational institutions (including seminary!), the workplace, recreation, and so on, many appear to be concerned about the efficacy of traditions and institutions that promote "segregation" rather than further integration. Claiming to be a nonethnic presentation of the gospel, evangelical Christianity appears to offer the integrative orientation sought by at least a few. African American hermeneutics challenges this misleading impression by exposing the cultural bias embedded in evangelical/fundamentalist claims. Even more, it calls attention to the richness of African American Christian traditions. Using these traditions, African American biblical scholars attempt to demonstrate that, although these resources were developed during a time of legally sanctioned segregation, they address universal existential and Christian concerns nevertheless. Rather than operating as a form of self-segregation, African American Christian tradition offers a way to reflect on and engage existential concerns that may begin with a distinctive historically conditioned cultural context but that move quickly to larger, widespread human concerns. In effect, what many scholars argue is that the African American context serves only as a point of entry to these larger concerns. In sum, although there are several compelling and legitimate ways to account for the rise of African American biblical hermeneutics, in my opinion, the specter that looms consistently in the background is that of fundamentalism and its increasing influence in the life of the black church.

Probing the Eclipse for Its Weaknesses

What African American biblical scholars have accomplished in the closing decades of the twentieth century has been nothing less than remarkable. Not only have they initiated an entirely new hermeneutical program, but they also have ignited a conversation as to the nature of hermeneutics itself. The burgeoning field of what is now called cultural hermeneutics has given voice to Afrocentric scholars as well as others who reject the disinterested claims of the historical-critical method. In such a short time, however, it has not been possible to reflect fully on the growth and implications of this new trajectory in biblical interpretation. I do not feign to offer such advice as may be needed to assess the program in its entirety. However, I do offer four areas of weakness that need to be addressed if African American biblical interpretation will continue to flourish.

First, African American biblical scholars must give a coherent account of the type of Eurocentric scholarship they seek to overturn. Fernando Segovia, a Latino biblical scholar, has urged Afrocentric interpreters to do this very thing. He says, "There are bits and pieces, here and there, but no coherent, comprehensive picture."[4] Calling the criticisms of African American biblical scholars "too scattered and unsystematic," Segovia believes a more defensible argument can be made for this form of interpretation if Afrocentric biblical interpreters would only supply a coherent picture of that against which they are arguing.[5] A fair number of mainstream scholars have rejected the African American enterprise entirely because it fails to provide such a picture.

In general, it appears that African American interpreters challenge the uncritical acceptance of the historical-critical method as it has been taught in our educational institutions. Still, these scholars have not been clear as to whether there is anything salvageable in the method at all. As we have seen, African American biblical scholars have continued to engage in historical criticism in one manner or another. Thus, historical criticism in itself may not be the culprit. I am inclined to believe that what African American biblical scholars reject is an implicit bias conveyed through historical criticism. As one of my students intimated recently, one would be inclined to believe that all individuals in the Bible and early Christianity were of European extraction by listening to historical critics. Of course, nothing could be further from the truth. Yet something about the way in which historical criticism developed has fostered this implicit bias.

In order to understand Eurocentrism, we may need to understand the development of Europe and Europeans. The traditional European cultures that have contributed to modern American biblical scholarship — France, Britain, Germany — all have connections to the ancient Roman Empire. The Germans, in particular, have an ongoing love affair with all things Greco-Roman. Such a

romanticized connection may have contributed to a sense of patri-
monial privilege from their Mediterranean predecessors. Contrary
to the notion of modernity, European scholars have not emphasized consistently the great historical distance that lies between
themselves and the ancient civilizations they study. Implicitly believing themselves to be the heirs of all things Greco-Roman, these
scholars have passed along this bias in their scholarship. Consequently, they have domesticated the ancient world and made it a
virtual extension of Europe.

The advent of historical criticism in the United States brought
this European bias along with it to American seminaries and other
educational institutions. American culture, which has never had a
direct connection to ancient Rome, did have one to Europe. Seeking to foster this historic relationship to the so-called Old World,
American scholars appear to have adopted this bias uncritically.
Modern biblical research, if it is to be effective and truthful, must
highlight the distance between these ancient civilizations and Europe, as we know it. This does not mean that there are no points
of contact between the modern context and the ancient world, but
they are not based as much as some suppose on any sort of direct historical connection. If African American biblical scholarship
seeks to be an effective voice in the larger enterprise of biblical studies, it should address this bias at the core of traditional
scholarship.

Second and related, African American hermeneutics appears to
be in need of stronger theoretical grounding. Again, Segovia is
instructive in his comments. He says, "[A] number of studies...
either subscribe to in part or argue for a certain continuing validity
for the traditional historical-critical method, even when the present
plurality of interpretive models is explicitly acknowledged."[6] With
the exception of a few womanist interpreters, African American
biblical scholars tend to revert to historical criticism as a model
for engaging the Bible. If historical criticism is bankrupt, as some
Afrocentric interpreters contend, then alternative methods of textual engagement need to be explored and applied consistently. If,
however, African American biblical scholars seek to retain the
historical-critical method, at least at some level, they need to
confront the implicit bias that I outlined above and demonstrate
biblical historiography's ability to surpass Eurocentrism. African
American interpreters have made strides along this line. For example, they have used Afrocentrism as a conceptual tool to de-center
the dominant Eurocentric historical narrative. More work needs to

be done in this area. Segovia encourages African American interpreters to engage methodological movements within and outside
the discipline of biblical studies:

> I would urge an ongoing conversation with contemporary
> currents in biblical interpretation both in the third world
> and among minority groups of the first world. Outside the
> discipline, I would urge, in addition to the wider world of lit-
> erary criticism, a similar conversation with such other fields
> as American black aesthetics, Caribbean studies, and cultural
> theory.[7]

Largely the products of the still dominant historical-critical pedagogy, African American interpreters may find it difficult to break
the chains of this method entirely. Still, it appears hypocritical to
denounce a method one employs in one's own engagement with
the Scriptures, at least without qualification. As we have seen, even
the most recent forms of African American engagement with the
Bible continue to rely heavily on historical reconstructions. Either
they will continue to embrace this method as instructive to the
Afrocentric enterprise, with the necessary conceptual fine-tuning,
or they will abandon it in favor of other models and methods of
textual interpretation.

Third, African American biblical scholars must revisit the issue
of Africans in the biblical world. As I pointed out in previous chapters, Afrocentric interpretation has moved quickly from corrective
historiography to a form of cultural hermeneutics that has virtually
ignored the presence of Africans in the text. Of course, it would
make little sense for African American interpreters to continue to
argue for the historical presence of black-skinned people in the
Bible. This would be difficult, if not impossible, to prove, given
the difficulties I have outlined previously. Still, Africans do occupy a considerable portion of the literature of the Hebrew Bible.
This fact in itself should compel African American interpreters
to engage the literary world of the Bible to analyze further the
ways in which Africans have been portrayed. Scholars have been
reluctant to offer critique, along with valorization, of the Egyptians and Ethiopians who appear in the narratives. To be sure,
some scholars have raised troubling questions (e.g., Weems, Kirk-
Duggan, Randall Bailey, Williams). Gale Yee, an Asian American
biblical scholar, has pointed to the absence of thoroughgoing critique as an ideological blind spot in the enterprise of Afrocentric
interpretation. She says, "[Nothing] is said about the imperialism,

militarism, despotism, and oppression upon which the so-called glory of these [African] civilizations [was] built."[8] Clearly, more exploration in this area needs to be done, especially with regard to modern African American tendencies to valorize and appropriate ancient examples of imperialism. To put it bluntly, if we were "kings and queens," then that glory came at the expense of others who were slaves and subordinates. If one of the goals of African American hermeneutics is to tell the truth about history and literature, then we must tell the entire truth.

Finally, African American biblical scholars must endeavor to include the voices, perspectives, and concerns of the African Americans who occupy the churches, parachurch organizations, suburbs, and inner cities of our nation. They are the real conversation partners in this enterprise. Part of the reluctance to include them may stem from a fear of what they will say. The experience of biblical scholars in Africa and South America demonstrates that we often will confront interpretations that are not liberatory (see chapter 1). To be sure, the oppressed are not always in the best position to reflect on the nature of their oppression. Nevertheless, true liberation is rarely, if ever, accomplished by the few on behalf of the many. If biblical interpretation in the African American religious community is becoming increasingly conservative, as some suggest, then it is having a deleterious effect on the lives of individual African Americans and the cohesiveness of the community in general. As a recent study by Allison Calhoun-Brown suggests, very few African Americans see Christianity through the liberatory paradigm of black theology, and those who do often fail to make the connection between this theological position and racial solidarity, which would include challenging interpretive paradigms that seek to divide, oppress, and marginalize.[9]

My own experience, although anecdotal, strongly suggests that African Americans are in search of a more meaningful form of biblical interpretation. Teaching and preaching in churches, I have been amazed at the number of adults who are afraid to admit that the Bible often contradicts some of their deepest existential convictions. Teaching and preaching among younger adults, I have consistently encountered a wall of resistance to interpretations of the Bible that attempt to deny the complexity and ambiguity of daily existence. Young adults often find the silence of their elders, and their unwillingness to challenge the validity of repeatedly unrefined interpretations of Scripture, to be hypocritical. Increasingly, young African Americans are looking elsewhere for guidance. Such a perception is borne out in a study conducted by Christopher Ellison and Darren Sherkat, which stated,

> The decline in the prestige of the black church may be linked with the increasing exposure of younger blacks to alternative value systems, from the materialistic "buppie" values eloquently anticipated by Frazier...to hedonistic urban streetwise values. Perhaps the young are rebelling against the black church's moral regulations....[10]

Biblical interpretation is at the heart of the African American community's present existential plight.[11] As the community's religious authorities increasingly espouse a fundamentalist interpretation of Scripture, they have become complicit in African American oppression. In effect, they have silenced their own constituency. Take, for example, the surge in HIV infections among an increasingly educated African American populace.[12] If African American males, who have long registered negative reactions to homosexuality, account for the majority of new HIV cases in the United States because of a phenomenon termed "being on the down low" (an expression that only serves to underscore the ambiguity and fear of stigmatization present in the African American community), then the black church has failed to provide the type of moral leadership necessary to promote human flourishing. It is not that the message has not been received — the silence and the surreptitious behavior of these men testify to that. The problem is a biblically mandated paradigm that is out of step with the realities of human sexual activity.[13]

Andrew Sung Park, another Asian American scholar, is undoubtedly correct when he argues that in African American biblical hermeneutics "emphasis should be equally given to the sociocultural analysis of present day African Americans as well as to that of the biblical Africans."[14] If the fear of Afrocentric interpreters is that fundamentalism will destroy the vitality of African American biblical interpretation, then efforts must be made to provide alternatives that liberate members of the community from a misguided biblical hegemony. In this instance, the model of ecclesial interpretive communities in which scholars and nonscholars read the Bible in dialogue may be useful (see chapter 1). If African American biblical hermeneutics remains a predominantly academic enterprise, it may fare no better than black theology when it comes to infiltrating the African American community.

Probing the Eclipse for Its Continued Potential

There is great potential in the enterprise of African American biblical hermeneutics. As one trajectory in cultural hermeneutics, it attempts to join method to context and agency. It is Afrocentric in that it embraces "an orientation to the world that privileges the position, values, and experiences of African and African American peoples."[15] Unlike that which it theoretically rejects, this mode of biblical engagement seeks to uncover the multiple truths that exist in a world almost silenced by the hegemonic forces that operate under the guise of Eurocentric tradition.

Having taken up the gauntlet laid down by black theology, African American interpreters have pursued the liberatory potential available in the Scriptures. To the chagrin of its earliest theological advocates, an African American reading of Scripture has served to complicate the idea that the Bible is a consistent and reliable source for human liberation. While Hebrew Bible scholars have found it difficult to use the Bible in this manner (e.g., Randall Bailey, Weems, Kirk-Duggan),[16] New Testament scholars, using Jesus as their hermeneutical paradigm, have been more successful in presenting the Bible as a manifesto for the marginalized (e.g., Felder, Wimbush, Blount). Yet more contemporary New Testament scholarship has called even the New Testament's liberatory orientation into question (e.g., Braxton and Williams). As increasing numbers of African Americans enter the discipline of biblical studies, one should expect further growth and challenge to what now appears to be a conundrum: that the Bible and the God portrayed in it display a clear preference for those living on the social margins (epistemological privilege). In contrast, what has become readily apparent is that the Bible is a complicated document. As Norman Gottwald has pointed out, "The most striking feature of [recent African American biblical scholarship] is the near unanimity with which [these scholars] caution against assuming that the Bible is uniformly and reliably supportive of liberation."[17] I offer the following four proposals in order to advance the enterprise even further.

Is God an Absentee Landlord?
The Complexity of Early Christianity

In the Synoptic Gospels, Jesus gives a parable that the church later dubbed "the parable of the wicked tenants" (Matt 21:33–46;

Mark 12:1–12; Luke 20:9–19). According to the narrative, a man plants a vineyard and leases it to a group of tenant farmers. He then departs to live somewhere far away. When the appropriate time arrives to collect his rent, he sends his slaves to the tenants. Instead of giving to the slaves what is supposedly due the land-owner, the tenants physically abuse them, even killing some (Matt 21:35–36; Mark 12:5). In response to this violent rejection, the landowner decides to send his son to the tenants, supposedly think-ing that they would respect his heir. This move proves senseless, as the tenants decide to kill the son in an attempt to claim the land as their own. Jesus then queries the audience as to the fate of these tenants. In the Lukan account, he concludes, "He will come and destroy those tenants and give the vineyard to others" (20:16). Ac-cording to the evangelists, God will deal with the Jewish religious authorities according to this model.

Form critical analysis has classified this parable as an allegory.[18] In its synoptic context, it functions as a not-so-veiled portent to the religious authorities that their divine patronage will be removed. However, there is some reason to question this classification. As some have pointed out, this parable also appears in the *Gospel of Thomas* 65, where no such allegorical classification appears war-ranted.[19] Bruce Malina and Richard Rohrbaugh accept the idea that, in the earliest gospel tradition, this parable was not an alle-gory, but then they oddly suggest that Jesus told the parable as "a warning to landowners expropriating and exporting the produce of the land."[20] This interpretive scenario, which I dub the "Robin Hood" scenario, argues that God will take away the "vineyard" from the "rich" (the Jewish religious authorities) and give it to the "poor" (the enigmatic others named in the gospels). There is an in-herent problem with this scenario, however. Unless it is viewed as an allegory, which means accepting to some degree the opponents named in the Synoptics, there is no reason to believe that Jesus champions anything other than the interests of the landowner.

The narrative components of the parable are equally disturb-ing. Even if taken as an allegory, the Robin Hood scenario fails to be compelling. Following the logic of the approach, God is repre-sented in the parable by the landowner, who planted the vineyard and leased it to tenants. This would have been accompanied by a written agreement, possibly to be understood as the Mosaic cove-nant (see, e.g., *SB* XIV 11279).[21] At the appropriate time, God sends slaves (possibly the prophets or other religious figures) to col-lect the rent from the tenants. The tenants, identified as the Jewish religious authorities, reject and even kill these slaves. Finally, God sends his Son, identified as Jesus in the gospels, to collect. Killing him, the religious authorities destroy any possibility of retaining their status. They will be overthrown in favor of other yet unidentified tenants (presumably Gentiles in most interpretations). Each of these components is disturbing to anyone who knows something of the phenomenon of absentee landlords in the first century.

Land ownership in the ancient world was concentrated in the hands of an elite few, who rarely lived near their holdings. Similar in many respects to the phenomenon of share cropping in the United States, this system relied on the exploitation of poor and vulnerable peasants forced to toil endlessly in order just to subsist.[22] The asymmetry of this economic arrangement begs the question of how the tenants could ever be identified as the rich in this parable. According to Malina and Rohrbaugh, after paying rent, taxes, and other various obligations, the tenant farmer would be left with less than 20 percent of his produce on which to survive.[23] Moreover, the landowner uses slaves to conduct his business. Although this was a customary arrangement at the time, the interpreter can never lose sight of the fact that slaves were considered property and not people. Their aberrant treatment at the hands of the tenants underscores this fact. In short, the parable portrays God as an absentee landlord who uses chattel property and ultimately his Son in an attempt to extract profit from those least capable of providing it. Contrary to the Robin Hood scenario, S. R. Llewelyn is correct to point out, "[The] import of the parable as a story to vindicate Jesus' mission to the poor would be confused by the audience, for the rich/poor distinction would be drawn between the landlord and his tenants rather than between the old and new tenants."[24]

To push my point even further, the parable is historically implausible on its face. Three problematic areas must be addressed and explained if the parable is to be considered anything other than fantastic. First, it is unlikely that any sane tenant would lease a newly planted vineyard.[25] It took at least five years for a vineyard to become productive, and it was customary to employ contract labor rather than tenants to cultivate vineyards prior to their full productivity.[26] Second, the behavior of the tenants toward the slaves, and their belief that they would inherit if they killed the son, is outrageous. In the past, scholars have argued that a provision in Jewish law, *ḥazaqah*, would have made such an assumption credible. This is highly unlikely. As Llewelyn says, "[The] land-lord's holding of a duly signed lease agreement would...preclude the tenants' claim, for the tenant was expressly excluded from acquisition by *ḥazaqah* under such circumstances."[27] Finally, the landowner's actions are as curious as those of his tenants. Although a great deal of legal procedure in antiquity relied on self-help, the landowner easily could have petitioned the authorities to assist in such an egregious situation (e.g., *P.Oxy.* XLIX 3464). There is no *prima facie* reason to believe that he would have been ignored, es-pecially given his higher social status.[28] In sum, when placed in historical context, the parable as presented provides a highly im-plausible scenario for a landowner's engagement with his tenants. Llewelyn makes this clear when he says, "If Jesus had intended the parable to deal with the exclusion of one social group and the in-clusion of a new group, then a simple story of the failure of the tenants to meet their contracted duties to the landlord might have sufficed."[29]

I have chosen this parable to highlight a pervasive bias in New Testament scholarship that deflects any criticism from the literary representations of Jesus. Such a pro-Jesus bias is equally true in African American biblical scholarship. For example, Blount refers to this parable twice in *Then the Whisper Put on Flesh*. In the first instance, he discusses it within the context of the gospel of Matthew. He argues that the parable describes "the kind of ethi-cal behavior necessary for entrance into the kingdom (e.g., 13:43; 21:43). To be sure," he says, "the kingdom is God's gift."[30] A de-cided halo effect appears to overshadow almost all readings of such passages. First, the parable outlines behavior that is questionable, if not implausible. Second, the parable is not about giving gifts. Giving, in the context of the parable, means the transference of a lease from one group of tenants to another. In the framework of tenant farming in antiquity, the only party that stood to benefit from the process was the landowner. Blount's reading, "an attempt to help readers who live outside of an oppressed circumstance read the New Testament through the circumstance of oppressed others," appears insensitive to all the oppressive elements of the parable I outlined above.[31] He has accepted the Robin Hood scenario.

The second instance occurs in Blount's discussion of Luke. He argues strongly that Jesus represents and advocates in the narrative a type of ethical reversal. He points to this parable explicitly as an example of God's preference for the poor. He says, "The foun-dation for the Lukan ethics of reversal in favor of the 'poor' starts right here."[32] Clearly, the only way to derive this meaning from the parable is to read it as an allegory, the Robin Hood scenario. To interpret this parable truthfully as a manifesto for the marginalized, in my estimation, is to twist it beyond all plausible recognition.

I propose that these and other New Testament texts be examined again with fresh eyes to see the ways in which they support or hinder the cause of liberation. New Testament scholars appear reluctant to interrogate such passages vigorously. If Tina Pippin is correct in her assertion that African American hermeneutics is guided by "a human-rights framework" that "sets high standards for what texts are authoritative," then it must be applied consistently and rigorously, even with texts attributed to Jesus.[33]

In truth, the development of early Christianity is far more complex and multifaceted than is represented in the preponderance of African American biblical scholarship. While criticism can be leveled against Paul and the early church, few apply a hermeneutic of suspicion to a reading of the Gospels. If R. Joseph Hoffmann is correct when he says, "[When] the gospel-tradition finally acquires written form, *it does so under the influence of specific doctrines about Jesus as the Christ,* and not out of any purely historical interest in preserving the facts of his existence," then what we encounter in the Synoptics and John is a theologically driven representation of Christianity's founder.[34] Earlier, Bultmann made a similar point, when he said, "The *message of Jesus* is a presupposition for the theology of the New Testament rather than a part of that theology itself."[35] In other words, what we encounter in the Gospels is a partisan presentation of the ministry of Jesus. To be sure, the evangelists preserved what they believed to be kerygmatic and essential to Christian discipleship, but that is not the same as direct access to Jesus. Willi Marxsen was correct when he said, "[We] can only ever ascertain how people understood Jesus, how they experienced him, how they heard him."[36] It stands to reason that if Paul's hearing of Jesus can fail to achieve the criterion of liberation at crucial points, then the gospel writers may fail the same test as well — even when the words are placed in the mouth of Jesus himself.

I recognize that my proposal, if pursued to its logical conclusion, will complicate further the task of developing a liberatory hermeneutic. If the gospel representations of Jesus cannot form a coherent and reliable center to promote the cause of human liberation, then what hope is there for an African American hermeneutic that will meet the needs of black theology? Before answering this question, let me state explicitly what cannot be the proper response. A liberatory African American hermeneutic cannot be based entirely or in part on any form of biblical interpretation that sanctions existing injustice and oppression. A liberating and liberated hermeneutic can be derived only from "a re-reading of the gospel from within the context of the liberating praxis that grows out of this commitment and is directed toward responding to the question of the oppressed by transforming existing conditions."[37]

The fundamental datum of scriptural authority lies not in the text but in that distinctive existential experience of human beings, commonly called faith in Christ. As Marxsen said quite cogently, "The only person who can call a savior *the* savior is one who knows something about his salvation."[38] Thus, the real authority that authorizes the authority of Scripture is Christ, as experienced primarily and distinctively by human beings.

Scripture is authoritative insofar as it stands under the authority of Christ. This is why, in deciding the contours of the canon, the church chose apostolicity as a necessary criterion. In effect, it asked whether a particular writing was authoritative "in the unique sense of being authored by someone directly authorized by Christ himself."[39] Since biblical criticism commonly acknowledges that none of the New Testament writings, to say nothing of the Hebrew Bible, was authored by a direct witness to the ministry of Jesus, it searches continually to identify, as best as it can, the original witness of the apostolic church, "of which all the canonical writings are, at one stage or another, later interpretations."[40] The result is that the true locus of authority for Scripture is not the canon determined by the church but the witness to Christ found in, but not identical with, that canon.

Martin Luther identified this witness in Scripture as that which "pushes Christ."[41] In a very real sense, the words of Scripture must always be understood as a repository for that witness to Christ grounded in the experience and testimony of its authors. In this sense, Scripture can only allow the interpreter to determine the appropriateness of a theological claim based on the testimony provided by its authors; it cannot assist the interpreter in determining the credibility of a theological claim, in the sense of its truth in terms of the contemporary, common existential experience of human beings as such. This determination of credibility requires a much larger conversation grounded in the ongoing yet distinctive experience of human beings called faith. This is why the church has maintained that the canon is "not the collection of writings recognized as authoritative by the early church, but whatever of or in those writings [that] is in fact authorized by Christ through the church's continuing experience under the guidance of the Holy Spirit."[42]

If African American biblical interpreters are looking for a clear, consistent, and reliable liberatory message in the Bible, they will be continually misled and disappointed. The Bible, particularly the New Testament Gospels, can only and at most supply the context in which the appropriateness of a theological assertion is tested. Optimally, the Bible can serve as the source from which the interpreter can derive the witness to Christ that gives it any authority at all. Interpretive appropriateness, however, does not begin to meet the criterion for the assertion's credibility. In black theology, African Americans have asserted that the Christian God desires the authentic existence of human beings represented symbolically as living in freedom. The credibility of this claim has been validated repeatedly in history, philosophy, and politics. The task remaining for African American interpreters is to explore the propriety of this claim as evidenced in the collection of documents they believe to be a witness to the liberatory activity of Christ.

In the end, the decision of Blount and others to read the parable of the wicked tenants as an allegory stems from a theological commitment grounded in the fundamental belief that oppressive religious structures must be overthrown. This reading has little or no connection to the actual parable itself, except that the evangelists chose to present it as such. More important, such an appropriation obscures the most disturbing elements of the parable in favor of a facile interpretation that lacks true liberatory content. If African American biblical interpretation will continue to flourish, it must examine rigorously its reading of the entire New Testament to unmask and expose the inconsistent nature of Christianity itself.

Was Jesus a Semitic Racist?
Engaging the Multifaceted Reality of Prejudices

In Matthew and Mark, we are given a somewhat unflattering portrait of Jesus and his encounter with a Gentile woman (Matt 15:21–28; Mark 7:24–30). In Matthew, the woman's ethnicity is given as Canaanite. In Mark, it is Syrophoenician. In both accounts

Jesus rebukes the woman, saying, "It is not fair to take the children's bread and throw it to the dogs" (Matt 15:26; Mark 7:27). Although the woman eventually succeeds in her request, Jesus' initial response to her plea makes him appear to be prejudiced against either Greeks or Canaanites.

Matthew presents this woman as an individual of great faith (15:28). The narrative, however, still paints Jesus as a person of prejudice. The study of prejudice in the United States has oscillated between psychological and sociological analysis. After World War II, the initial studies on prejudice that emerged were decidedly psychological in nature. The central focus of such analysis was anti-Semitism. Not long afterwards, social science rushed in with its own explanation of prejudice. The focus here was more often racism as it developed in the once slaveholding American context. Both attempts had their strengths and weaknesses. Looking at the results of the social-scientific approach, Elisabeth Young-Bruehl says, "The very liberal social scientists who rushed to alter attitudes of prejudice with behavior-shaping institutions were slow to realize that applying the behavior-changes-attitudes formula to victim groups was dangerous."[43] She argues that a "both/and" approach is more desirable.

Young-Bruehl argues that prejudice, contrary to the widespread conception, is not a singular thing that displays itself in a variety of forms. Not all prejudices have the same root. In fact, it is improper to speak of prejudice. It is more accurate to speak of prejudices. She explains, "To avoid essentializing, one should speak of prejudices, not of prejudice, or, at least, one should give the various prejudices their due as distinct forms."[44]

According to Young-Bruehl, the realization that prejudices stem from multiple sources and thus should be confronted with multiple analyses and solutions marks a breakthrough in research on the nature of prejudice. Her insight into the multiple natures of prejudices coincides well with the womanist outlook and its hermeneutical project. Whether it is racism, sexism, classism, sexual orientation, or another form of social oppression, womanists have acknowledged consistently the multiple and interrelated structures that impose themselves on human beings. Young-Bruehl goes on to argue that the language of ideology, liberation, and public/private arises as a response to the experience of prejudice.[45]

Overseeing the complex and multiple forms of prejudice that exist in the world, Young-Bruehl bemoans the lack of an equally sophisticated engagement with its roots:

There is no tradition within the history of studies and theories of prejudice for looking at people as the victims of multiple prejudices. Nor is there much attention to the prejudices of victims of prejudice — to the sexism of black males, the racism of white females, to the antisemitism of black females, and so forth — or to the ways in which intragroup prejudices relate to these cross-group prejudices: how the attitudes of white males toward Blacks, male and female, are related to their attitudes toward white women, for example.[46]

She goes on to lay out a possible solution for the absence of a sophisticated theory to account for this phenomenon in her book *The Anatomy of Prejudices.*

According to Young-Bruehl, three broad and overlapping social psychologies can be identified and related to the phenomenon of prejudices. They are the obsessional, hysterical, and narcissistic. Take, for example, the hysterical form of prejudice. By this, she means "a prejudice that a person uses unconsciously to appoint a group to act out in the world forbidden sexual and sexually aggressive desires that the person has repressed."[47] It is a form of prejudice that most commonly transfixes on bodily features. In societies in which hysterical trends can be found, one often encounters the rhetoric of equality and fairness. Yet, at the same time, they are societies prone to "courtly and carefully coded and elaborately theatrical ways of life."[48] Of course, Young-Bruehl is addressing a phenomenon as it exists in a modern society like the United States. I was struck, however, at how potentially relevant Young-Bruehl's work may be for studies such as the recent one conducted by Gay L. Byron.

Her book *Symbolic Blackness and Ethnic Difference in Early Christian Literature* examines the literary representations of color symbolism and ethnic "othering" in the New Testament, apostolic, monastic, and later patristic writings.[49] Although this book represents a fine study of what Byron calls "ethno-political rhetorics," I wonder how much more nuanced and insightful her work could have been if it were informed by the insights of Young-Bruehl. For example, in her discussion of hysterical prejudice, she describes the role of the "other" as one of love and hate.[50] Unlike an obsessional form of prejudice, hysterical prejudice does not seek the complete destruction of the object. It seeks, rather, that the object of the prejudice be kept in its place.[51]

Byron points out that one of the functions of Christian rhetoric regarding Egyptians and Ethiopians involved the slandering of them as threats. Such slander, however, was not intended to eliminate them. It was intended to "other" them — to keep them in their rhetorical place. Moreover, she argues, "Greco-Roman authors were consumed with ethnic difference."[52] Byron contends that Christians adopted the larger Greco-Roman fixation with ethnic difference and adapted it into their social psychology as a mechanism for constructing and reinforcing an acceptable Christian identity. In such circumstances, Young-Bruehl says, "Hypocrisy is normal."[53]

I know that my proposal that African American interpreters explore again the nature of prejudices to develop a more comprehensive understanding of the phenomenon will unsettle some. As I said earlier, however, the central value of Young-Bruehl's contribution is how well it coincides with the claims and insights that womanist interpreters have already made. If anything, Young-Bruehl's proposal gives theoretical backing and, arguably, clinical grounding for the womanist claim. Recognizing and appreciating the multiple and interrelated structures of oppression involves an analogous recognition of the multiple sources of prejudices.

To return to our initial illustration, Jesus displays an orientation toward the Canaanite or Syrophoenician woman that is neither idiosyncratic nor socially determined in its entirety. Prejudices frequently are acquired in complex ways and do not always represent some form of pathology. Young-Bruehl points out, "There is, in fact, no empirical evidence at all that people who are prejudiced are any more pathological than the general population, and also no evidence that particular pathologies subtend either prejudice as 'generalized attitude' or specific prejudices."[54] Without a more realistic conception of prejudices, it becomes impossible to confront and address them in a manner that promotes generalized human flourishing.

Is the God of the Oppressed the God of All? Engaging Neoclassical or Process Thought

An African American law professor at the University of Pennsylvania is thrown up against her car and handcuffed over a speeding violation. She blames racial profiling.[55] New Jersey officials claim that African American drivers speed more often than others do, according to a forty-eight-hour study. In the report, African Americans made up 16 percent of the drivers on the New Jersey turnpike and 25 percent of the speeders.[56] African Americans join Euro-Americans and others in supporting the racial profiling of Arabs. Daniel L. Feder, an attorney for an Arab-American bumped from a flight, says, "When pilots put people off planes because of how they look, I don't think there is any issue of profiling, per se. It's the public humiliation."[57] Adrienne T. Washington, a reporter for the *Washington Times,* complains,

> For all those television executives who are so pleased with their reality television shows, I've got a great idea: Forget the Australian outback; try sending some soul to survive as a black man or black woman for just one day in America, where racial profiling is practiced on many fronts. I bet they couldn't pay people $1 million to engage in that living color adventure.[58]

Whether it is in small towns in the South or large urban centers in the Northeast and Midwest, oppression lives on. No longer confined to lynchings, segregated education, and cross burnings in the South, oppression takes on a nuanced and sinister form when it is practiced by those who refuse to acknowledge their complicity. The experience of oppression that lies at the heart of black theology is its most basic existential claim (datum).

Oppression can be characterized as a power that potentially delivers death.[59] As Theodore Walker, Jr., relates in a story from Howard Thurman, the fundamental existential reaction to oppression in any form is the struggle for freedom. He says, "Thurman reasoned that it is divinely given to the nature of all creatures, even little green snakes, to struggle and protest against oppression."[60] Thus, the desire for liberation is the corollary to the experience of oppression.

Black theology has developed the fundamental existential datum of oppression and connected it to two other affirmations. First, human experience becomes divine experience. Human suffering becomes divine suffering, since black theologians maintain that God experiences the experiences of human beings. Second, that God desires and strives for the liberation of the oppressed. This theological affirmation flows from the aforementioned of oppression and the divine experience of suffering. If Thurman's claim regarding liberation is correct, as black theologians believe it is, then the eminent example of freedom is God. Freedom, an essential aspect of God that makes God who God is, is a property of existence that God bestows on all living beings as such. Even plants seek the "light" of freedom.

The problem of black theology has always been the monopolar conception of the deity in classical Western theism. The notion of the entirely absolute, invariable, and eminently transcendent God is a staple of Western Christian theological reflection. This concept of deity is incongruent with the African American cultural experience of the Christian God. The more normative understanding held by African Americans is the perception of the deity as a co-sufferer, a God who not only "feels" our pain but also is affected by it as a real experience — in short, a God who is altered by our suffering. This affirmation, I believe, opens up the possibility for a dynamic understanding of God, one that aligns more with how African Americans and others truly experience God than with how classical Western theologians have attempted to portray God.

Theodore Walker has suggested that African Americans adopt the neoclassical or Hartshornean process understanding of God. Unlike the classical Western conception of deity, process thought, Walker implies, offers African Americans a way to think of God that coincides with their collective cultural understanding. A co-suffering God, he reasons, would be more compatible with the dynamic of process than with the stagnancy of traditional theology. He says,

> Where traditional theology says God is absolute and absolute only, process theology says God is both absolute and relative (unsurpassably absolute in some respects and unsurpassably relative in other respects), not just absolute. Where a traditional theology says God is unchanging and unchanging only, process theology says God is both unchanging and changing (unsurpassably unchanging in some respects and unsurpassably changing/responsive in others); that God is both being and becoming, not just being. Where a traditional theology says God is abstract, process theology says God is both abstract and concrete. Where a traditional theology says God is transcendent, process theology says God is both transcendent and immanent; both spiritual and physical, active and passive, independent and dependent, simple and complex, necessary and contingent, each in its respective and unsurpassable way.[61]

Such a dipolar conception of deity provides a basis for the claim of black theologians that God suffers with the oppressed. As John Cobb and David Ray Griffin point out, process theology does not merely claim that God knows of our suffering. As they understand it, God's emotional state is dependent on worldly actualizations, which include feelings. Thus, they say, "God enjoys our enjoyments, and suffers with our sufferings."[62]

This vision of God, although attractive, has been rejected repeatedly by black theologians because they find this God to be anemic. Although Cobb and other process theologians claim that God loves all persons equally, they also believe that God "is directly acting in the world to create just conditions."[63] More importantly, process thinkers such as Charles Hartshorne would argue more pointedly for a vigorous understanding of deity within which God takes sides. As Walker says, "[The] logic of Hartshorne's conception of divine love is such as to place God decisively on the side of the oppressed in their struggle for liberation."[64] Unlike the sentimental faith that many black theologians attach to process theology, Hartshorne and others consistently argue that an ethic of love does not exclude the possibility of violence. As Walker makes clear, "Difficult though it is for humans with imperfect love, the demands of perfect love may, nonetheless, require that we kill an oppressor with whom we have sympathy."[65] A God who cares for all is the same God who supports freedom for the sake of all.

I know that my proposal that African American biblical scholars engage process thought in their attempt to explicate a liberated and liberating hermeneutic will appear odd to some. Many believe that African American biblical hermeneutics is adequately served by the enterprise of black theology. I am not arguing against such a view. Black theology provides African American biblical interpretation with its theological center. Yet, as we have seen, the implications of liberation take on many, often unexpected, forms. A process perspective would provide the African American hermeneutical paradigm with some agility with respect to these unexpected implications of liberation.

Novelty is at the core of how God acts in the world, according to process theologians. This means that some of the ongoing strife that erupts in human social relations is due to God's activity. As Cobb and Griffin maintain,

> [No] type of social order is to be maintained if it no longer tends to maximize the enjoyment of the members of the

society. Also, it is impossible for any form of social order to continue indefinitely to be instrumentally good. God, far from being the Sanctioner of the Status Quo, is the source of some of the chaos in the world.[66]

The idea that God may be behind the repeated challenges to our attempts to construct a stable understanding of human social relationships can go a long way toward tempering our fears about the unknown, yet emerging, new social order, which includes, by necessity, new hermeneutical implications and possibilities.

Unheard Voices in the Margin: The Possibility of a Neo-Womanist Perspective

I recently read the story of Detra (not her real name), a thirty-year-old African American, born and raised in a large city called Jefferson (a pseudonym, I believe, for Chicago).[67] The oldest of four children, she has one brother and two sisters. One of her earliest childhood memories was the return of her father from prison. They lived in the projects at the time, and one day her father just knocked on the door. This was sometime before she was six. Her paternal grandmother, Caroline Jones, who viewed Detra as the light of her life, was mysteriously and brutally killed when Detra was eight.

Around the age of nine, Detra began to feel as though she was different from other children. She couldn't quite explain what it was, but she remembers it distinctly. Around the same time that Detra began to ponder her sense of identity, her father was shot coming home from work. She remembers her mother crying herself to sleep for months afterward. They had been married for over ten years.

Her mother was determined to keep her children's lives normal and so insisted that they play and live life. Detra would frequent the local community center, going to arts and drama classes. One day, another frequent visitor to the community center, Timmy, stopped her on her way home from arts class. He played ball with the other teenagers at the center. He was nineteen. As she describes the episode,

> He...stopped me and told me that I had to give up something. At the time I was thinking, I thought he was talking about money or something. And I told him I didn't have no money. So he said you have to give up something, and he

patted me on my butt. I still didn't know what he was talking about, but I was scared to death. And then he grabbed
me by my collar and took me down in the boy's bathroom.
The boy's bathroom was situated where there was these steps
that goes down underground, right, and he ripped my jean
open and laid me down. And when he entered me, the hol-
lering, because it was real painful, so he put his hands over
my mouth, and then he did his little thing, right. When I got
home I didn't tell nobody, but I took a bath. I was bleeding.[68]

She had not even reached the age of eleven. Reflecting back on this
event years later, she called it "violent," "painful," and "terror-
izing."[69] Timmy continued to rape her over the course of several
months, until one day she ran screaming in front of the police and
he was arrested.

In the next two years, Detra began to experiment sexually. She
had sex with a young man named Nicky — originally on a dare,
but then on a regular basis. Shortly after, she began another sexual tryst with a gang member called Duke. He caught her coming
out of Nicky's house late one night, and this encounter began their
relationship.

Between the ages of twelve and thirteen, during this time of
sexual experimentation, Detra attempted suicide. The rape had a
greater effect than she had imagined. She felt worthless. She says,

I think the rape confirmed that. Subconsciously, I think so.
Yeah, that I wasn't important, you know. I was obsolete.
I could be what... anything could be done to me. It didn't
make no difference.... In the eyes of these people you're very
immaterial. That these little pieces of immaterial things you
can do what you want to do to them.[70]

Thankfully, the attempt failed, and she never told anyone about it.

When Detra was fourteen, her mother began a relationship with
a drug user named Jeff. She called this period of her life "the
Decline of the Roman Empire."[71] Her family, which had been relatively stable, was beginning to fall apart. Her mother became a
drug addict and became increasingly involved in illegal activities,
and slowly they lost everything. By the time Detra was sixteen, her
family was scattered across the city, and she and her mother were
living in a house with no furniture or utilities.

She met her first real boyfriend, Mookie, at age fifteen. He
taught her and her close friends how to hustle. Sixteen marked a

turning point in her life. Not only had her family life hit rock bottom, but she also was arrested for being underage at an adult party. She had to confide to her mother things about her life that she had always tried to hide.

It was also around this time that she began to take heroin like her mother. She was involved with a man who was a drug dealer. He got her high in exchange for sex. By the time he was arrested, she was hooked. She began hustling on the streets to feed her habit. She was seventeen.

At eighteen, she clipped a John for around eighteen hundred dollars. With this money, she got her first apartment. A couple of years later, she met a man named Curt in a nearby town. They would be a couple for the next three years. He supported their union through burglary, and she supplemented it with continued hustling. Eventually, Curt was arrested for violating probation, and the relationship ended.

Detra moved backed to Jefferson. Her mother, who by this time had lost the house, moved in with her, and they lived together for eight months. Fortunately, after fourteen years, her mother finally won her claim for survivor's benefits. The money she received allowed her to restart her life, and she moved into her own home again.

Unfortunately, Detra's drug use compelled her to take unhealthy risks. One day, she missed injecting the heroin in her vein. An abscess ensued, and Detra was hospitalized. They thought she would lose her leg, but as she described it, God intervened and her leg was spared. Her sister Betty was not so lucky. She died a drug addict when Detra was twenty-eight.

Detra is a drag queen.[72] Her story and those of others have been chronicled by Leon Pettiway, a criminologist, in his provocative book *Honey, Honey, Miss Thang: Being Black, Gay, and on the Streets*. Pettiway wrote the book to evoke questions, to prod our common understanding of "deviants" and their value. Those whom criminologists label "deviants," theologians often have labeled "the marginalized." They are those whom society has rejected. Many would say they are not even human. Not physically female, not psychosocially male, they simply do not fit. As one journalist wryly observed, "If you're poor, black, feminine and gay, life is the wrong place."[73]

In truth, these people challenge the core of what we mean by liberation. Cornel West once observed that the construction of Afrocentrism meets its limit here:

Afrocentrism, a contemporary species of black nationalism, is
a gallant yet misguided attempt to define an African identity
in a white society perceived to be hostile. It is gallant because
it puts black doings and sufferings, not white anxieties and
fears, at the center of discussion. It is misguided because —
out of fear of cultural hybridization and through silence on
the issue of class, retrograde views on black women, gay men,
and lesbians, and a reluctance to link race to the common
good — it reinforces the narrow discussions about race.[74]

Womanists have challenged the "retrograde views" of many forms
of Afrocentrism, as we have seen. Their voices challenge the mainstream, even in the African American community, to "critique all
rationalizations for domination and exploitation," and to concede
"that as human beings we are all mutually connected to each other
and dependent upon one another for our emancipation and for our
survival."[75]

I chose to tell Detra's story in the manner I did, playing on the
gender ambiguity, to highlight the resonance her story has with
that of many African American women in a similar context. I was
struck in reading her story that her experiences often reminded me
of women, gays, and lesbians I have known through the years.
Pettiway is correct when he says, "[These women's stories] demonstrate that lived experiences are complex and move between and
include times of triumph and defeat, humiliation and pride. They
reveal what we always knew — that life is filled with ambivalence
and ambiguity."[76]

I know that my proposal, that the stories of transvestites like
Detra could form the core of a neo-womanist hermeneutic, will
offend some within and outside the womanist theological community. Please believe, however, that my purpose is not to offend but
to challenge and expand. I could have asserted that African American biblical hermeneutics needed to include the distinctive social
location of black gays and lesbians, transvestites and the trans-
gendered, into their interpretive program, and many would have
nodded in assent. If, however, the possibility of the actual inclusion
of such a hermeneutical perspective rests entirely on the presence
of these individuals in the guild, then their voices may never be
heard. The discipline of biblical studies, as Cone and Wilmore have
pointed out, has been reluctant until recently to include the voices
of African Americans at all, much less those who are transvestites.
Couple this with the avoidance of a frank and open discussion

of sexuality in the African American community in general, and the thought of an African American transvestite expounding an Afrocentric hermeneutic is phantasmagorical.

The tactic of advocating a neo-womanist hermeneutic grew out of the analogies I saw between the womanist hermeneutical program and the plight of individuals like Detra. I was specifically reminded of Alice Walker's words, "When we have pleaded for understanding, our character has been distorted; when we have asked for simple caring, we have been handed empty inspirational appellations, then stuck in the farthest corner."[77] If imitation is the sincerest form of flattery, it also signifies that one is doing something correctly.[78] The complexity and fecundity of the womanist hermeneutical paradigm bespeaks a human existential intricacy that can capture and elucidate the multiple and often contradictory oppressive structures that negate the authentic existence of transvestites like Detra. Let me explain.

Womanist thinkers have advocated a hermeneutical strategy of being "broad in the concrete." In the lives of Detra and other marginalized African American transvestites, we see the struggles of human existence as such. As Pettiway says, "The private troubles of being black, poor, gay, transvestite, and drug using should be transformed into the public issues of homosexuality, drug addiction, sexual identity, poverty, crime control, and race relations."[79] He goes on to give a very personal account of how in studying their lives, Pettiway found resonances with his own.

> There are countless examples of this dichotomy [between social insiders and outsiders] and its effect. For example, the lives of Shontae, China, Detra, Keisha, and Monique have not been very different from my own. I am an Afro-American male born at a time when there were basic questions as to the humanity of black folks. I grew up in Durham, North Carolina, and I recall at the age of five my mother dragging me to the back of the bus because even little black boys and girls could not sit in the front. I remember separate rest rooms and water fountains. I heard of those awful deeds committed further South, in Alabama, Georgia, Mississippi, and Louisiana where sojourners of justice fell victims at the hands of klansmen and ignorance. I was bused from one side of the county to the other side because that was where black students had to attend high school. I remember

how some black men dropped their heads as a sign of defer-
ence to whites regardless of who they were. It was "yes, sir"
and "no, sir" for whites and "Helen," "Mary," "John," or
just simply "nigger" for us. To the wider culture, we were
irresponsible and inept children. But within our own communities, to each other, we were infinitely complex, interesting
and full of potential and possibility.[80]

Pettiway is pointing to an idea that Felder raised with respect
to African Americans in chapter 2: the idea of subjugated knowl-
edges. Like women and African Americans generally, the insights,
voices, perceptions, and contributions of persons like Detra have
been distorted "because they did not fit into 'a unitary body of
theory which would filter, hierarchise and order them in the name
of some true knowledge and some arbitrary idea of what constitutes a science and its objects.' "[81] Over against Felder's assertion,
which was based on race, womanists and individuals like Detra
understand that subjugation is much more complicated.

Detra measures her life in terms of her connectedness to others.
She speaks of "when my father did this" or "when my sister said
that." It is an implicit acknowledgment that time is important only
insofar as it assists us in measuring and appreciating our connections to other human beings. As Pettiway says of the entire group,
"Time exists [for them] in relation to experiences. It is not marked
by fleeting hours of the days and months but rather by the 'feel'
of being black, gay, and a transvestite as well as the experiences of
courage, resilience, resistance."[82] The concrete occurrences of Detra's life provide a lens through which we can reflect on existential
issues that confront us all. Her sense of time as relationship reminds us, often disturbingly, that all life — especially in the forms
that challenge us most — is interconnected and that the idea that
we are isolated is not only an illusion but also one lacking any
redemptive value.

Another theme found in some womanist theology is an innate
sense of dignity in the face of oppressive social structures. In the
presence of taunts, slurs, and physical abuse, these women "are
unanimous in their belief that they are human beings who deserve respect."[83] Monique's plea may be the most poignant: "Let
me be."[84]

Such dignity keeps them from being alienated from God. Whether
they hold to the notion of a "higher power" or a more traditional

notion of the Christian God, individuals like Detra refuse to allow others to dictate their ultimate worth to the deity. Keisha says,

> I mean the Lord made everybody. So something He doing, you know, for…they may say…well, some people say, "You going to hell" and "Change your life over and everything." But I don't believe that. 'Cause nobody don't know where they going at. I can't say right now if I die where I'm going at. I was raised up on one person, the Lord.[85]

Individuals like Detra and Keisha demonstrate continually an innate belief that they are important to God. As Pettiway says, "They insist that even His eyes can be amazed by them, amazed by what they have done with what He has given them when He created them."[86]

Detra recognizes that the oppression she encounters is multiple and simultaneous. Reflecting on her early life — the rape, poverty, drug abuse, alienation, identity questions, race issues — she says, "Okay, the fact is that it was very difficult but I feels as though I was in quicksand and I found a branch to hold on and pull myself out of it."[87] Against these structures of oppression, Detra arrived at the hard-won conclusion that God made her who she is.

The most disturbing aspect of the structures of oppression arrayed against individuals like Detra is our commonplace notion of gender. What I found surprising, however, is how much their ideas of gender identification correspond to womanist notions of the "grown" African American female. As Keisha explains:

> Well, when I was growing up, only person I looked up to… was women. I was going to be a woman right. I looked in the mirror, in East Jefferson, and I said, "Ooh, I wanna be a woman." And I don't know if it's foolish or what, I just said, "I wanna be woman. I know God didn't make me no woman, but I wanna look like a woman." And bam! I start throwing makeup. Start looking like a woman. Arch my eyes. Hair started growing like a woman. Perm. My nails. Then I started taking female hormones. Taking pills. I started just taking them. Then I started getting more effeminate. Then people start mistaking me as a real woman in the world. See, I went in the world to test it, see. Just like I was walk into a store and they was like, "Excuse me, miss. You can go ahead." A gentleman would say that. Then I knew, right

then and there, I'm on the right track, you know. Not acting. See, you gotta be yourself in order to be a woman also.
You can't just act out "I'm gonna be a woman" and get
and be all flaming. Yeah. You can't be all like this. 'Cause
a woman is not like this. She's natural. She's unique. That's
her, you know.[88]

In many ways, Detra and Keisha are improvisers of gender who
undermine the distinction between male and female. They trouble the once stable categories of "gay," "straight," "man," and
"woman." Our commonplace certainty in meaning unravels and
becomes blurred after we encounter them. In this and other ways,
they force us to confront our ideology of gender as a natural and
given "set of binarily constructed differences between human beings."[89] In short, they call us back to the critical posture that
womanism embraces from the start.

   As a proposal to advance the enterprise of African American
biblical hermeneutics, I hope this neo-womanist perspective receives some consideration. Clearly, our constructions of gender
are challenged in my overture to consider this peculiar aspect of
African American existence as a cohort to the otherwise stable enterprise of womanist hermeneutics. As I said previously, I could
have suggested that Afrocentric interpretation include the voices of
gays and lesbians and left it at that. In choosing persons like Detra,
I sought to reinscribe the idea that a liberated and liberating hermeneutic involves the recognition that even the most marginalized in
our society deserve the possibility of authentic human existence. I
am reminded of yet another story Pettiway tells in his provocative
book. He says,

   There is a point in the liturgy just prior to the readings
   from the Bible when the priest stands with his hands out-
   stretched, and says, "Let us pray." Ordinarily, after a brief
   pause, the priest would proceed to read the appropriate
   prayers from the prayer book being held for him by his al-
   tar person. On this particular Sunday, however, there was a
   homeless person in attendance who was apparently not familiar with the liturgy. Consequently, when the priest said,
   "Let us pray," he obediently stood and began, loudly, to pray
   the "Our Father." His voice reverberated through the assembly and throughout the congregation you could hear faint
   gasps or see embarrassed smiles. The priest, however, simply waited until the man had finished praying. Then he said,

"Amen," adding, "I'm not the only person who knows how to pray."

The voices from the margins not only continue to speak but also struggle to continue to eclipse the powers that would banish them back to the supposed margins — where there is weeping and gnashing of teeth (cf. Matt 8:12).

Notes

Preface

1. Michael Joseph Brown, "Are We Missing a Truly Multicultural Moment?" *Teaching Theology and Religion* (1998), 165–68.

Chapter 1: The Eclipse of a Eurocentric Enterprise

1. Mark Golden and Peter Toohey, eds., *Inventing Ancient Culture: Historicism, Periodization, and the Ancient World* (New York: Routledge, 1997), 3.

2. See Michael Joseph Brown, *What They Don't Tell You: A Survivor's Guide to Biblical Studies* (1st ed.; Louisville: Westminster John Knox, 2000), 66.

3. See, e.g., Joseph Childers and Gary Hentzi, eds., *The Columbia Dictionary of Modern Literary and Cultural Criticism* (New York: Columbia University Press, 1995), 9–10.

4. For a definition of culture, see Mark C. Taylor, ed., *Critical Terms for Religious Studies* (Chicago: University of Chicago Press, 1998), 70–93.

5. See, e.g., Childers and Hentzi, eds., *The Columbia Dictionary of Modern Literary and Cultural Criticism*, 85–86.

6. Vincent L. Wimbush, "Biblical Historical Study as Liberation: Toward an Afro-Christian Hermeneutic," in *African American Religious Studies: An Interdisciplinary Anthology* (ed. Gayraud Wilmore; Durham: Duke University Press, 1989), 140.

7. See Edgar Krentz, *The Historical-Critical Method* (Guides to Biblical Scholarship; Philadelphia: Fortress, 1975), esp. 16–22.

8. Ibid., 13.

9. Ibid., 41. Emphasis mine.

10. Ibid., 55.

11. See John Barton, "Historical-Critical Approaches," in *The Cambridge Companion to Biblical Interpretation* (ed. John Barton; Cambridge Companions to Religion; Cambridge: Cambridge University Press, 1998), 9–20.

12. Taken from the online edition of *The Columbia World of Quotations*. Online: http://www.bartleby.com/66/25/37025.html.

13. Barton, "Historical-Critical Approaches," 13.

14. See Walter Dietrich and Ulrich Luz, eds., *The Bible in a World Context: An Experiment in Contextual Hermeneutics* (Grand Rapids: Eerdmans, 2002), vii–xii.

15. Ibid., vii.

16. Ibid.

17. Ibid., viii.

18. Ibid.

19. Ibid., ix.

20. See ibid.

21. Ibid.

22. Ibid.

23. Ibid.

24. Gerald West, "Reading the Bible Differently: Giving Shape to the Discourses of the Dominated," *Semeia* 73 (2001): 21.

25. Ibid., 22.

26. Ibid.

27. Ibid., 23.

28. Ibid.

29. Ibid., 24.

30. Ibid., 25.

31. Ibid.

32. Ibid., 37.

33. Carlos Mesters, ed., *The Use of the Bible in Christian Communities of the Common People* (Maryknoll, N.Y.: Orbis, 1993), 5.

34. See ibid., 4.

35. See ibid., 11.

36. Ibid., 4.

37. Ibid., 7.

38. Ibid., 11.

39. Ibid., 12.

40. See ibid., 10.

41. Ibid., 14.

42. Ibid.

43. Ibid., 15.

44. Ibid.

45. See Justin S. Ukpong, "Inculturation Hermeneutics: An African Approach to Biblical Interpretation," in *The Bible in a World Context: An Experiment in Contextual Hermeneutics* (ed. Walter Dietrich and Ulrich Luz; Grand Rapids: Eerdmans, 2002), 17–32.

46. Ibid., 17. Emphasis mine.

47. Ibid., 20.

48. Ibid., 21.

49. Ibid., 22.

50. Ibid., 23.

51. See ibid., 24–25.

52. See ibid., 26–27.

53. Ibid., 27.

54. Ibid., 28.

55. Ibid., 30.

56. See William Baird, *History of New Testament Research* (2 vols.; Minneapolis: Fortress, 1992), 1:165–70.

57. Edward Antonio, "Black Theology," in *The Cambridge Companion to Liberation Theology* (ed. Christopher Rowland; Cambridge Companions to Religion; Cambridge: Cambridge University Press, 1999), 63.

58. See ibid., 64.

59. See ibid., 65.

60. Ibid., 66.

61. See ibid., 69.

62. See ibid., 68–69.

63. Ibid., 72–73.

64. Ibid., 78.

65. See James H. Cone, "Biblical Revelation and Social Existence," in *Black Theology: A Documentary History* (ed. James H. Cone and Gayraud Wilmore; 2 vols.; Maryknoll, N.Y.: Orbis, 1993), 1:159–76.

66. James H. Cone and Gayraud Wilmore, eds., *Black Theology: A Documentary History* (2 vols.; Maryknoll, N.Y.: Orbis, 1993), 2:177.

67. See Randall C. Bailey, "Academic Biblical Interpretation among African Americans in the United States," in *African Americans and the Bible: Sacred Texts and Social Textures* (ed. Vincent L. Wimbush; New York: Continuum, 2001), 696.

68. Ibid.

69. Ibid.

70. Ibid., 697.

71. Ibid., 698.

72. Ibid., 702.

73. Ibid., 703.

74. Ibid., 704.

Chapter 2: Dark and Prophetic Voices in the Wilderness

1. Quoted in Cain Hope Felder, *Troubling Biblical Waters: Race, Class, and Family* (ed. James H. Cone; The Bishop Henry McNeal Turner Studies in North American Black Religion; Maryknoll, N.Y.: Orbis, 1989), xii.

2. See, e.g., Edgar Krentz, *The Historical-Critical Method* (Guides to Biblical Scholarship; Philadelphia: Fortress, 1975); John Barton, "Historical-Critical Approaches," in *The Cambridge Companion to Biblical Interpretation* (ed. John Barton; Cambridge Companions to Religion; Cambridge: Cambridge University Press, 1998).

3. Charles B. Copher, "Three Thousand Years of Biblical Interpretation with Reference to Black Peoples," in *African American Religious*

Studies: An Interdisciplinary Anthology (ed. Gayraud Wilmore; Durham: Duke University Press, 1989), 105.

4. Charles B. Copher, "The Black Presence in the Old Testament," in *Stony the Road We Trod: African American Biblical Interpretation* (ed. Cain Hope Felder; Minneapolis: Fortress, 1991), 164.

5. Copher, "Three Thousand Years," 105–25; Copher, "Black Presence," 146–64.

6. Copher, "Three Thousand Years," 105–28.

7. Ibid., 107.

8. Ibid., 123.

9. Ibid., 109.

10. Ibid., 111–12.

11. Ibid., 112.

12. Ibid.

13. Ibid.

14. Cf. Gay L. Byron, *Symbolic Blackness and Ethnic Difference in Early Christian Literature* (New York: Routledge, 2002).

15. Copher, "Three Thousand Years," 115.

16. See ibid., 115–16.

17. Ibid., 117.

18. Ibid., 122.

19. See ibid., 122–23.

20. Ibid., 120.

21. Ibid., 123.

22. E.g., Cain Hope Felder says, "Lest we be accused of anti-Jewishness or being anti-Israeli, let us remember that today's Palestinians are racially more Semitic than the Ashkenazic Jews of Israel" (Felder, *Troubling Biblical Waters,* 20). See also Cain Hope Felder, "The Bible, Re-Contextualization and the Black Religious Experience," in *African American Religious Studies: An Interdisciplinary Anthology* (ed. Gayraud Wilmore; Durham: Duke University Press, 1989), 168.

23. Copher, "Black Presence," 146–64.

24. Ibid., 149.

25. See ibid., 149 n. 110.

26. Ibid., 151.

27. Ibid., 152.

28. Ibid.

29. Ibid., 151.

30. Ibid., 154–55.

31. Ibid., 156; see also n. 123.

32. Ibid., 157.

33. Ibid.

34. Ibid., 158.

35. Ibid., 160–62.

36. Ibid., 163.

37. Ibid., 164.
38. Ibid., 152.
39. Ibid., 154.
40. Ibid.
41. Ibid.
42. Ibid., 157.
43. On the subject of race, see Dave Unander, *Shattering the Myth of Race: Genetic Realities and Biblical Truths* (Valley Forge, Pa.: Judson, 2000). On the subject of slavery in the ancient world, see Muhammad A. Dandamayev, "Slavery (ANE)," in *The Anchor Bible Dictionary* (ed. D. N. Freedman; 6 vols.; New York: Doubleday, 1992), 6:58–62; and I. Mendelsohn, "Slavery in the OT," *The Interpreter's Dictionary of the Bible* (ed. G. A. Buttrick; 4 vols.; Nashville: Abingdon, 1962), 4:383–91. Neither article suggests that persons of the ancient Near East enslaved Europeans in large numbers. And since Copher has argued that persons of the ancient Near East were of mixed ethnic stock, or black, his claim that the majority of slaves would have been white seems incredible.
44. Copher, "Black Presence," 159.
45. Ibid.
46. Ibid.
47. Ibid., 161.
48. Ibid.
49. Felder, *Troubling Biblical Waters,* 53.
50. For a discussion of what William Beardslee calls "the ethics of transformation," see William A. Beardslee, "Ethics and Hermeneutics," in *Margins of Belonging: Essays on the New Testament and Theology* (ed. William A. Beardslee; AAR Studies in Religion; Atlanta: Scholars Press, 1991), 181–96.
51. See, e.g., Felder, "The Bible, Re-Contextualization, and the Black Religious Experience"; Felder, *Troubling Biblical Waters*; Cain Hope Felder, "Race, Racism, and the Biblical Narratives," in *Stony the Road We Trod: African American Biblical Interpretation* (ed. Cain Hope Felder; Minneapolis: Fortress, 1991); Cain Hope Felder, "Cultural Ideology, Afrocentrism, and Biblical Interpretation," in *Black Theology: A Documentary History* (ed. James H. Cone and Gayraud Wilmore; 2 vols.; Maryknoll, N.Y.: Orbis, 1993), 184–95.
52. Felder, *Troubling Biblical Waters,* xi.
53. Felder, "Race, Racism, and the Biblical Narratives," 136.
54. Ibid.
55. Felder, *Troubling Biblical Waters,* 16.
56. Ibid., 20.
57. Ibid., 5.
58. Ibid., 6.
59. See my discussion in chapter 6, as well as Theodore Walker, Jr., "Theological Resources for a Black Neoclassical Social Ethics," in *Black*

Theology: A Documentary History (ed. James H. Cone and Gayraud Wilmore; 2 vols.; Maryknoll, N.Y.: Orbis, 2003), 2:37.

60. Felder, *Troubling Biblical Waters*, 15.

61. Ibid., 14.

62. See, e.g., Peter J. Gomes, *The Good Book: Reading the Bible with Mind and Heart* (1st ed.; New York: Morrow, 1996).

63. Schubert Miles Ogden, *On Theology* (1st ed.; San Francisco: Harper & Row, 1986), 57.

64. See also Felder, "Cultural Ideology, Afrocentrism and Biblical Interpretation," 188.

65. See Felder, *Troubling Biblical Waters*, 7–8; Felder, "Cultural Ideology, Afrocentrism, and Biblical Interpretation," 189.

66. Felder, *Troubling Biblical Waters*, 10.

67. Ibid., 11, emphasis mine.

68. See, in contrast, David Frankfurter, *Religion in Roman Egypt: Assimilation and Resistance* (Princeton: Princeton University Press, 1998), 97–144.

69. Felder, *Troubling Biblical Waters*, 17.

70. See Antony Flew, *A Dictionary of Philosophy* (rev. 2d ed.; New York: St. Martin's, 1984), 11–12.

71. Felder, *Troubling Biblical Waters*, 12.

72. Ibid., 18–19.

73. E.g., Felder, "Cultural Ideology, Afrocentrism, and Biblical Interpretation," 192.

74. Ibid.

75. For such a noncanonical account, see R. Joseph Hoffmann, *Jesus Outside the Gospels* (Buffalo: Prometheus, 1984), 36–53.

76. Felder, "Cultural Ideology, Afrocentrism, and Biblical Interpretation," 194.

77. Felder, *Troubling Biblical Waters*, 38.

78. Ibid.

79. Ibid., 39.

80. Felder, "Race, Racism, and the Biblical Narratives," 131.

81. Felder, *Troubling Biblical Waters*, 41.

82. Ibid.

83. Ibid., 42.

84. See Felder, "Race, Racism, and the Biblical Narratives," 135–36.

85. Felder, *Troubling Biblical Waters*, 46.

86. Ibid., 47.

87. Ibid., 48.

88. Felder, "Race, Racism, and the Biblical Narratives," 143.

89. See, e.g., Richard Alston, *Soldier and Society in Roman Egypt: A Social History* (London: Routledge, 1995).

90. Felder, *Troubling Biblical Waters*, 55.

91. Ibid., 61.

92. Ibid., 71.
93. Ibid., 72.
94. Ibid., 73.
95. Ibid., 77.
96. Ibid., 102.
97. Ibid.
98. Ibid., 113.
99. Ibid., 114.
100. For an alternative understanding of the Pauline concept of freedom, see Hans Dieter Betz, *Paulinische Studien* (Tübingen: Mohr [Paul Siebeck], 1994), 110–25.
101. Felder, *Troubling Biblical Waters*, 115.
102. See Betz, *Paulinische Studien*, 118.
103. Felder, *Troubling Biblical Waters*, 134.
104. Ibid., 137.
105. Ibid.
106. Ibid., 139.
107. Ibid., 140.
108. Ibid., 143.
109. Ibid., 147.
110. Ibid., 159.
111. Ronald N. Liburd, "'Like...a House upon the Sand': African American Biblical Hermeneutics in Perspective," *Journal of the Interdenominational Theological Center* 22 (1994): 77.
112. Ibid., 81.
113. Ibid., 90.
114. Robert A. Bennett, "Biblical Theology and Black Theology," in *Black Theology: A Documentary History* (ed. James H. Cone and Gayraud Wilmore; 2 vols.; Maryknoll, N.Y.: Orbis, 1993), 1:185. A similar, but more forceful, claim is made in Robert A. Bennett, "Black Experience and the Bible," in *African American Religious Studies: An Interdisciplinary Anthology* (ed. Gayraud Wilmore; Durham: Duke University Press, 1989), 129–39.
115. Thomas Hoyt, "Interpreting Biblical Scholarship for the Black Church Tradition," in *Stony the Road We Trod: African American Biblical Interpretation* (ed. Cain Hope Felder; Minneapolis: Fortress, 1991), 24.

Chapter 3: Afrocentrism and the Blackening of the Bible

1. Vincent L. Wimbush, "Reading Texts as Reading Ourselves: A Chapter in the History of African-American Biblical Interpretation," in *Reading from This Place: Social Location and Biblical Interpretation in the United States* (ed. Fernando Segovia and Mary Ann Tolbert; Minneapolis: Fortress, 1994), 103.

2. See Randall C. Bailey, "Beyond Identification: The Use of Africans in Old Testament Poetry and Narratives," in *Stony the Road We Trod: African American Biblical Interpretation* (ed. Cain Hope Felder; Minneapolis: Fortress, 1991), 165–94.

3. Ibid., 169.

4. Ibid., 170.

5. Ibid., 171.

6. Ibid., 173.

7. Ibid., 178.

8. Ibid., 181.

9. Ibid., 182.

10. Randall C. Bailey, "They're Nothing but Incestuous Bastards: The Polemical Use of Sex and Sexuality in Hebrew Canon Narratives," in *Reading from This Place: Social Location and Biblical Interpretation in the United States* (ed. Fernando Segovia and Mary Ann Tolbert; Minneapolis: Fortress, 1994), 121–38.

11. Ibid., 124.

12. Ibid., 123 n. 124.

13. Ibid., 124.

14. Bailey uses a phrase first coined by Mary Ann Tolbert in this instance. See ibid., 125.

15. Ibid.

16. Ibid., 127.

17. Ibid.

18. Ibid., 131.

19. Ibid., 133.

20. Ibid., 134.

21. Ibid., 135.

22. Ibid., 137.

23. Ibid., 136.

24. Ibid., 138.

25. Ibid.

26. Ibid., 123.

27. See Joseph Childers and Gary Hentzi, eds., *The Columbia Dictionary of Modern Literary and Cultural Criticism* (New York: Columbia University Press, 1995), 150.

28. See Edgar Krentz, *The Historical-Critical Method* (Guides to Biblical Scholarship; Philadelphia: Fortress, 1975), 34.

29. See, e.g., Schubert Miles Ogden, *On Theology* (1st ed.; San Francisco: Harper & Row, 1986), 45–68.

30. Ronald N. Liburd, "'Like...a House upon the Sand': African American Biblical Hermeneutics in Perspective," *Journal of the Interdenominational Theological Center* 22 (1994): 90.

31. Attributed to the poet Sterling Brown, quoted in Vincent L. Wimbush, ed., *African Americans and the Bible: Sacred Texts and Social Textures* (New York: Continuum, 2001), 3.

32. Ibid., 31–32 n. 15. Emphasis mine.

33. Ibid.

34. See ibid., 33 n. 25.

35. See ibid.

36. Vincent L. Wimbush, "Interrupting the Spin: What Might Happen If African Americans Were to Become the Starting Point for the Academic Study of the Bible," *Union Seminary Quarterly Review* 52 (1998): 68.

37. Ibid.

38. See Wimbush, ed., *African Americans and the Bible*, 31 n. 12.

39. See ibid., 25.

40. Vincent L. Wimbush, "A Meeting of Worlds: African Americans and the Bible," in *Teaching the Bible: The Discourses and Politics of Biblical Pedagogy* (ed. Fernando Segovia and Mary Ann Tolbert; Maryknoll, N.Y.: Orbis, 1998), 198.

41. See Vincent L. Wimbush, "The Bible and African Americans: An Outline of an Interpretative History," in *Stony the Road We Trod: African American Biblical Interpretation* (ed. Cain Hope Felder; Minneapolis: Fortress, 1991), 82–83.

42. See Wimbush, "A Meeting of Worlds," 196.

43. Ibid., 197.

44. Wimbush, "Bible and African Americans," 83.

45. Ibid., 84.

46. Vincent L. Wimbush, "Biblical Historical Study as Liberation: Toward an Afro-Christian Hermeneutic," in *African American Religious Studies: An Interdisciplinary Anthology* (ed. Gayraud Wilmore; Durham: Duke University Press, 1989), 150.

47. Ibid., 141. Emphasis mine.

48. Wimbush, "Bible and African Americans," 81–97.

49. Ibid., 85.

50. Ibid., 84.

51. Ibid., 88.

52. See ibid., 89.

53. Wimbush, "Reading Texts," 97.

54. Wimbush, "Bible and African Americans," 92.

55. See ibid., 91–92.

56. Ibid., 92.

57. Wimbush, "Reading Texts," 106.

58. Ibid., 107.

59. Wimbush, "Bible and African Americans," 93.

60. Ibid., 94.

61. Ibid.

62. Wimbush, "Reading Texts," 96.

63. Vincent L. Wimbush, " 'Rescue the Perishing': The Importance of Biblical Scholarship in Black Christianity," in *Black Theology: A Documentary History* (ed. James H. Cone and Gayraud Wilmore; 2 vols.; Maryknoll, N.Y.: Orbis, 1993), 2:210–15.

64. Ibid., 2:213.

65. Ibid., 2:212.

66. Ibid.

67. Ibid., 2:214.

68. Ibid.

69. Ibid.

70. Wimbush, "Reading Texts," 102.

71. Ibid., 95.

72. Ibid., 100.

73. Ibid., 101.

74. Wimbush, "Interrupting the Spin," 61–76.

75. Ibid., 67. Emphasis mine.

76. See Ibid., 64–67.

77. Ibid., 69.

78. Ibid., 70–71.

79. Ibid. 71.

80. Ibid.

81. Ibid.

82. Ibid., 72.

83. Ibid.

84. See Ibid., 72–73.

85. Wimbush, ed., *African Americans and the Bible,* 26.

86. Ibid., 37 n. 53.

87. Ibid., 21.

88. Ibid., 31 n. 10.

89. Wimbush, "Bible and African Americans," 81–97.

90. For a discussion of this idea, see Ogden, *On Theology,* 45–68.

Chapter 4: The Womanization of Blackness

1. Quoted in Jacquelyn Grant, "Womanist Theology: Black Women's Experience as a Source for Doing Theology, with Special Reference to Christology," in *Black Theology: A Documentary History* (ed. James H. Cone and Gayraud Wilmore; 2 vols.; Maryknoll, N.Y.: Orbis, 1993), 2:277.

2. See Alice Walker, *In Search of Our Mothers' Gardens* (San Diego: Harcourt Brace Jovanovich, 1983), xi–xii.

3. See, e.g., Grant, "Womanist Theology," 2:273, 279; Diana L. Hayes, "Feminist Theology, Womanist Theology: A Black Catholic Perspective," in *Black Theology: A Documentary History* (ed. James H. Cone and Gayraud Wilmore; 2 vols.; Maryknoll, N.Y.: Orbis, 1993), 2:329.

4. bell hooks, *Feminist Theory: From Margin to Center* (Boston: South End, 1984), 3.

5. Quoted in Kelly Delaine Brown Douglas, "Womanist Theology: What Is Its Relationship to Black Theology?" in *Black Theology: A Documentary History* (ed. James H. Cone and Gayraud Wilmore; 2 vols.; Maryknoll, N.Y.: Orbis, 1993), 2:294.

6. Ibid.

7. A phrase first coined by Anna Julia Cooper, quoted in Grant, "Womanist Theology," 2:277.

8. Howard Thurman, *Jesus and the Disinherited* (Nashville: Abingdon, 1949), 30–31.

9. Another phrase coined by Anna Julia Cooper, quoted in Renita J. Weems, "Womanist Reflections on Biblical Hermeneutics," in *Black Theology: A Documentary History* (ed. James H. Cone and Gayraud Wilmore; 2 vols.; Maryknoll, N.Y.: Orbis, 1993), 2:219.

10. Joseph Childers and Gary Hentzi, eds., *The Columbia Dictionary of Modern Literary and Cultural Criticism* (New York: Columbia University Press, 1995), 253.

11. Ibid., 257.

12. See Weems, "Womanist Reflections on Biblical Hermeneutics," 2:216–24.

13. Cain Hope Felder, *Troubling Biblical Waters: Race, Class, and Family* (ed. James H. Cone; The Bishop Henry McNeal Turner Studies in North American Black Religion; Maryknoll, N.Y.: Orbis, 1989), 146.

14. See, e.g., the discussion in Jo-Ann Shelton, *As the Romans Did: A Sourcebook in Roman Social History* (2d ed.; New York: Oxford University Press, 1998), 288–306.

15. Weems, "Womanist Reflections on Biblical Hermeneutics," 2:217.

16. Ibid.

17. Ibid.

18. See ibid.

19. Ibid., 220.

20. Ibid., 219.

21. Charles Hartshorne, *The Divine Relativity: A Social Conception of God* (New Haven: Yale University Press, 1948), 27. For the idea of the organic interconnectedness of systems of oppression, see Weems, "Womanist Reflections on Biblical Hermeneutics,"2:219.

22. See Weems, "Womanist Reflections on Biblical Hermeneutics," 2:220.

23. Ibid., 2:219.

24. Ibid., 2:223 n. 228.

25. Ibid., 2:220.

26. Ibid., 2:218.

27. Schubert Miles Ogden, *On Theology* (1st ed.; San Francisco: Harper & Row, 1986), 85.

28. Renita J. Weems, "Reading *Her Way* through the Struggle: African American Women and the Bible," in *Stony the Road We Trod: African American Biblical Interpretation* (ed. Cain Hope Felder; Minneapolis: Fortress, 1991), 57–77.

29. See Ibid., 58.

30. Quoted in ibid., 58 n. 51.

31. Ibid., 59.

32. Ibid., 59 n. 54.

33. Ibid., 59–60 n. 54.

34. Ibid., 61.

35. See ibid., 60.

36. Ibid., 61.

37. Ibid., 60.

38. Ibid., 62.

39. See ibid., 63.

40. Ibid.

41. Ibid.

42. Ibid., 64.

43. Ibid., 65.

44. Ibid., 66.

45. Ibid., 67.

46. See ibid., 71.

47. Ibid., 68.

48. Ibid., 66.

49. Ibid., 69.

50. Ibid., 69 n. 20.

51. Quoted in ibid., 70 n. 25.

52. Ibid., 72.

53. Ibid., 73.

54. Ibid., 74.

55. Ibid., 76.

56. Clarice J. Martin, "Womanist Interpretations of the New Testament: The Quest for Holistic and Inclusive Translation and Interpretation," in *Black Theology: A Documentary History* (ed. James H. Cone and Gayraud Wilmore; 2 vols.; Maryknoll, N.Y.: Orbis, 1993), 2:225–44.

57. Ibid., 2:226.

58. Ibid., 2:227.

59. Ibid., 2:229.

60. See ibid., 2:231–32.

61. Ibid., 2:233.

62. Ibid., 2:234.

63. Ibid., 2:235.

64. Ibid., 2:238.

65. Ibid., 2:239.

66. Clarice J. Martin, "The *Haustafeln* (Household Codes) in African American Biblical Interpretation: 'Free Slaves' and 'Subordinate Women,' " in *Stony the Road We Trod: African American Biblical Interpretation* (ed. Cain Hope Felder; Minneapolis: Fortress, 1991), 206–31.

67. Ibid., 206.

68. Ibid., 207.

69. Ibid., 208.

70. Ibid., 210.

71. Ibid.

72. Ibid., 211.

73. Ibid., 213.

74. Ibid., 217. Emphasis mine.

75. Ibid., 218.

76. Ibid., 218 n. 255.

77. Ibid., 225.

78. Ibid., 227.

79. Ibid.

80. Ibid., 228.

81. Ibid., 230.

82. Ibid., 231.

83. Wilma Ann Bailey, "The Sorrow Songs: Laments from Ancient Israel and the African American Diaspora," in *Yet with a Steady Beat: Contemporary U.S. Afrocentric Biblical Interpretation* (ed. Randall C. Bailey; Semeia Studies; Atlanta: Society of Biblical Literature, 2003), 61–83.

84. Ibid., 61.

85. Ibid.

86. Ibid., 75.

87. Quoted in ibid., 77.

88. Ibid., 83.

89. Cheryl A. Kirk-Duggan, "Let My People Go! Threads of Exodus in African American Narratives," in *Yet with a Steady Beat: Contemporary U.S. Afrocentric Biblical Interpretation* (ed. Randall C. Bailey; Semeia Studies; Atlanta: Society of Biblical Literature, 2003), 123–43.

90. Ibid., 143.

91. See ibid., 124.

92. Ibid., 127.

93. See ibid.

94. Ibid., 128.

95. Ibid., 129.

96. Ibid., 129–30.

97. Ibid., 139.

98. Ibid., 140.

99. Ibid., 141.

100. Ibid., 142.

Chapter 5: A Dark Enterprise Redolent
with Political Implications

1. Gayraud S. Wilmore, quoted in Ronald N. Liburd, "Textual Harassment? A Hermeneutical Perspective on African American Preaching," in *Yet with a Steady Beat: Contemporary U.S. Afrocentric Biblical Interpretation* (ed. Randall C. Bailey; Semeia Studies; Atlanta: Society of Biblical Literature, 2003), 93.

2. Brian K. Blount, *Cultural Interpretation: Reorienting New Testament Criticism* (Minneapolis: Fortress, 1995), 23.

3. Ibid., viii.

4. See ibid., 7.

5. Ibid., vii.

6. See ibid., 7.

7. Ibid.

8. Ibid., 11–12.

9. Ibid., 85.

10. See ibid., 13–14.

11. Ibid., 17.

12. Ibid.

13. Ibid.

14. Ibid., 21.

15. Ibid., 29.

16. Ibid., 30–31.

17. Ibid., 34.

18. Ibid., 56.

19. Ibid., 60.

20. Ibid., 69.

21. Ibid., 71.

22. See ibid., 76.

23. Ibid.

24. Ibid.

25. Ibid., 79.

26. Ibid., 90.

27. Ibid.

28. See ibid., 94.

29. Ibid., 181.

30. Ibid., 182–83.

31. Ibid., 177.

32. See Vincent L. Wimbush, "Interrupting the Spin: What Might Happen If African Americans Were to Become the Starting Point for the Academic Study of the Bible," *Union Seminary Quarterly Review* 52 (1998), 61–76.

33. See Vincent L. Wimbush, ed., *African Americans and the Bible: Sacred Texts and Social Textures* (New York: Continuum, 2001), 1–43.

34. Blount, *Cultural Interpretation*, 14.

35. Brian K. Blount, *Then the Whisper Put on Flesh: New Testament Ethics in an African American Context* (Nashville: Abingdon, 2001).

36. Ibid., 24.

37. Ibid., 29.

38. Ibid., 189.

39. Randall C. Bailey, ed., *Yet with a Steady Beat: Contemporary U.S. Afrocentric Biblical Interpretation* (Semeia Studies; Atlanta: Society of Biblical Literature, 2003), 2.

40. See Harold V. Bennett, *Injustice Made Legal: Deuteronomic Law and the Plight of Widows, Strangers, and Orphans in Ancient Israel* (Bible in Its World; Grand Rapids: Eerdmans, 2002); Harold V. Bennett, "Triennial Tithes and the Underdog: A Revisionist Reading of Deuteronomy 14:22–29 and 26:12–15," in *Yet with a Steady Beat: Contemporary U.S. Afrocentric Biblical Interpretation* (ed. Randall C. Bailey; Semeia Studies; Atlanta: Society of Biblical Literature, 2003), 7–18.

41. See Bennett, "Triennial Tithes and the Underdog," 8.

42. Ibid.

43. Ibid., 11.

44. Ibid., 13.

45. Ibid., 15.

46. Ibid.

47. Ibid.

48. Ibid., 17.

49. Ibid., 18.

50. Ibid.

51. Ibid., 11.

52. See Cain Hope Felder, *Troubling Biblical Waters: Race, Class, and Family* (ed. James H. Cone; The Bishop Henry McNeal Turner Studies in North American Black Religion; Maryknoll, N.Y.: Orbis, 1989), 61.

53. Herbert R. Marbury, "Regulating Bodies and Boundaries: A Reading of the Dodecalogue" (Nashville: unpublished manuscript, 2004), 1.

54. Ibid., 2.

55. Ibid.

56. Ibid., 4.

57. Ibid.

58. Ibid., 5.

59. Ibid., 6.

60. Ibid.

61. Ibid., 7.

62. Ibid.

63. Ibid., 9.

64. Ibid., 13.

65. See Brad Ronnell Braxton, *The Tyranny of Resolution: 1 Corinthians 7:17–24* (Dissertation Series No. 181; Atlanta: Society of Biblical Literature, 2000).

66. Brad Ronnell Braxton, "The Role of Ethnicity in the Social Location of 1 Corinthians 7:17–24," in *Yet with a Steady Beat: Contemporary U.S. Afrocentric Biblical Interpretation* (ed. Randall C. Bailey; Semeia Studies; Atlanta: Society of Biblical Literature, 2003), 22.

67. Ibid., 23. Emphasis mine.

68. Ibid., 24.

69. Ibid.

70. Ibid., 25.

71. See ibid., 25–26.

72. See, e.g., Naphtali Lewis, *Greeks in Ptolemaic Egypt: Case Studies in the Social History of the Hellenistic World* (Classics in Papyrology; Oakville, Conn.: American Society of Papyrologists, 2001), 104–23.

73. Braxton, "The Role of Ethnicity," 27.

74. Ibid., 28.

75. Ibid., 29.

76. Ibid.

77. Ibid., 30.

78. Ibid., 32.

79. See Brad Ronnell Braxton, *No Longer Slaves: Galatians and African American Experience* (Collegeville, Minn.: Liturgical Press, 2002).

80. Even when the term *Greek* is used, it does not necessarily function as a precise ethnic designation. More often than not, it carries the same semantic significance as *Gentile.*

81. See, e.g., Margaret Mary Mitchell, *Paul and the Rhetoric of Reconciliation: An Exegetical Investigation of the Language and Composition of 1 Corinthians* (Hermeneutische Untersuchungen Zur Theologie 28; Tübingen: J. C. B. Mohr [Paul Siebeck], 1991).

82. Demetrius K. Williams, *An End to This Strife: The Politics of Gender in African American Churches* (Minneapolis: Fortress, 2004). Please note, however, that this work was not published at the time of the writing of this book.

83. See Theophus Harold Smith, *Conjuring Culture: Biblical Formations of Black America* (New York: Oxford University Press, 1994).

84. Demetrius K. Williams, "The Bible and Models of Liberation in the African American Experience," in *Yet with a Steady Beat: Contemporary U.S. Afrocentric Biblical Interpretation* (ed. Randall C. Bailey; Semeia Studies; Atlanta: Society of Biblical Literature, 2003), 38.

85. Ibid., 41.

86. Ibid., 42.

87. Ibid.

88. See ibid., 48.

89. Ibid., 49.

90. See ibid., 50–54.

91. Ibid., 54.

92. Ibid., 55.

93. Ibid., 57.
94. Ibid., 58.
95. Ibid.
96. Ibid., 59.
97. Ibid.
98. To see how Marbury's literary methods are based on social scientific models, see Steven L. McKenzie and Stephen R. Haynes, eds., *To Each Its Own Meaning: An Introduction to Biblical Criticisms and Their Application* (rev. and expanded ed.; Louisville: Westminster John Knox, 1999), 284–306.
99. By saying this, I do not mean to suggest that earlier forms of Afrocentric interpretation did not have political agendas. Clearly, they do. What I am attempting to relate is that the political has become the driving purpose behind Afrocentric interpretation in a way that outdistances prior scholarship. Not only are modern Afrocentric interpreters "troubling biblical waters," they are troubling the idea that the Bible can say anything directly that is liberatory at all.

Chapter 6: Can the Eclipse Continue?

1. A lyric from *Porgy and Bess,* quoted in Randall C. Bailey, ed., *Yet with a Steady Beat: Contemporary U.S. Afrocentric Biblical Interpretation* (Semeia Studies; Atlanta: Society of Biblical Literature, 2003), 178.
2. Vincent L. Wimbush, " 'Rescue the Perishing': The Importance of Biblical Scholarship in Black Christianity," in *Black Theology: A Documentary History* (ed. James H. Cone and Gayraud Wilmore; 2 vols.; Maryknoll, N.Y.: Orbis, 1993), 2:210–15.
3. This is somewhat distinct from the issue of black/liberation theology discussed above. Although they share significant similarities, especially when it comes to identity, one need not be interested in liberation to appropriate African American Christian traditions. Take, for example, my own background. African Methodism has been struggling for years between so-called traditionalists and Pentecostals/evangelicals, who believe that AME tradition has become traditionalism. The promise of conservative evangelical Christianity, a non-ethnically based understanding of Christianity, appeals to some who believe that one can adopt a "pure" gospel uninfluenced by the traditions of "man," the always convenient pejorative employed to denigrate some aspect of Christian faith with which the speaker disagrees. Although I disagree sharply with the idea that one can appropriate such a "pure" gospel, I recognize it can be seductive to individuals who have attempted (or are attempting) to integrate into the larger society.
4. Fernando Segovia, "The Stony Road as the Road of the Future and the Road of Liberation: Critical Reflections," *Journal of the Interdenominational Theological Center* 22 (1994): 141.

5. Ibid.

6. Ibid., 142.

7. Ibid., 143.

8. Gale A. Yee, "Review of Cain Hope Felder, Ed., *Stony the Road We Trod: African American Biblical Interpretation*," *Journal of the Interdenominational Theological Center* 22 (1994): 151.

9. See Allison Calhoun-Brown, "The Image of God: Black Theology and Racial Empowerment in the African American Community," *Review of Religious Research* 40 (1999): 197–213.

10. Christopher G. Ellison and Darren E. Sherkat, "The Politics of Black Religious Change Disaffiliation from Black Mainline Denominations," *Social Forces* 70 (1991): 447.

11. I say this in contradiction to the conservative message promulgated by many. See, e.g., Glenn Loury and Linda Datcher Loury, "Not by Bread Alone: The Role of the African-American Church in Inner-City Development," *Brookings Review* 15 (1997): 10–13.

12. See, e.g., Peter Leone, "HIV/AIDS Epidemiology; AIDS Rising in Black Male College Students," *Medical Letter on the CDC & FDA*, 7 March 2004, 40.

13. See my forthcoming essay, Michael Joseph Brown, "Constructing a Doctrine for the Ecclesia Militans," in *Loving the Body: Black Religious Studies and the Erotic* (ed. Dwight Hopkins and Anthony B. Pinn; New York: Palgrave, 2004).

14. Andrew Sung Park, "African American Biblical Interpretation: Reflections on *Stony the Road We Trod*," *Journal of the Interdenominational Theological Center* 22 (1994): 131.

15. Karen Strother-Jordan, "On the Rhetoric of Afrocentricity," *The Western Journal of Black Studies* 26 (2002): 193.

16. I am aware, as I have stated earlier in this book, that Cheryl Kirk-Duggan is not a formally trained biblical scholar. I group her here with other Hebrew Bible scholars for the sake of convenience.

17. Norman K. Gottwald, "African American Biblical Hermeneutics: Major Themes and Wider Implications," in *Yet with a Steady Beat: Contemporary U.S. Afrocentric Biblical Interpretation* (ed. Randall C. Bailey; Semeia Studies; Atlanta: Society of Biblical Literature, 2003), 178.

18. See Joachim Jeremias, *The Parables of Jesus* (2d rev. ed.; New York: Scribner, 1972), 70–77, and the host of others who follow him.

19. See, e.g., Bruce J. Malina and Richard L. Rohrbaugh, *Social Science Commentary on the Synoptic Gospels* (Minneapolis: Fortress, 1992), 133.

20. Ibid.

21. See *New Documents Illustrating Early Christianity: A Review of the Greek Inscriptions and Papyri* (ed. G. H. R. Horsley and S. R. Llewelyn; North Ryde, N.S.W.: Macquarie University, 1981), 6:86–88.

22. I am thankful to Dr. Marcia Allen Owens, a former student, for making the connection between tenant farming in antiquity and share cropping in the United States.

23. See Malina and Rohrbaugh, *Social Science Commentary,* 134.

24. *New Documents,* 6:94.

25. For an explanation of why I assume the vineyard was newly planted, see ibid., 9:95 n. 105.

26. See ibid., 6:105.

27. Ibid., 6:96.

28. See the discussion in ibid., 6:98–100.

29. Ibid., 6:94.

30. Brian K. Blount, *Then the Whisper Put on Flesh: New Testament Ethics in an African American Context* (Nashville: Abingdon, 2001), 67.

31. Ibid., 9.

32. Ibid., 83.

33. Tina Pippin, "On the Blurring of Boundaries," in *Yet with a Steady Beat: Contemporary U.S. Afrocentric Biblical Interpretation* (ed. Randall C. Bailey; Semeia Studies; Atlanta: Society of Biblical Literature, 2003), 172.

34. R. Joseph Hoffmann, *Jesus Outside the Gospels* (Buffalo: Prometheus, 1984), 34.

35. Rudolf Karl Bultmann, *Theology of the New Testament* (New York: Scribner, 1951), 3. Emphasis mine.

36. Willi Marxsen, *Jesus and the Church: The Beginnings of Christianity* (trans. Philip E. Devenish; Philadelphia: Trinity, 1992), 57.

37. Schubert Miles Ogden, *On Theology* (1st ed.; San Francisco: Harper & Row, 1986), 137.

38. Marxsen, *Jesus and the Church,* 22.

39. Ogden, *On Theology,* 56.

40. Ibid.

41. See ibid., 54.

42. Ibid.

43. Elisabeth Young-Bruehl, *The Anatomy of Prejudices* (Cambridge: Harvard University Press, 1996), 91.

44. Ibid., 22.

45. See ibid., 23–26.

46. Ibid., 115.

47. Ibid., 34.

48. Ibid.

49. Gay L. Byron, *Symbolic Blackness and Ethnic Difference in Early Christian Literature* (New York: Routledge, 2002).

50. See, e.g., Young-Bruehl, *The Anatomy of Prejudices,* 34.

51. See ibid., 34–35.

52. Byron, *Symbolic Blackness,* 42.

53. Young-Bruehl, *Anatomy of Prejudices,* 35.

54. Ibid., 32.

55. David Boyer, "Civil Rights Group Accuses N.Y. Police of Racial Profiling," *Washington Times*, 17 June 2000, 2.

56. Jerry Seper, "N.J. Says Blacks Biggest Speeders; Vows to Help End Racial Profiling," *Washington Times*, 28 March 2002, A04.

57. Frank J. Murray, "Profiling by Airlines Gets Public Support," *Washington Times*, 1 November 2001.

58. Adrienne T. Washington, "To See Racial Profiling in Action, Just Turn on the TV," *Washington Times*, 22 May 2001, 2.

59. See, e.g., Frederick Ferre and Rita H. Mataragnon, eds., *God and Global Justice: Religion and Poverty in an Unequal World* (New York: Paragon, 1985), 20.

60. Theodore Walker, Jr., "Theological Resources for a Black Neo-classical Social Ethics," in *Black Theology: A Documentary History* (ed. James H. Cone and Gayraud Wilmore; 2 vols.; Maryknoll, N.Y.: Orbis, 2003), 2:48.

61. Ibid., 2:36.

62. John B. Cobb and David Ray Griffin, *Process Theology: An Introductory Exposition* (Philadelphia: Westminster, 1976), 48.

63. Ibid., 49.

64. Walker, Jr., "Theological Resources for a Black Neoclassical Social Ethics," 2:40.

65. Ibid.

66. Cobb and Griffin, *Process Theology*, 60.

67. This story is adapted from the one found in Leon E. Petti-way, *Honey, Honey, Miss Thang: Being Black, Gay and on the Streets* (Philadelphia: Temple University Press, 1996), 111–71.

68. Ibid., 119–20.

69. Ibid., 121.

70. Ibid., 152, 153.

71. Ibid., 134.

72. Although the term *transvestite* is the more politically correct way to describe Detra, I have chosen to describe her with the terms she uses to describe herself — just as I use feminine pronouns to reference her because she thinks of herself as a woman.

73. Anthony Tommasini, "An Honest, Funny Look at Gay Black Men," *Boston Globe*, 5 July 1992, 27.

74. Cornel West, *Race Matters* (Boston: Beacon, 1993), 4.

75. Renita J. Weems, "Womanist Reflections on Biblical Hermeneu-tics," in *Black Theology: A Documentary History* (ed. James H. Cone and Gayraud Wilmore; 2 vols.; Maryknoll, N.Y.: Orbis, 1993), 2:219, 218.

76. Pettiway, *Honey, Honey, Miss Thang*, xii.

77. Alice Walker, "In Search of Our Mothers' Gardens," in *Black Theology: A Documentary History* (ed. James H. Cone and Gayraud Wilmore; 2 vols.; Maryknoll, N.Y.: Orbis, 2003), 1:343.

78. Attributed to C. C. Colton (1780–1832), *Lacon: Or, Many Things in Few Words, Addressed to Those Who Think* (New York: Burtsell, 1821).

79. Pettiway, *Honey, Honey, Miss Thang,* xl.

80. Ibid., xix.

81. Ibid., xiii.

82. Ibid., xxiv.

83. Ibid., xxxii.

84. Ibid., xxxiii.

85. Ibid., xxxix.

86. Ibid.

87. Ibid., 153.

88. Ibid., xxx.

89. Daniel Boyarin, "Gender," in *Critical Terms for Religious Studies* (ed. Mark C. Taylor; Chicago: University of Chicago Press, 1998), 117.

Bibliography

Chapter 1: The Eclipse of a Eurocentric Enterprise

Antonio, Edward. "Black Theology." Pages 63–88 in *The Cambridge Companion to Liberation Theology*. Edited by Christopher Rowland. Cambridge: Cambridge University Press, 1999.

Bailey, Randall C. "Academic Biblical Interpretation among African Americans in the United States." Pages 696–711 in *African Americans and the Bible: Sacred Texts and Social Textures*. Edited by Vincent L. Wimbush. New York: Continuum, 2001.

Baird, William. *History of New Testament Research*. 2 vols. Minneapolis: Fortress, 1992.

Barton, John. "Historical-Critical Approaches." Pages 9–20 in *The Cambridge Companion to Biblical Interpretation*. Edited by John Barton. Cambridge: Cambridge University Press, 1998.

Brown, Michael Joseph. *What They Don't Tell You: A Survivor's Guide to Biblical Studies*. 1st ed. Louisville: Westminster John Knox, 2000.

Childers, Joseph, and Gary Hentzi, eds. *The Columbia Dictionary of Modern Literary and Cultural Criticism*. New York: Columbia University Press, 1995.

Cone, James H. "Biblical Revelation and Social Existence." Pages 159–76 in *Black Theology: A Documentary History*. 2 vols. Edited by James H. Cone and Gayraud Wilmore. Maryknoll, N.Y.: Orbis, 1993.

Cone, James H., and Gayraud Wilmore, eds. *Black Theology: A Documentary History*. 2 vols. Maryknoll, N.Y.: Orbis, 1993.

Dietrich, Walter, and Ulrich Luz, eds. *The Bible in a World Context: An Experiment in Contextual Hermeneutics*. Grand Rapids: Eerdmans, 2002.

Krentz, Edgar. *The Historical-Critical Method*. Guides to Biblical Scholarship. Philadelphia: Fortress, 1975.

Mesters, Carlos, ed. *The Use of the Bible in Christian Communities of the Common People*. Edited by Norman K. Gottwald and Richard A. Horsley. Maryknoll, N.Y.: Orbis, 1993.

Taylor, Mark C., ed. *Critical Terms for Religious Studies*. Chicago: University of Chicago Press, 1998.

Ukpong, Justin S. "Inculturation Hermeneutics: An African Approach to Biblical Interpretation." Pages 17–32 in *The Bible in a World Context: An Experiment in Contextual Hermeneutics*. Edited by Walter Dietrich and Ulrich Luz. Grand Rapids: Eerdmans, 2002.

West, Gerald. "Reading the Bible Differently: Giving Shape to the Discourses of the Dominated." *Semeia* 73, no. 1 (2001): 21–41.

Wimbush, Vincent L. "Biblical Historical Study as Liberation: Toward an Afro-Christian Hermeneutic." Pages 140–54 in *African American Religious Studies: An Interdisciplinary Anthology*. Edited by Gayraud Wilmore. Durham: Duke University Press, 1989.

Chapter 2: Dark and Prophetic Voices in the Wilderness

Alston, Richard. *Soldier and Society in Roman Egypt: A Social History*. London: Routledge, 1995.

Barton, John. "Historical-Critical Approaches." Pages 9–20 in *The Cambridge Companion to Biblical Interpretation*. Edited by John Barton. Cambridge: Cambridge University Press, 1998.

Beardslee, William A. "Ethics and Hermeneutics." Pages 181–96 in *Margins of Belonging: Essays on the New Testament and Theology*. Edited by William A. Beardslee. Atlanta: Scholars Press, 1991.

Bennett, Robert A. "Black Experience and the Bible." Pages 129–39 in *African American Religious Studies: An Interdisciplinary Anthology*. Edited by Gayraud Wilmore. Durham: Duke University Press, 1989.

———. "Biblical Theology and Black Theology." Pages 177–92 in *Black Theology: A Documentary History*. Edited by James H. Cone and Gayraud Wilmore. 2 vols. Maryknoll, N.Y.: Orbis, 1993.

Betz, Hans Dieter. *Paulinische Studien*. Tübingen: Mohr (Paul Siebeck), 1994.

Copher, Charles B. "Three Thousand Years of Biblical Interpretation with Reference to Black Peoples." Pages 105–28 in *African American Religious Studies: An Interdisciplinary Anthology*. Edited by Gayraud Wilmore. Durham: Duke University Press, 1989.

———. "The Black Presence in the Old Testament." Pages 146–64 in *Stony the Road We Trod: African American Biblical Interpretation*. Edited by Cain Hope Felder. Minneapolis: Fortress, 1991.

Felder, Cain Hope. "The Bible, Re-Contextualization, and the Black Religious Experience." Pages 155–71 in *African American Religious Studies: An Interdisciplinary Anthology*. Edited by Gayraud Wilmore. Durham: Duke University Press, 1989.

———. *Troubling Biblical Waters: Race, Class, and Family*. Edited by James H. Cone. The Bishop Henry McNeal Turner Studies in North American Black Religion. Maryknoll, N.Y.: Orbis, 1989.

————. "Race, Racism, and the Biblical Narratives." Pages 127–45 in *Stony the Road We Trod: African American Biblical Interpretation.* Edited by Cain Hope Felder. Minneapolis: Fortress, 1991.

————. "Cultural Ideology, Afrocentrism and Biblical Interpretation." Pages 184–95 in *Black Theology: A Documentary History.* Edited by James H. Cone and Gayraud Wilmore. 2 vols. Maryknoll, N.Y.: Orbis, 1993.

Flew, Antony. *A Dictionary of Philosophy.* Rev. 2d ed. New York: St. Martin's, 1984.

Frankfurter, David. *Religion in Roman Egypt: Assimilation and Resistance.* Princeton, N.J.: Princeton University Press, 1998.

Gomes, Peter J. *The Good Book: Reading the Bible with Mind and Heart.* 1st ed. New York: Morrow, 1996.

Hoffmann, R. Joseph. *Jesus Outside the Gospels.* Buffalo: Prometheus, 1984.

Hoyt, Thomas. "Interpreting Biblical Scholarship for the Black Church Tradition." Pages 17–39 in *Stony the Road We Trod: African American Biblical Interpretation.* Edited by Cain Hope Felder. Minneapolis: Fortress, 1991.

Krentz, Edgar. *The Historical-Critical Method.* Guides to Biblical Scholarship. Philadelphia: Fortress, 1975.

Liburd, Ronald N. " 'Like...a House upon the Sand': African American Biblical Hermeneutics in Perspective." *Journal of the Interdenominational Theological Center* 22, no. 1 (1994): 71–91.

Ogden, Schubert Miles. *On Theology.* 1st ed. San Francisco: Harper & Row, 1986.

Unander, Dave. *Shattering the Myth of Race: Genetic Realities and Biblical Truths.* Valley Forge, Pa.: Judson, 2000.

Chapter 3: Afrocentrism and the Blackening of the Bible

Bailey, Randall C. "Beyond Identification: The Use of Africans in Old Testament Poetry and Narratives." Pages 165–84 in *Stony the Road We Trod: African American Biblical Interpretation.* Edited by Cain Hope Felder. Minneapolis: Fortress, 1991.

————. "They're Nothing but Incestuous Bastards: The Polemical Use of Sex and Sexuality in Hebrew Canon Narratives." Pages 121–38 in *Reading from This Place: Social Location and Biblical Interpretation in the United States.* Edited by Fernando Segovia and Mary Ann Tolbert. Minneapolis: Fortress, 1994.

Childers, Joseph, and Gary Hentzi, eds. *The Columbia Dictionary of Modern Literary and Cultural Criticism.* New York: Columbia University Press, 1995.

Krentz, Edgar. *The Historical-Critical Method.* Guides to Biblical Scholarship. Philadelphia: Fortress, 1975.

Liburd, Ronald N. " 'Like...a House upon the Sand': African American Biblical Hermeneutics in Perspective." *Journal of the Interdenominational Theological Center* 22, no. 1 (1994): 71–91.

Ogden, Schubert Miles. *On Theology*. 1st ed. San Francisco: Harper & Row, 1986.

Wimbush, Vincent L. "A Meeting of Worlds: African Americans and the Bible." Pages 190–99 in *Teaching the Bible: The Discourses and Politics of Biblical Pedagogy*. Edited by Fernando Segovia and Mary Ann Tolbert. Maryknoll, N.Y.: Orbis, 1998.

———. "Biblical Historical Study as Liberation: Toward an Afro-Christian Hermeneutic." Pages 140–54 in *African American Religious Studies: An Interdisciplinary Anthology*. Edited by Gayraud Wilmore. Durham: Duke University Press, 1989.

———. "The Bible and African Americans: An Outline of an Interpretative History." Pages 81–97 in *Stony the Road We Trod: African American Biblical Interpretation*. Edited by Cain Hope Felder. Minneapolis: Fortress, 1991.

———. " 'Rescue the Perishing': The Importance of Biblical Scholarship in Black Christianity." Pages 210–15 in *Black Theology: A Documentary History*. Edited by James H. Cone and Gayraud Wilmore. Maryknoll, N.Y.: Orbis, 1993.

———. "Reading Texts as Reading Ourselves: A Chapter in the History of African-American Biblical Interpretation." Pages 95–108 in *Reading from This Place: Social Location and Biblical Interpretation in the United States*. Edited by Fernando Segovia and Mary Ann Tolbert. Minneapolis: Fortress, 1994.

———. "Interrupting the Spin: What Might Happen If African Americans Were to Become the Starting Point for the Academic Study of the Bible." *Union Seminary Quarterly Review* 52, nos. 1–2 (1998): 61–76.

———, ed. *African Americans and the Bible: Sacred Texts and Social Textures*. New York: Continuum, 2001.

Chapter 4: The Womanization of Blackness

Bailey, Wilma Ann. "The Sorrow Songs: Laments from Ancient Israel and the African American Diaspora." Pages 61–84 in *Yet with a Steady Beat: Contemporary U.S. Afrocentric Biblical Interpretation*. Edited by Randall C. Bailey. Atlanta: Society of Biblical Literature, 2003.

Brown Douglas, Kelly Delaine. "Womanist Theology: What Is Its Relationship to Black Theology?" Pages 290–99 in *Black Theology: A Documentary History*. Edited by James H. Cone and Gayraud Wilmore. 2 vols. Maryknoll, N.Y.: Orbis, 1993.

Childers, Joseph, and Gary Hentzi, eds. *The Columbia Dictionary of Modern Literary and Cultural Criticism.* New York: Columbia University Press, 1995.

Grant, Jacquelyn. "Womanist Theology: Black Women's Experience as a Source for Doing Theology, with Special Reference to Christology." Pages 273–89 in *Black Theology: A Documentary History.* Edited by James H. Cone and Gayraud Wilmore. 2 vols. Maryknoll, N.Y.: Orbis, 1993.

Hartshorne, Charles. *The Divine Relativity: A Social Conception of God.* New Haven: Yale University Press, 1948.

Hayes, Diana L. "Feminist Theology, Womanist Theology: A Black Catholic Perspective." Pages 325–35 in *Black Theology: A Documentary History.* Edited by James H. Cone and Gayraud Wilmore. 2 vols. Maryknoll, N.Y.: Orbis, 1993.

hooks, bell. *Feminist Theory: From Margin to Center.* Boston: South End, 1984.

Kirk-Duggan, Cheryl A. "Let My People Go! Threads of Exodus in African American Narratives." Pages 123–44 in *Yet with a Steady Beat: Contemporary U.S. Afrocentric Biblical Interpretation.* Edited by Randall C. Bailey. Atlanta: Society of Biblical Literature, 2003.

Martin, Clarice J. "The *Haustafeln* (Household Codes) in African American Biblical Interpretation: 'Free Slaves' and 'Subordinate Women.'" Pages 206–31 in *Stony the Road We Trod: African American Biblical Interpretation.* Edited by Cain Hope Felder. Minneapolis: Fortress, 1991.

———. "Womanist Interpretations of the New Testament: The Quest for Holistic and Inclusive Translation and Interpretation." Pages 225–44 in *Black Theology: A Documentary History.* Edited by James H. Cone and Gayraud Wilmore. 2 vols. Maryknoll, N.Y.: Orbis, 1993.

Ogden, Schubert Miles. *On Theology.* 1st ed. San Francisco: Harper & Row, 1986.

Shelton, Jo-Ann. *As the Romans Did: A Sourcebook in Roman Social History.* 2d ed. New York: Oxford University Press, 1998.

Thurman, Howard. *Jesus and the Disinherited.* Nashville: Abingdon, 1949.

Walker, Alice. *In Search of out Mothers' Gardens.* San Diego: Harcourt Brace Jovanovich, 1983.

Weems, Renita J. "Reading Her Way through the Struggle: African American Women and the Bible." Pages 57–77 in *Stony the Road We Trod: African American Biblical Interpretation.* Edited by Cain Hope Felder. Minneapolis: Fortress, 1991.

———. "Womanist Reflections on Biblical Hermeneutics." Pages 216–24 in *Black Theology: A Documentary History.* Edited by James H. Cone and Gayraud Wilmore. 2 vols. Maryknoll, N.Y.: Orbis, 1993.

Chapter 5: A Dark Enterprise Redolent with Political Implications

Bailey, Randall C., ed. *Yet with a Steady Beat: Contemporary U.S. Afrocentric Biblical Interpretation.* Semeia Studies. Atlanta: Society of Biblical Literature, 2003.

Bennett, Harold V. *Injustice Made Legal: Deuteronomic Law and the Plight of Widows, Strangers, and Orphans in Ancient Israel.* Bible in Its World. Grand Rapids: Eerdmans, 2002.

———. "Triennial Tithes and the Underdog: A Revisionist Reading of Deuteronomy 14:22–29 and 26:12–15." Pages 7–18 in *Yet with a Steady Beat: Contemporary U.S. Afrocentric Biblical Interpretation.* Edited by Randall C. Bailey. Atlanta: Society of Biblical Literature, 2003.

Blount, Brian K. *Cultural Interpretation: Reorienting New Testament Criticism.* Minneapolis: Fortress, 1995.

———. *Then the Whisper Put on Flesh: New Testament Ethics in an African American Context.* Nashville: Abingdon, 2001.

Braxton, Brad Ronnell. *The Tyranny of Resolution: 1 Corinthians 7:17–24.* SBL Dissertation Series No. 181. Atlanta: Society of Biblical Literature, 2000.

———. *No Longer Slaves: Galatians and African American Experience.* Collegeville, Minn.: Liturgical Press, 2002.

———. "The Role of Ethnicity in the Social Location of 1 Corinthians 7:17–24." Pages 19–32 in *Yet with a Steady Beat: Contemporary U.S. Afrocentric Biblical Interpretation.* Edited by Randall C. Bailey. Atlanta: Society of Biblical Literature, 2003.

Felder, Cain Hope. *Troubling Biblical Waters: Race, Class, and Family.* Edited by James H. Cone. The Bishop Henry McNeal Turner Studies in North American Black Religion. Maryknoll, N.Y.: Orbis, 1989.

Lewis, Naphtali. *Greeks in Ptolemaic Egypt: Case Studies in the Social History of the Hellenistic World.* Classics in Papyrology. Oakville, CT: American Society of Papyrologists, 2001.

Liburd, Ronald N. "Textual Harassment? A Hermeneutical Perspective on African American Preaching." Pages 85–102 in *Yet with a Steady Beat: Contemporary U.S. Afrocentric Biblical Interpretation.* Edited by Randall C. Bailey. Atlanta: Society of Biblical Literature, 2003.

Marbury, Herbert R. "Regulating Bodies and Boundaries: A Reading of the Dodecalogue." Unpublished manuscript. Nashville, 2004.

McKenzie, Steven L., and Stephen R. Haynes, eds. *To Each Its Own Meaning: An Introduction to Biblical Criticisms and Their Application.* Rev. and expanded ed. Louisville: Westminster John Knox, 1999.

Mitchell, Margaret Mary. *Paul and the Rhetoric of Reconciliation: An Exegetical Investigation of the Language and Composition of 1 Corinthians.* Hermeneutische Untersuchungen Zur Theologie 28. Tübingen: J. C. B. Mohr (Paul Siebeck), 1991.

Smith, Theophus Harold. *Conjuring Culture: Biblical Formations of Black America.* New York: Oxford University Press, 1994.

Williams, Demetrius K. "The Bible and Models of Liberation in the African American Experience." Pages 33–60 in *Yet with a Steady Beat: Contemporary U.S. Afrocentric Biblical Interpretation.* Edited by Randall C. Bailey. Atlanta: Society of Biblical Literature, 2003.

————. *An End to This Strife: The Politics of Gender in African American Churches.* Minneapolis: Fortress, 2004.

Wimbush, Vincent L. "Interrupting the Spin: What Might Happen If African Americans Were to Become the Starting Point for the Academic Study of the Bible." *Union Seminary Quarterly Review* 52, nos. 1–2 (1998): 61–76.

————, ed. *African Americans and the Bible: Sacred Texts and Social Textures.* New York: Continuum, 2001.

Chapter 6: Can the Eclipse Continue?

Bailey, Randall C., ed. *Yet with a Steady Beat: Contemporary U.S. Afrocentric Biblical Interpretation.* Semeia Studies. Atlanta: Society of Biblical Literature, 2003.

Blount, Brian K. *Then the Whisper Put on Flesh: New Testament Ethics in an African American Context.* Nashville: Abingdon, 2001.

Boyarin, Daniel. "Gender." Pages 117–35 in *Critical Terms for Religious Studies.* Edited by Mark C. Taylor. Chicago: The University of Chicago Press, 1998.

Boyer, David. "Civil Rights Group Accuses N.Y. Police of Racial Profiling." *Washington Times,* 17 June 2000, 2.

Brown, Michael Joseph. "Constructing a Doctrine for the Ecclesia Militans." In *Loving the Body: Black Religious Studies and the Erotic.* Edited by Dwight Hopkins and Anthony B. Pinn. New York: Palgrave, forthcoming.

Bultmann, Rudolf Karl. *Theology of the New Testament.* New York: Scribner, 1951.

Byron, Gay L. *Symbolic Blackness and Ethnic Difference in Early Christian Literature.* New York: Routledge, 2002.

Calhoun-Brown, Allison. "The Image of God: Black Theology and Racial Empowerment in the African American Community." *Review of Religious Research* 40, no. 3 (1999): 197–213.

Cobb, John B., and David Ray Griffin. *Process Theology: An Introductory Exposition.* Philadelphia: Westminster, 1976.

Ellison, Christopher G., and Darren E. Sherkat. "The Politics of Black Religious Change: Disaffiliation from Black Mainline Denominations." *Social Forces* 70 (1991): 431–55.

Ferre, Frederick, and Rita H. Mataragnon, eds. *God and Global Justice: Religion and Poverty in an Unequal World.* New York: Paragon, 1985.

Gottwald, Norman K. "African American Biblical Hermeneutics: Major Themes and Wider Implications." Pages 177–82 in *Yet with a Steady Beat: Contemporary U.S. Afrocentric Biblical Interpretation.* Edited by Randall C. Bailey. Atlanta: Society of Biblical Literature, 2003.

Hoffmann, R. Joseph. *Jesus Outside the Gospels.* Buffalo: Prometheus, 1984.

Jeremias, Joachim. *The Parables of Jesus.* 2d rev. ed. New York: Scribner, 1972.

Leone, Peter. "HIV/AIDS Epidemiology: AIDS Rising in Black Male College Students." *Medical Letter on the CDC & FDA,* 7 March 2004, 40.

Llewelyn, S. R., ed. *New Documents Illustrating Early Christianity: A Review of the Greek Inscriptions and Papyri Published in 1980–81.* Vol. 9. Macquarie University, N.S.W.: The Ancient History Documentary Research Centre Macquarie University, 1992.

Loury, Glenn, and Linda Datcher Loury. "Not by Bread Alone: The Role of the African-American Church in Inner-City Development." *Brookings Review* 15, no. 1 (1997): 10–13.

Malina, Bruce J., and Richard L. Rohrbaugh. *Social Science Commentary on the Synoptic Gospels.* Minneapolis: Fortress, 1992.

Marxsen, Willi. *Jesus and the Church: The Beginnings of Christianity.* Translated by Philip E. Devenish. Philadelphia: Trinity, 1992.

Murray, Frank J. "Profiling by Airlines Gets Public Support." *Washington Times,* 1 November 2001, 1.

Ogden, Schubert Miles. *On Theology.* 1st ed. San Francisco: Harper & Row, 1986.

Park, Andrew Sung. "African American Biblical Interpretation: Reflections on Stony the Road We Trod." *Journal of the Interdenominational Theological Center* 22, no. 1 (1994): 126–34.

Pettiway, Leon E. *Honey, Honey, Miss Thang: Being Black, Gay, and on the Streets.* Philadelphia: Temple University Press, 1996.

Pippin, Tina. "On the Blurring of Boundaries." Pages 169–76 in *Yet with a Steady Beat: Contemporary U.S. Afrocentric Biblical Interpretation.* Edited by Randall C. Bailey. Atlanta: Society of Biblical Literature, 2003.

Segovia, Fernando. "The Stony Road as the Road of the Future and the Road of Liberation: Critical Reflections." *Journal of the Interdenominational Theological Center* 22, no. 1 (1994): 135–46.

Seper, Jerry. "N.J. Says Blacks Biggest Speeders; Vows to Help End Racial Profiling." *Washington Times,* 28 March 2002, 1.

Strother-Jordan, Karen. "On the Rhetoric of Afrocentricity." *The Western Journal of Black Studies* 26, no. 4 (2002): 193+.

Walker, Alice. "In Search of Our Mothers' Gardens." Pages 339–46 in *Black Theology: A Documentary History.* Edited by James H. Cone and Gayraud Wilmore. 2 vols. Maryknoll, N.Y.: Orbis, 2003.

Walker, Theodore, Jr. "Theological Resources for a Black Neoclassical Social Ethics." Pages 35–52 in *Black Theology: A Documentary History.* Edited by James H. Cone and Gayraud Wilmore. 2 vols. Maryknoll, N.Y.: Orbis, 2003.

Washington, Adrienne T. "To See Racial Profiling in Action, Just Turn on the TV." *Washington Times,* 22 May 2001, 2.

Weems, Renita J. "Womanist Reflections on Biblical Hermeneutics." Pages 216–24 in *Black Theology: A Documentary History.* Edited by James H. Cone and Gayraud Wilmore. 2 vols. Maryknoll, N.Y.: Orbis, 1993.

West, Cornel. *Race Matters.* Boston: Beacon, 1993.

Wimbush, Vincent L. " 'Rescue the Perishing': The Importance of Biblical Scholarship in Black Christianity." Pages 210–15 in *Black Theology: A Documentary History.* Edited by James H. Cone and Gayraud Wilmore. 2 vols. Maryknoll, N.Y.: Orbis, 1993.

Yee, Gale A. "Review of Cain Hope Felder, Ed., *Stony the Road We Trod: African American Biblical Interpretation.*" *Journal of the Inter-denominational Theological Center* 22, no. 1 (1994): 147–52.

Young-Bruehl, Elisabeth. *The Anatomy of Prejudices.* Cambridge: Harvard University Press, 1996.

Index